"WHEN THE DRUMMERS WERE WOMEN *adds a valuable dimension to our understanding of the ancient Goddess religions. Redmond, herself a brilliant drummer, documents that these instruments have long been played by women in ritual. Her own experience as a musician gives her insight into the ways drumming can be used to affect consciousness and opens our imagination to envision the actual ceremonies of the Goddess. As a drummer and priestess myself, I loved this book!"*

STARHAWK,
author of Dreaming the Darkness

◎ ◎ ◎

"*Wow! Through Layne's fabulous book, my own intuitive experience with drumming has been made more clear and has been grounded in 'Her-story.' I'm sure this learning will deepen and enlarge my personal and group work. I highly recommend this well-documented treatise to EVERYONE, and especially those who are drawn to the power and magic of the drum.*"

BROOKE MEDICINE EAGLE,
author of Buffalo Woman Comes Singing

◎ ◎ ◎

"*. . . Redmond evokes the certainty that there is a parallel shamanic and mystery tradition for women. Since time immemorial, she shows, through carefully presented images, that women were aware of and attuned to the rhythms of being. This book instructs us, through myth and legend, through archaeological images, maps, and tables, and the integrity of Redmond's own search, that since ancient times, Drummers Were Women.*"

STEPHEN LARSEN,
Center for Symbolic Studies

"*It is important that this information is available and being talked about.*"

OLYMPIA DUKAKIS

◎ ◎ ◎

"*By searching out the lost, early history of the frame drum, Layne Redmond has uncovered an important missing chapter in the history of humanity—a chapter in which goddesses ruled beside gods and in which women's spirituality, wisdom, and sexuality were affirmed through rituals involving drumming. In an age where people are rediscovering the communal and healing powers of rhythm,* WHEN THE DRUMMERS WERE WOMEN *establishes the link between ancient knowledge and the contemporary emphasis on the importance of passion and soulfulness to life.*"

RICK MATTINGLY,
editor, Percussive Notes *magazine*

◎ ◎ ◎

"*As a scholar Redmond traces the history of the frame drum from its former exalted position, through its centuries of suppression, down to its current intense revival; as a virtuoso performer she speaks with authority on the drum's real and readily accessible powers. Women reading this book will want to jump up and start playing Layne Redmond's drum; men will get a valuable lesson in what they have been missing these past 5000 years or so.*"

JOHN ANTHONY WEST,
author of Serpent in the Sky

a spiritual

history of

rhythm

WHEN
THE DRUMMERS
WERE WOMEN

LAYNE
REDMOND

THREE RIVERS PRESS, NEW YORK

Published by Three Rivers Press, a division of Crown Publishers, Inc., 201 East 50th Street, New York, New York 10022. Member of the Crown Publishing Group.

Random House, Inc. New York, Toronto, London, Sydney, Auckland
http://www.randomhouse.com/

THREE RIVERS PRESS and colophon are trademarks of Crown Publishers, Inc.

Design by Lauren Dong

Printed in the United States of America

Library of Congress Cataloging-in-Publication Data is available upon request.

ISBN 0-609-80128-7

10 9 8 7 6 5 4 3 2 1

First Edition

For my niece Sheeva,

 and her mother, my sister Susan,

 and her mother, my mother Sue,

 and her mother, my grandmother Lucy,

 and her mother, my great-grandmother Mama Charlotte,

 and her mother, and her mother, back through the beat of the blood

 of all the mothers and grandmothers to the very first Great Mother of us all.

Acknowledgments

There are two people whose creative talents dramatically shaped the form of this book. Tommy Brunjes created all the drawings for the book and functioned as my primary sounding board for all the decisions of what to keep and what to save for the next project. His support, humor, and belief in my ability to complete this project kept me going when the light at the end of the tunnel was out. Marilyn Bowden edited, wrote, and rewrote much of the manuscript with me, at times taking my raw notes and literally turning them into the final polished form. There is simply no way this book would exist without their energy and effort, and they have my deepest gratitude and appreciation for their considerable talents.

Also, very special thanks and gratitude are due to my teacher, Glen Velez, who first introduced me to the frame drum and its history. My assistant, Christine Uberti, who for a year did everything from editing to obtaining photographic permissions, contributed immensely to this project. Maria Epes worked with many versions of this manuscript, and her feedback and support were invaluable to me. Dr. Wendy Griffin thoroughly reviewed and critiqued the manuscript in an extraordinarily supportive and helpful manner. My first assistant, Arianna Staruch, showed me that I didn't have to do everything myself. John Wieczorek escorted me from museum to museum in Syria, Turkey, Cyprus, and Greece, as we searched for representations of frame drummers. Evelyne Pouget translated and wrote many letters for me in French and Italian. To all of these friends and everyone else who helped along the way, I'm forever grateful for your inspirational support.

At Three Rivers Press, my editor Leslie Meredith's vision, support, and inspiring loyalty to this project were the driving force that brought *When the Drummers Were Women* into being. Sherri Rifkin edited and Joanna Burgess cheerfully shepherded this book to fruition.

Finally, endless thanks to all the women who have studied the frame drum and sent wonderful words of support to me, some of which are reprinted in this book. This book is for you.

Contents

You may not remember,
but let me tell you this,
someone in some future time
will think of us.

SAPPHO, SEVENTH CENTURY B.C., POET, COMPOSER,
MUSICIAN, TEACHER, PRIESTESS OF APHRODITE

Greek priestesses of Dionysos
celebrating the preparation
of wine for ritual use, circa
420 B.C.

WHEN
the DRUMMERS
WERE WOMEN

İntroduction

HANDHELD FRAME DRUMS are among the oldest known musical instruments. They are hoop-shaped drums with a diameter that is much greater than the depth of their shell. In prehistoric times, their rhythms helped shamans and seers attain the sacred trance state necessary for healing and prophecy. The rituals of the earliest known religions evolved around the beat of frame drums.

These religions were founded on the worship of female deities —Mother Goddesses who evolved into the many goddesses of Mediterranean cultures in classical times. In the oldest times women's bodies were considered holy, because they had the seemingly magical ability to give birth; to create new human beings. As a result, women became the first technicians of the sacred, performing religious functions we would today associate with the clergy or priesthood. Sacred drumming was one of their primary skills. It remained a powerful tool for communal bonding and individual transformation until the fall of the Roman Empire.

Though the existence of cultures whose primary deity was a goddess has been well documented in the last twenty-five years in popular and influential works by scholars such as Marija Gimbutas, Buffie Johnson, Merlin Stone, Rianne Eisler, and Joseph Campbell, the role of women as custodians of the spiritual life of these cultures is not as well known. Perhaps for this reason, the significance of the frame drum as the focus of women's spiritual power has been virtually overlooked.

In modern times, drummers have been almost exclusively men, but more and more women are rediscovering their ancient birthright. Every year there are more professional women percussionists.

Cybele/Astarte with drum. From the necropolis of the ancient Phoenician city of Carthage, circa fifth–third century B.C.

And yet at the same time many women are returning to the drum not for a profession but to recover an important spiritual connection to health and to one another that has been lost—a connection long buried but somehow instantly familiar.

When the Drummers Were Women is the story of a buried and forgotten aspect of women's spiritual heritage. It traces the use of the frame drum as a ritual instrument from the sacred caves of Old Europe through the mystery cults of Rome. It demonstrates that banning women's drumming from religious life was central to the disempowerment of women in Western culture. Finally, it shows how drumming is again becoming a tool for individual and cultural healing and transformation.

Twelve-inch bendir from Morocco and fourteen-inch tar made in North America after Middle Eastern design.

The return of the drum into our culture is not yet recognized by the scientific community or the major media, but droves of ordinary people are being captivated by its sound, power, and magic. Across the country, executives in Fortune 500 companies attend workshops in rhythm that are designed to boost managerial development and cooperation. Members of the Christian clergy are turning to the

Various tambourines, which belong to the family of frame drums, from Germany, Egypt, India, and a contemporary design from America.

entraining properties of drumming to generate a communal sense of spiritual power (I once drummed for two days while a group of Catholic nuns meditated). Dr. Oliver Sacks, author of a number of popular books on neurological disorders, has helped to set up drumming circles in nursing homes. Testifying before the Senate Special Committee on Aging, he hypothesized that Alzheimer's disease can be ameliorated by the healing effects of rhythm. In Topeka, therapists are experimenting with drumming in the treatment of dementia.

I've been teaching and performing with the frame drum for many years now, and I'm continually amazed by its enthusiastic reception. Its voice inspires instant communion with everyone who hears it. I am convinced that the new drumming phenomenon answers a deep cultural need to reestablish our rhythmic links with nature and with one another.

FOLLOWING PAGE: Egyptian goddess Hathor sitting in lotus playing to Horus, the hawk god. Dendera, Ptolemaic period.

PART I

THE DIVINE FEMININE

The sky and its stars make music to you.
The sun and the moon praise you.
The gods exalt you.
The goddesses sing to you.

INSCRIPTION ON A WALL OF THE TEMPLE OF HATHOR,
DENDERA, EGYPT, SECOND CENTURY B.C.

CHAPTER ONE
....

IN SEARCH
OF THE
SACRED

WOMEN TODAY ARE on a tremendous spiritual search. About 80 percent of participants at transformational centers, continuing education classes, therapy groups, and New Age centers are women. Behind this surging feminine energy is a yearning to understand who they are and what their purpose in life is. They long to live meaningful lives in harmonious rhythm with the sacred energies of the earth and heavens. Many have an underlying intuition that women have been dispossessed of a heritage, tradition, and sense of identity that was once uniquely their own. They suspect that women's real history has been disguised and distorted. Many women believe that locked in that history is an ancient wisdom transmitted by long-vanished sages and benevolent deities that may speak to the problems of contemporary life, such as how to live individually with a sense of spiritual connectedness and belonging each day, and, most important, how to live with one another and share a sense of community and purpose.

The legend of a lost paradise is as old as humankind. It surfaces in nearly every religious text. Centuries before the Biblical account of Adam and Eve's expulsion from the Garden of Eden, texts from Mesopotamia evoked a Garden Paradise. The ancient Hindus whispered of the first Golden Age. The Greek poet Hesiod sang of a Golden Race. This deep-seated sense that life was better at some long-distant time and place also suggests that, far from advancing, we are in fact losing ground.

Women often feel that, along with a portion of their history, they're missing a part of their psyches. They've lost access to important regions of their minds. Until they can reclaim those parts of themselves, they are not whole.

The original Mob of Angels,
New York City, 1990.

THE LEGACY OF THE GODDESS

Recent scientific investigations into prehistory suggest that there is indeed a rich vein of feminine wisdom at the core of Western civilization. Due to technological advances in the field of archaeology and extensive excavations, a wealth of new information about the past has come to light. This century has witnessed a literal unearthing of an ancient Great Goddess and her mythologies. Thousands of images of this Divine Feminine, relics of the societies that revered her and rediscovered sacred sites where she was worshiped, bear witness to a history that has lain buried for millennia.

As long-cherished beliefs about the nature of the past are challenged by archaeological evidence, a massive and often controversial reassessment of prehistory and ancient history is currently under way. Scholars are divided about everything from dates to the meaning of symbols and mythologies. Egyptologists quarrel over the correlation of Pharaonic tables to European calendars. Stone Age markings once dismissed as meaningless are being reinterpreted as the earliest evidence of religious symbolism.

A number of scholars, many of them women, have turned their minds and intuition toward piecing together the bones of the goddess's existence and the extensive religions centered around her. Ground-breaking work by scholars such as Marija Gimbutas, James Mellaart, Alexander Marshack, Jane Ellen Harrison, and William Irwin Thompson have made it clear that man's famous inhumanity to man is not our only heritage. From the Neolithic city of Çatal Hüyük in present-day Turkey to the palaces of Minoan Crete, scholars found traces of societies that based their religious structures around a goddess, who lived in peace for thousands of years, with role models for the sexes very different from those now the norm.

Greek hellenistic sculpture of enthroned and crowned goddess Cybele, holding her frame drum and lotus libation bowl, with a lion on her lap.

THE ETERNAL FEMALE

In Egypt the goddess was known as Hathor, Isis, Sekhmet. In Sumerian, Syro-Palestinian, and Cypriot cultures she was called Inanna, Ishtar, Astarte, Astoreth, Anat, Aphrodite. In Anatolia, Asia Minor, Crete,

Greece, and Rome she was Cybele, Rhea, Demeter, Artemis, Ariadne, Persephone. All these historical goddesses sprang from an archetypal Great Goddess of the Paleolithic Age, when cultures throughout the European and western Asian world worshiped forms of a Divine Mother.

This Divine Mother should not be imagined as the female equivalent of the Judeo-Christian God the Father. She is more fluid, capable of assuming many forms. She is a powerful mythological symbol who speaks to something basic in human consciousness. As an archetype of the eternal female, she transmits, simultaneously, layer upon layer of meaning—some of it seemingly contradictory or disparate. Bypassing the intellect, often inaccessible to conscious thought, these multidimensional images strike to the heart of awareness. They vibrate within our psyches, oscillating between various levels of meaning. They are the unconscious source of our thoughts and emotions.

Crowned goddess with drum, found in burial goods, Spain, circa fourth–third century B.C.

Think of this great fount of archetypes as a stream of energy that assumes whatever form our consciousness can understand. Because there are so many different levels of comprehension, the goddess appears in myriad forms. The archetype of compassion, for example, is reflected in our own mothers (regardless of the nature of each particular mother/child relationship). In its most ancient form, it is embodied in the archetype of the Great Mother, who created her children and nourished them on the fluids of her body, devoting herself to maintaining and guiding their existence. As we are drawn deeper into each form and expression of the archetype, we begin to assimilate the primordial energy that creates it.

Consciousness-transforming practices such as rhythmic drumming or meditation can put us in touch with the archetypal patterns of consciousness inherent in human beings—archetypes once represented by the various forms of the goddess. As patterns of behavior are brought up from unconsciousness into the light of conscious awareness, we can begin to change distorted or unhealthy behavior.

For thousands of years, this nurturing Divine Feminine represented the ultimate spiritual example. Her mythology was a storehouse of human experience and recollection conveying an archaic technology of psychological and spiritual wisdom. This archetypal knowledge enabled women and men to understand who they were, within themselves and in relation to their families, communities, and environment.

PRIESTESSES OF THE SACRED SOUND

The goddess and those who performed her sacred rituals were female. These oldest of rituals were earth-based. The earth itself was revered as the Great Mother of All That Is. Because new life came from women's bodies as it did from the earth, women were celebrated as the embodiment of the divine. Human beings were not separate from their environment. They saw themselves as the earth in human form. In caring for the earth, people cared for themselves. Women's rites preserved the sanctity of this nourishing bond.

Rhythmic music seems to have been particularly important in the rites associated with the ancient goddesses. In the oldest cultures, rhythm was revered as the structuring force of life—so much so that historian William H. McNeill argues that "learning to move and give voice [rhythmically], and the strengthened emotional bonds associated with this sort of behavior, were critical prerequisites for the emergence of humanity."

Human, plant, and animal evolved in a rhythmic web. The daily cycles of the sun initiated the primary rhythms of activity and rest. Its seasonal cycles governed growth and decay. Human communities survived by understanding the natural rhythms of their environment. The need to predict cyclical patterns—the ebb and flow of tides, the growth and fruiting of plants, the migration and mating patterns of animals and birds—gave rise to the earliest timekeeping systems. In fact, there is some evidence that the first calendar makers were women. The readily observable correspondence between menstrual and lunar cycles would have made women particularly sensitive to their intimate connection with the natural world.

Woman with frame drum found in southern Italy, circa 300–275 B.C.

Female performance ensembles of musicians, singers, and dancers appear in some of the earliest representations of religious rituals. The frame drum was at the musical and psychic center of these rituals. One of the oldest known sacred ritual instruments, it first appears painted on a shrine room wall in ancient Anatolia (present-day Turkey) from the sixth millennium B.C. It is mentioned in the earliest surviving written texts from Sumer in the Tigris-Euphrates River Valley. From Egypt to the Indus River Valley, from Cyprus and Crete to Greece and Rome, priestesses and other worshiping women used the frame drum to celebrate their goddesses as the endlessly rhythmic energy of life.

Sacred drumming probably began as an echo of the human pulse. The pulse of our mother's blood was our first continuous experience as we quickened in the womb. Our physical being formed in response to

Procession of priestesses playing to an enthroned goddess. Nimrud, Mesopotamia, circa ninth century B.C.

Phoenician, found in burial goods at Carthage, circa fourth–third century B.C.

the rhythms of her body. No other sensation is so basic. The beat of the priestesses' frame drums articulated this process of creation, bonding the individual with the rhythms of the community, the environment, and the cosmos.

As McNeill's work demonstrates, however, the rhythmic synchronization of human movements that he calls "keeping together in time" is double-edged. It is a tremendous power and in human history it has been used in two major ways: for spiritual transformation and for organizing for war. Driven by the goddess's drums, it was a spiritual tool directed toward beneficial and peaceful means. In the hands of warlike invaders seeking to dominate, it became a grimly effective tool for military organization.

BURYING THE GODDESS

Around five thousand years ago, a new power elite doomed the goddess to eventual oblivion. Marija Gimbutas and other scholars have found evidence of several major incursions of warlike nomads in European prehistory. These invaders, referred to as either Kurgans or Aryans or Indo-Europeans, rode horse-drawn chariots and brandished swords. The peaceful goddess-based cultures were no match for them.

The Kurgans worshiped angry storm gods of vengeance and battle. They imposed their fiercely patriarchal social system on the indigenous tribes they conquered. Riane Eisler, who details the social and religious upheavals caused by these invasions in *The Chalice and the Blade*, describes Kurgan culture as a dominator model of social organization in which "male dominance, male violence, and a generally hierarchic and authoritarian social structure was the norm." She points out that the way these groups acquired wealth was "not by developing technologies of production, but through ever more effective technologies of destruction."

These people destroyed the peaceful cultures of the Neolithic that were based on the sacred female. Mythologies replete with tales of gods raping goddesses and mortal women, and of forced marriages of indigenous goddesses to newer gods, show how the invaders' patriarchal religion was grafted onto the old beliefs. Gradually, the symbols of the goddesses were demonized and imbued with evil connotations.

Though her myths were distorted and her power forcibly shared with male deities, the goddess did not disappear from Mediterranean culture until much later. In Crete and Anatolia, Egypt, India, Greece, and Rome, people continued to worship her in many forms. It took another large-scale social upheaval—the fall of the Roman Empire—for the storm god to complete his triumph.

The excesses and corruption that destroyed the Empire also created a fertile environment for the growth of Christianity. At first, this new religion offered a caring and powerful alternative to the state religions of Rome. But the early Roman church fathers used their growing political and military power to eradicate all traces of the Divine Feminine. They insisted on the exclusive worship of one male deity, served by a celibate, all-male priesthood. Because they recognized its intimate connection with women's spiritual power, they banned the sacred frame drum. Eventually, women were not even allowed to speak in church.

Today, the Western world is still living with the consequences of the rape of the goddess by the storm god. Our major religions—Judaism, Christianity, and Islam—are based on the belief that one-half of the human race is made in the image of divinity and the other is not, and therefore should not have access to religious power. Cultures driven by belief systems like these are dangerously out of balance. The desacralization of women has contributed to the terrible inequalities and violence that women struggle against every day. A cosmology that admits of only one male god limits women's capacity to envision their full potential as human beings. Men, cut off from aspects of their own psyches considered soft or "feminine" in our culture, also suffer.

Clearly, history itself is a form of mythmaking. The official version of our mytho-history colors our comprehension of the world and our place in it. It filters our perceptions of reality. It defines what is acceptable and what is not. It shapes our sense of self. Restoring our history of

Cybele from Miletus, ancient Turkey, Roman work, circa fourth century A.D.

goddess-based societies that functioned peacefully for centuries in accordance with more democratic religious beliefs than those now in existence helps women and men to cut through oppressive and destructive cultural stereotypes. This restored knowledge is helping women and men to transform themselves and therefore their culture.

Our present social and religious structures are clearly breaking down. Escalating environmental and political crises are forcing a reevaluation of our cultural assumptions about everything from a nation's right to deplete the resources within its boundaries to a woman's right to control her own body.

In re-visioning the past we envision the future. We are faced with the necessity of evolving a new social structure. If we are to survive, we're going to have to resurrect the values once associated with female-based religious systems—values of compassion and healing, of providing and sheltering, of nourishing, of holding all life sacred.

Cultural transformation begins with individual transformation. Though many of the rites channeling the energy of the Divine Feminine have been lost in the West, her symbols and mythologies have endured in the goddess traditions of some Eastern religions like Hinduism and Tibetan Buddhism. Using these traditions and the spiritual practices associated with them as a guide, we can illuminate the ancient symbols and mythology of the Mediterranean goddesses and explore the lost path of the Divine Feminine.

Maenad leading procession of Dionysos and Ariadne. Roman, circa 110–130 A.D.

SACRED DRUMMING

Sixteen years ago, I began to learn to play the frame drum. I was amazed at the spiritual power of rhythmic disciplines. Mental and physical concentration on rhythm connects me at times with a universal energy, both internally and externally. This energy conveys a feeling of timelessness. Drumming engages the conscious mind, and like meditation, cuts back on its continual chatter. As a result, as happens after practicing meditation, the habitual patterns of thinking that drive behavior become less powerful.

When I began to teach other women to drum, I became more deeply convinced of the healing and transforming power of this ancient sacred technology. There is power in drumming alone but that power recombines and multiplies in a group of drummers. It creates the deep sense of group solidarity that McNeill calls "muscular bonding." Women who drum together can connect to their own rhythms, form a healthier collective view of their own potential, and loosen the unconscious grip of dominant cultural beliefs.

I am convinced that the role of women's sacred drumming in the past served these same functions. This is why I believe that the ancient path of the goddess is still valid—in fact, essential—today. Women need the archetypal image of a Divine Female. We need to reconnect with the inherent sacredness of woman as creator and nourisher, rather than accept a vision of ourselves as less-than-divine inferiors.

I'm not advocating a return to the past, but the recovered wisdom of traditions focused on the frame drum can help us break free of negative cultural conditioning, live in greater harmony with the natural world, and create a spiritual life for ourselves.

All humans are sacred beings, each of us an expression of ultimate reality or divinity. Personally, I no longer belong to a formal religious organization. My spiritual goal is to fulfill and express my full potential as a human being. But many who choose to remain within traditional religions, including nuns and ordained clergywomen, have found sacred drumming to be a beneficial supplement to their own religious practices. Now, as in ancient times, the path of the goddess is not restrictive. It offers a channel for spiritual energy, and a sense of unity through rhythmic movement, for all people.

CHAPTER TWO

FIRST-PERSON FEMININE

IN 1980, on a whim, I joined a conga-drumming class.

Perhaps I was fulfilling an old wish, for I had asked for a drum set once as a teenager. My parents found this so absurd that they didn't even bother to respond. I might just as well have asked to go to Venus. Many women in my drum classes have come to me with similar stories. When I was growing up, women played the piano or maybe the flute. They didn't drum.

I had almost no musical background. I grew up in a very small, isolated community in western Florida where musical experience was hard to come by. The high-school band was poorly trained. My church didn't even have a choir.

I was fortunate enough to be able to study ballet and tap dance with a great teacher from New York who had retired to our small town. I also spent five years as a cheerleader. Later in my life, I realized that cheerleading was a very important part of my training. In the rural South, the football game is the biggest thing going in the county. I was using rhythmic movement and chanting to rouse and shape the group energies of hundreds of people. This early training helped me to develop my ability to create community rituals.

Once I came to New York to study art in the early seventies, I got very involved in the Manhattan art scene, and my musical horizons began to expand beyond the standard Top 40 fare. I'd go to the library and check out recordings of any kind of music I didn't know about. I listened to John Cage, Native American chants, music from India, Africa, Bali.

Taking conga lessons soon taught me that listening didn't come close to active music-making. I experienced for the first time the trance-union of people drumming in rhythm with one another. I had a sense of connecting, a sense of being one with the other players. It was an ecstatic, joyously communal feeling.

After only eight weeks, before I'd even managed to buy my own conga, classes ended. My teacher was moving to California. At one of our last classes, he introduced a guest performer, Glen Velez, who played a Brazilian tambourine in a duet with the conga teacher. He explained briefly that he was studying different types of drums like these, which he called frame drums, and also gave lessons. I jotted down his address but let the drumming go for a while.

Pandeiro.

Much as I enjoyed music, my concentration lay elsewhere. I was very involved in my work as a performance artist. My performance work was evolving out of my immersion in the works of scholars such as Joseph Campbell, Robert Graves, and Carl Sagan. Mythology fascinated me. Using my training in photography and filmmaking, I created multimedia installations within which I enacted archetypal images of the World Tree, the Cosmic Egg, and Medusa against a backdrop of deep space. As my interest in alternative music grew, I included unusual, obscure tape recordings of traditional music from around the world in my performances.

Through these performances, I was exploring ways of awakening some forgotten connection or recollection that could replace an indefinable "something" I sensed was missing from modern life. I was convinced that what I was searching for was in some way related to ancient mythologies. I wanted to present audiences with scenes they had never seen or heard before, but which at the same time would seem familiar.

A number of months after the conga classes had ended, I discovered that Glen Velez would be performing in a concert at a small downtown music studio, which I attended. About twenty people showed up. We sat in a circle around Glen as he played one type of frame drum after another. They come from many different cultures and most of them are portable and can be held in one hand.

As Velez performed, I was enchanted by the power and beauty of these unusual instruments. The rhythmic music transported me. It seemed to lead me closer to what I was searching for than anything else I had experienced. I knew I had to learn to play these drums myself—a reaction I've since witnessed over and over again in many women.

Glen wasn't teaching extensively at that time but I convinced him to take me on as a student. Among the drums he'd played at the concert was a *doumbek*, a ceramic drum from the Middle East shaped like an hourglass. I chose it to begin with, thinking it might be closest to the conga drums with which I was familiar.

But when I arrived at Glen's for my first lesson, he had some bad news. That morning, he'd dropped and broken the *doumbek*. He glanced around his studio apartment, which was jammed with frame drums of every description. Grabbing an Egyptian tambourine off the wall, he said, "Hey, how about this?"

It wasn't what I had planned. But, not wanting to lose this opportunity to learn from such a skilled drummer, I agreed. I held my first tambourine in my hands. Without ever really knowing why, I started on a disciplined regimen of learning to play the frame drum, which eventually changed my life completely.

At that time I was living a romantic myth of my own—that of the starving artist. I lived in a tenement in Hell's Kitchen on the west side of Manhattan, made my living as a waitress, and had no intention of looking for a "real job." Creating art was my life. There was no room for any other serious interest.

Once a week, I went for a lesson, tape-recorded it and used it to practice with every day at home. I quickly realized that, with no prior musical training, I had embarked on the study of a very difficult instrument. I had no time for this! But I loved the rhythmic sounds—I was hooked.

I was an eager pupil, and I now realize a talented one. In some ways my lack of experience served me well. Glen was beginning to create complex pieces that centered around unusual rhythmic patterns— cycles of ten, nine, and eight beats, within which he could cue me, using another rhythm, to move to a cycle of seven beats, six beats, sixteen beats, and so on. If I had spent years playing music based on traditional four-beat rhythms, I might have had a hard time adjusting, conceptually as well as musically. Instead, I found that seven-, five-, or even thirty-seven-beat cycles weren't that tough for me.

DRUM ROLES

After a couple of years, Glen and I began performing together in the avant-garde music scene in New York and Europe. We earned some serious attention and good press. We started to record for several different music labels.

When I first began studying with Glen, he would sometimes play in my performance-art pieces as well. Gradually, though, the music took over, and I was just playing his music in his concerts. I was now working as a freelance computer programmer to make ends meet. The music I was performing was so complex and difficult to master that I had to devote more and more time to rehearsing it. The starving-artist routine was losing its appeal, and besides, I had very little time for making art. Glen was also playing in other bands, traveling, and becoming well-known as a virtuoso percussionist.

I was confused about the way my life was going. Some days I felt like I'd always be tied to jobs I didn't like. Drumming didn't seem to offer an answer. For one thing, most drummers begin playing during childhood. I was twenty-seven years old when I had my first lesson. For another, the professional world of percussion is predominantly male, although it is slowly changing. But drumming had become the center of my life. In 1985, Glen and I formed a group with Steve Gorn, a gifted flutist. Glen is often described as a "master drummer," and Steve a "master musician," so I wondered what I could bring to our trio to complement their years of training, expertise, and virtuosity. One thing I did have was a radiant feminine energy and I set my mind on conveying that through my drumming.

Now I am sometimes described as a "master drummer" myself since there is no appropriate feminine counterpart. The phrase doesn't quite fit, since "master," correctly used, describes a dominant man. And "mistress drummer" obviously doesn't cut it or do justice to the ancient connection of primordial feminine energy and drumming.

In learning to express this connection through my drumming, I had no idea that I was embracing one of the world's oldest traditions. As I studied various styles of frame drumming, I also learned something of their history. Glen had collected hundreds of images of frame drummers from the ancient Mediterranean world. Almost all of them were women. As I helped him organize his slides and studied the images more closely, I realized that many of them were representations of goddesses or their priestesses.

Because of my interest in mythology, I could name quite a few ancient goddesses, but I had never associated

Mesopotamian, found at Diqdiqqeh, circa 2300–2000 B.C.

Cybele from West Anatolia, Roman period, first century A.D.

THE DIVINE FEMININE

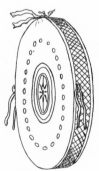

Cybele, found in West Anatolia, end of fifth century B.C.

any of them with drums. I vaguely recalled angels playing tambourines in renaissance religious art, but nothing else.

I began to read the large new body of scholarship about ancient religions, stretching back to the Paleolithic era, and about a Great Mother Goddess. No one had focused on the fact that in many cases the goddesses were portrayed with frame drums. I didn't need an expert to tell me that drumming hadn't always been a male prerogative. The archaeological evidence shows plainly that at one time the drummers were women.

Who were these women? Why had they been associated with drums for so many thousands of years? Why don't we know anything about them now? Why don't women play drums today?

My life became more focused and I saw my unique purpose: I had to find out what had happened when the drummers were women and why they stopped drumming. Over the next decade, my search for answers to questions like these led me to museums and temple ruins throughout the ancient Mediterranean world. One reason for the magnitude of my quest was the antiquity of the instrument itself.

THE FRAME DRUM

Roman frame drums.

The ancient frame drum of the trans-Mediterranean cultures that prefigure our own is primarily a wheel-shaped drum whose diameter is much wider than the depth of its shell. It is round and shaped like a grain sieve, and both the drum and the sieve probably share the same origin. Both are symbolic of the feminine, fertility, grain, the moon, the sun, and the primordial first body of water. Ritual and symbolic connections between the two reach back into prehistory.

The frame drum most often has a skin on only one side but sometimes it may have skins stretched across both sides. Bells or jingling and rattling implements may be attached to the inside rim, and in ancient times were believed to add to the drum's power to purify, dispel, and summon. The drums were often painted red, the color of blood, or sometimes green, the color of vegetation. Throughout the ancient world, these were the primordial colors of life. Mystical designs and symbols might also be painted on the skin head or the wooden frame. Threads or ribbons knotted with ritual prayers or chants often hung from them.

Although this frame drum is similar in appearance to the shaman's drum found throughout Asia and North America, there is a major difference in how they are played. The shaman's drum is struck with a bone, horn, or stick, whereas the Mediterranean frame drum is played with the bare hands. While striking a drum with a stick gives a single deep, resonant sound, finger techniques allow more variety: a deep, open tone, a slap, a high-pitched rim sound, a soft brushing sound. This difference in stroke technique has led to differences in construction. The inner edge of the rim of the Mediterranean frame drum is beveled, and its skin is usually thinner, to enhance the sounds produced by fingers and hands.

Hand or stick? I have not been able to determine which technique is older—the shaman's drum played with a stick or the frame drum of the goddess played with bare hands. The use and basic construction of the drums are so similar that they probably both grew from the same root techniques of altering consciousness.

Italian tambourine with jingles and bells, early twentieth century.

Tibetan shaman's drum.

ANCIENT RHYTHMS

In every ancient Mediterranean civilization I studied, it was a goddess who transmitted to humans the gift of making music. In Sumer it was Inanna; in Egypt, Hathor; in Greece, the nine-fold goddess called the Muses. Musical, artistic, and poetic inspiration was always thought to

Egyptian drummers from a tomb painting at Thebes necropolis, Eighteenth Dynasty (1504–1450 B.C.).

Included with burial goods in the ancient Phoenician necropolis of Utica, in Tunisia, circa fifth–third century B.C.

spring from the Divine Feminine. One of the main techniques for connecting to this power of inspiration was drumming.

The drum was the means our ancestors used to summon the goddess and also the instrument through which she spoke. The drumming priestess was the intermediary between divine and human realms. Aligning herself with sacred rhythms, she acted as summoner and transformer, invoking divine energy and transmitting it to the community.

The drum was the primary trance-inducing instrument in transition rites. Initiates who concentrated on its rhythmic patterns could transcend ordinary consciousness. In rituals invoking the archetypal pattern of death and rebirth, the drum signaled the release of outmoded behavior patterns and the transition to a new status in life.

Death-and-rebirth rituals were often symbolic reenactments of the death-and-resurrection myths found in many ancient mythologies. Inanna, Osiris, Persephone, Adonis, and Dionysos were among many deities recalled from the underworld to renewed life by the power of the frame drum. Funeral rites took their shape from these metaphorical resurrections. Throughout the Mediterranean world, the beat of a drum guided the passage of ordinary mortals through the realms of the afterlife and was believed to hasten their rebirth. In many areas, the dead were buried with figurines of goddesses or women playing the frame drum.

Invoking the elemental powers of the deities, the voice of the drum called forth the cyclical rebirth of nature. Its vibrational force woke the sleeping life within the earth. Drummers played over freshly sown seeds to quicken their ripening, and later over the burgeoning vegetation to protect and enhance its growth.

The drum's association with fertility encompassed human sexuality. In many ancient cultures, frame drums were particularly associated with feminine sexual energy. As instigator of creation, the goddess manifested in sexual desire and union. The drum she held identified her with the primal rhythms of life apparent in the sexual act. Sacred sexual priestesses of Inanna, Hathor, Aphrodite, and Cybele all played the frame drum to increase the energy of sexual attraction and the powers of femininity. In menstruation and birthing rites, certain drum rhythms caused the womb to contract, aiding the flow of menstrual blood or facilitating labor in childbirth.

The forceful beat of the drum drove away evil spirits that spread confusion and disease and created a purified space where health and well-being could flourish. This ancient tradition survived into quite recent days, when somber drumbeats marked time at executions or expulsions (for instance, from military service), as people who were considered a negative influence were driven from this world and from their communities.

It is thought that drumbeats were the earliest form of long-distance communication. Telegraphic rhythms imitating patterns of speech conveyed complex messages throughout communities and even from village to village, much as they still do today in parts of rural Africa.

Finally, drum rhythms measured the tempo of everyday life. Drums linked individuals together in communal labor, coordinating and energizing them to work for hours in a trancelike, rhythmic flow of physical activity. The rhythm of music and song wafted from home and field, workshops and passing boats. Bands of soldiers or camel drivers drummed and chanted as they traveled. Some of these traditions survived until the Industrial Revolution, when the grinding, discordant clang of heavy machinery destroyed the peaceable synchronization of natural rhythms and work.

My geographic and scholarly travels had become a quest for more than the his-

Aphrodite from Carthage, Roman period.

Women playing frame drums seated in camel saddle. A Roman sculpture found at Salamiya, ancient Syria, circa A.D. 1–100.

tory of a musical instrument. My search for historical uses of the frame drum was a path into our mythological history and origins as a primal people. It was a path that led into a complex of archetypal energies at whose heart lies women's lost spiritual legacy—the most powerful spiritual traditions of the ancient world.

Each of these traditions centered around a goddess or goddesses. Like moons that spin around the larger planet from which they emerged, these historical deities proved to be aspects derived from the primordial Great Goddess.

The rhythms of the drum would lead me back and back, through ancient historical civilizations, through the Neolithic, and finally deep into the Paleolithic—into the very genesis of human symbolic thought.

Egyptian boat scene with woman frame drummer, Saite period, circa 589–404 B.C.

FOLLOWING PAGE: Priestess playing the frame drum to draw the vegetation up from the underworld. Fifth century B.C.

Part II

In the Beginning

She is none other than the Great Goddess,
source and mistress of all life, the creatress,
the Great Mother, the symbol of life itself.

JAMES MELLAART, *THE GODDESS FROM ANATOLIA*

Cultural Stages
Paleolithic   500,000–10,000
Mesolithic   10,000–8,000
Neolithic   8,000–4,000

100,000
Neanderthal burials with flowers.

40,000–35,000
Appearance of modern humans, Homo Sapiens Sapiens.

33,000–27,000
Aurignacian Cultures. The earliest manifestations of art.
Body ornaments of shells and perforated teeth appear in
graves, along with the use of red ocher. First vulvas.
Ideophones (scrapers, rattles), bone flutes, and bull-
roarers appear.

27,000–19,000
Gravettian Cultures. Painted, engraved, and
sculpted images. Goddesses of Willendorf,
Laussel, and Kostenki.

20,000–15,000
Solutrean Cultures. Animals rendered with
artistic mastery. The height of flint tool making.
Sewing needles appear.

15,000–10,000
Magdalenian Cultures. Height of the wall paintings in
the cave sanctuaries. Shamanistic scene in Lascaux.

10,000–8,000
Mesolithic. Major climatic changes. Deterioration
in cultural forms.

8,000–4,000
Neolithic. Çatal Hüyük, frame drum appears,
5600 B.C. Skin-covered ceramic drums, 3500 B.C.

4,000–1,000
Rise of Mesopotamian, Nile, and Indus Valley Cultures.
First named drummer in history, Lipushiau, 2380 B.C.

TIMELINE

CHAPTER THREE

PRIMEVAL GODDESS OF RHYTHM

AMONG THE EARLIEST historical cultures of the Mediterranean world, women were spiritual leaders. Priestesses and other holy women played the frame drum in the rituals of their goddesses. From the visual evidence I found in ancient sculptures and wall paintings, it is clear that the link between drums and spiritual power had already been established before the invention of written language. I found symbols painted on the heads of ancient frame drums that I traced back further and further into the very earliest periods of human history. My search for the meaning and origins of female drumming led me finally into an examination of the nomadic people who inhabited Europe and West Asia almost forty thousand years ago. Information about this distant time is at best conjectural, based on obscure clues gleaned from incomplete archaeological evidence. Still, our Paleolithic ancestors left behind fascinating glimpses into their world.

During the Upper Paleolithic, a vast period of time stretching from 40,000 B.C. to 10,000 B.C., nomadic tribes roamed across the Eurasian land mass, foraging in rhythm with the plants, animals, and seasons. The climate was still fluctuating with the recurring glaciations of the most recent ice age. The survival of these tribes depended upon their keen awareness of the immediate environment and the forces operating in it.

It was a period of relative leisure. Scholar and author William Irwin Thompson has estimated that adult members of historical hunting and gathering economies expended an average of fifteen hours a week collecting food. In the Paleolithic, people lived in small groups that did not tax the capacity of the environment, which sustained everyone.

The Paleolithic was also apparently a time of peace. There is no undisputed archaeological evidence of large-scale, organized violence; in no art form are human beings depicted in aggressive postures, or bearing weapons. Evidently, Paleolithic humankind did not make war.

THE BIRTH OF THE SPIRIT

The graves of Paleolithic people tell us something about their spiritual beliefs. Our prehistoric ancestors began burying their dead sometime around a hundred thousand years ago. By 34,000 B.C., human interment had become ceremonial. The dead were buried in the earth or in caves, often in a fetal position. They were adorned with body ornaments and jewelry made of shells, beads, ivory, and perforated animal teeth. Their headdresses or hoods were decorated with rows of cowrie shells. The cowrie shell, which resembles a vulva, is a very ancient and widespread symbol of rebirth. Both sexes were buried with tools, vessels, and food offerings, indicating a belief in continuing existence after death. We don't know whether the afterlife envisioned by Paleolithic people involved the survival of individual souls or the recycling of the materials of the body in the animate earth, yet these ritual burials demonstrate that they shared a belief in *some* form of continuance after death—a belief that is the cornerstone of most religious traditions.

The cowrie shell has been a sacred image of the vulva since the Paleolithic period. Contemporary African amulet for well-being and protection of the life force.

Very often, Paleolithic human remains were heavily painted with red ocher. This pigment, produced by grinding hematite or other iron oxides, has been used for ritual purposes by cultures around the world. In the Upper Paleolithic, it was used to redden graves, corpses, cave and shelter walls, engraved objects, and sculptures of women. Possibly it also served as body paint in ritual ceremonies.

In *A History of Religious Ideas*, Mircea Eliade notes, "Belief in a survival after death seems to be demonstrated from the earliest times, by the use of red ocher as a ritual substitute for blood, hence as a symbol of life." The presence of red ocher in Paleolithic burial sites suggests that it is indeed among our oldest religious symbols. As we will see, Paleolithic art makes clear that ocher had a special association with the blood of women.

Vulva carved in cave wall, Paleolithic period, circa 30,000 B.C.

CARVED IN STONE

Paleolithic people are the earliest humans known to have created works of art. These works, which included sculpture, carving, and cave drawings, appear to have been created less for aesthetic pleasure than to embody religious concepts or to transmit accumulated information and wisdom. In a preliterate world, they acted as a visual language. They are the earliest surviving expression of abstract thought.

Around 30,000 B.C., representations of the vulva of a human female, carved in stone and painted with red ocher, turned up all over Europe. They appear in relief on cave walls and as small, amulet-sized sculptures, often polished from wear. Some have been found in graves. These vulval images are the oldest known examples of representative art.

The sculptured or inscribed vulvae vary in size and shape. Some are oval or round, others are downward-pointing triangles. Some are realistic representations, some are abstract. A mammoth ivory pendant from Dolni Vestonice, close to present-day Brno in the Czech Republic, is shaped like a wishbone, with a vulva incised between its "legs." Sometimes these images appear alone, but often they are associated with images of a Mother Goddess or her symbols, or seem to represent an aspect of her story.

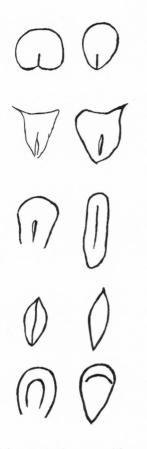

Vulvae incised or carved from the Upper Paleolithic.

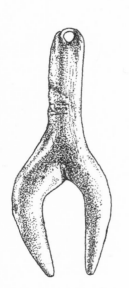

Paleolithic mammoth ivory pendant from Dolni Vestonice, Czech Republic, circa 25,000 B.C.

"It is not the anatomic 'sexual' organ that is being symbolized, but the storied characters and processes with which the symbol had become associated," Alexander Marshack emphasizes. The vulva is pre-eminently a symbol of birth, representing beginnings, fertility, the gateway to life itself. It is the primordial matrix from which everything arises. As the female power to give birth gradually gave rise to the idea of a woman's power to invoke rebirth, the vulva came to symbolize this power of regeneration as well.

Vulval imagery may also have represented initiation into a new phase of existence. For many thousands of years, people gathered ceremonially in caves whose dark, damp, womblike interiors, painted with shamanistic images of animals, were almost certainly the sites of initiation rites. At the mouths of these caves excavators frequently find carvings of vulvae.

Vulval images have also been found on some of the Paleolithic carved sticks called *batons de commandement*. Abbe Breuil, a Catholic scholar who dominated the study of the Magdalenian painted caves of France, gave them this name because he thought they resembled military batons. Their true function is a matter of conjecture among archaeologists. Marshack, Eliade, and Thompson recognize them as lunar calendars. A baton of the Middle Magdalenian period, toward the end of the Paleolithic, is engraved with a series of markings on its shaft that appear to represent a lunar count. The presence of a vulva on this baton may further indicate that it was in some way related to menstruation or pregnancy. Thompson compares them to the pregnancy calendars still kept by Siberian tribal women. Regarding its use as a ritual implement, he calls the *baton de commandement* "the most ancient symbol of feminine power." Interestingly, archaeologist Horst Kirchner concluded they might be drumsticks. If he is right, and the batons, with their vulval imagery and lunar associations, were sometimes employed as drumsticks, the connection between women and drumming would be very old indeed.

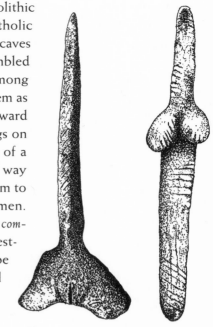

LEFT: Possible drumstick. Carved and engraved Middle Magdalenian baton with vulva from the cave of Le Placard (Charente, France), 15,000–13,000 B.C.

RIGHT: Paleolithic baton with breasts, carved from mammoth ivory from Dolni Vestonice, Czech Republic, circa 25,000 B.C. The "batons" were sacred ritual objects worn hung on a belt or thong, used as amulets or holders of power and divinity. When worn on the body, the energy-generating rituals used to create the baton became operative. The batons then acted as portable shrines, forming a field of protection around the wearer, imbuing her with the magical powers of the symbol.

GREAT MOTHER OF THE STONE AGE

Between 27,000 B.C. and 19,000 B.C., Paleolithic artists began to carve female figurines that contemporary art historians call Paleolithic Venuses. These artifacts, skillfully carved in bone, ivory, or stone, are the oldest known examples of sculpture in the round. They have been discovered at sites in Italy, France, Austria, and as far north as Siberia, yet they are remarkably homogeneous in style— mute testimony to the cultural unity of Paleolithic peoples.

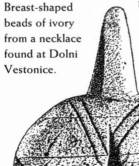

Breast-shaped beads of ivory from a necklace found at Dolni Vestonice.

Paleolithic Venuses focus on the maternal organs. Breasts and hips are rendered enormous; other features seem dwarfed or stunted by comparison. The arms are thin, the legs taper to nothing; hands and feet are absent altogether. These women are faceless, and most appear pregnant, though there is more variation than was at first realized. Prudence C. Rice, who comprehensively studied the figurines, found that they represent women at every stage of life—as young girls, pregnant women, nonpregnant women of childbearing age, and women past the age of childbirth.

Although hundreds of Venus figures have been discovered, only a few roughly made male figures have been found. By calling attention to the reproductive and nourishing functions of a woman's body, these figures tell us Paleolithic people viewed her ability to create new life out of her own body with religious awe. Birth was the earliest sacred mystery. The broad hips and full buttocks of the goddess suggest her powerful ability to procreate. From her large, luxurious, pendulous breasts flows the nourishing milk of life. In many cultures, milk still represents the sacred, divine love of a Great Mother.

Venus of Willendorf, limestone, circa 25,000 B.C.

The Venus of Willendorf, named for the place in Austria where she was unearthed, was carved out of limestone around 25,000 B.C. Like most Paleolithic Venuses, she has no feet. The legs were intentionally polished off at the ends of her calves by the original artist. Art historian George Weber suggested a plausible explanation for this: She is not standing but floating on her back. Her feet are under the surface of the water. A close examination of the sculpture reveals other anatomical hints to substantiate this idea. Her head is tilted forward, a position that would be natural to floating but awkward in any other stance. Her mountainous breasts and vast buttocks don't hang as they would if she were standing; they seem buoyant.

The theme that all life arose out of the primal waters of creation is woven through the creation myths of almost every culture. It reflects an intuitive knowledge of the origins of life in the shallow primordial sea that once covered the earth.

Linguistic evidence shows that, in early religious systems, water

Venus of Kostenki, ivory, western Ukraine, circa 20,000 B.C.

was considered the life-inducing, fertilizing fluid of conception, supporting the sacred seeds of life. Eliade notes that in the ancient Sumerian language the symbol for water also represents "sperm, conception and generation." Gerald Massey points out that Adam, the name of the Biblical first human, signifies blood, and "*adamu* is now known to signify the principle of female matter . . . that is the mystical water, or matter of life and the red earth of mythology." Thus water symbolized the source of all things, harboring all potentiality. It purified and regenerated; it healed and restored.

As the creator and nourisher of life, woman was also revered as the universal source. In a simple metaphorical transfer, the symbolic properties of water became properties of an idealized divine woman, the rain-bearing, milk-giving Great Goddess embodied in these Paleolithic sculptures. Her womb is the primordial sea from which life first arose. As the faceless first mother, she is the mythical ancestress, beyond time, place, and identity, whose power echoed down through the centuries into historical time.

Most of these sculptures, including the Venus of Willendorf, are coated with red ocher. This symbol of a floating woman painted blood red represents the first religious transformation mystery—woman's mystical transformation of water into blood. She bleeds in rhythm with the moon. When she doesn't bleed for ten cycles of the moon, her blood is transformed into a new being—her waters break and she brings forth new life in blood. A woman past the age of childbearing retains that lunar flow as "wise blood," the wisdom of the crone.

Venus of Laussel, circa 25,000 –20,000 B.C., carved into an entrance of a cave in southern France.

MOON GODDESS

The Venus of Laussel, about six thousand years younger than her sister found at Willendorf, guards the entrance to a cave in southern France. She, too, has a large, fertile body painted blood red. In her right hand she holds a bison's horn in the shape of a crescent moon. This is the oldest image so far discovered associating a Paleolithic goddess with a moon symbol.

The horn is a very ancient symbol of the new moon; two horns together represent the moon's

Moon vulva from Brno, Moravi, carved from a mammoth tooth, found in a male burial, circa 25,000 B.C., painted with red ocher. The circular moon-shaped vulva represented the goddess as the great round of rhythmic birth, life, and death. It was the symbol of the beginning, of wholeness and perfection, the moon, and her drum.

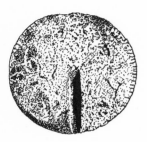

The moon is the primordial symbol of rhythm, for as it waxes and wanes, it exerts real physical influence on the earth and on all who live on the earth, controlling the rhythms of the tides and the blood cycles of women. It is the ultimate symbol of rhythm and the oldest way of marking time.

entire cycle. Its cornucopia shape relates it metaphorically to the sacred vulva symbol. The bison horn is also one of the oldest known musical instruments. In the later Biblical tradition, the *shofar,* a ram's horn, was used to call people to worship and to invoke the power of the deity. It was the horn Joshua used to blow down the walls of Jericho.

The Venus of Laussel's horn is marked with thirteen or possibly fourteen strokes. The number thirteen represents the number of days in the lunar cycle from new moon to full—or the number of days to ovulation in a woman's menstrual cycle. It has further significance in both senses: Thirteen lunar months and thirteen menstrual periods make a year.

Many studies now confirm what almost every woman knows from her own experience—that women who live or work closely together end up synchronizing their menstrual periods. Women living near the equator tend to ovulate during the full moon. It is quite possible that in ancient cultures that were firmly and neatly in tune with the cycles of nature, women menstruated in sync with the moon's cycle as well. In classical mythology, women's menstrual periods are associated with the dark of the moon. In any case, the similarity of lunar and menstrual cycles would have been obvious to women especially. The Venus of Laussel gives us clear evidence that this was understood. Her right hand holds the crescent-shaped horn; her left hand rests on her womb.

In early historical civilizations, lunar symbols wove together three major metaphorical concepts. The first is the idea of fertility. The moon controls the tides of both water and blood—the sacred fluids of early religions. The second is the concept of periodic rebirth, symbolized by the moon's monthly waning and renewal. The third is the notion of continually repeating cycles of change. The five phases of the moon mirror the natural cycle of birth, growth, fruition, dissolution, and death, which is always followed by a new cycle, initiated with birth.

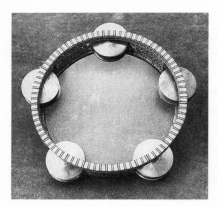

Watching the phases of the moon is our oldest way of marking time. The sun's rising and setting set the daily rhythm of work and rest, but the moon's waxing and waning became a means of counting and marking the cycles of sundays. In *The Roots of Civilization*, Marshack posited the invention of a calendar system based on the rhythm of the moon's phases some fifteen thousand years before the development of agriculture. Once again, linguistic analysis lends support to archaeological theory. Eliade noted that "the oldest Indo-Aryan root connected with the heavenly bodies is the one that means 'moon': it is the root *me*, which in Sanskrit becomes *mami*, I measure."

Traditional Middle Eastern tambourine, with five sets of moon-shaped jingles, representing the five phases of the moon: birth, growth, fruition, dissolution, and death. A five-pointed star within a circle is an ancient Egyptian symbol for the womb of the earth. In the Hindu system of geometrical symbols it represents the element earth and the magic of transformation, which is contained in the power of the womb.

As the primordial symbol of rhythm, the moon stood at the center of an intricate web of meaning tying many different phenomena— water, blood, women, vegetation, fertility, death, rebirth, and rhythm—into a single coherent system. All these symbols were embodied not only in the moon in the heavens but also in the earth-bound Great Mother. That is why, in many traditions, the moon is represented as a goddess playing on her moon-shaped frame drum, spinning and weaving the rhythms of human lives.

MISTRESS OF THE WILD BEASTS

Toward the end of the Upper Paleolithic, during the period from 16,000 to 10,000 B.C., known as the Magdalenian, a cultural revolution swept across the plains of Europe. This may have been due partly to a sharp warming trend between 15,000 and 13,500 B.C., when the climate of western Europe was only slightly cooler than it is today.

Magdalenian culture produced the celebrated cave art of Europe. The cave at Lascaux in central France is perhaps the most famous site,

Cybele with crescent moon from ancient Macedonia.

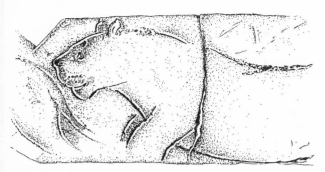

Lioness carved on a fragment of bone from La Vache, late Magdalenian.

but more than a hundred and fifty other painted caves have been discovered so far, mainly in Spain and France.

In dim chambers deep in the womb of the earth, the Magdalenians drew and carved Stone Age bestiaries. Most frequently represented are horses, bison, and aurochs, the ancestors of domesticated cattle, but the cave artists also sketched felines, deer, fish, birds, and serpents, as well as some images of plants.

Most of the decorated caves lie on or near the seacoast or coastal rivers. Since Magdalenian culture appears to have been fairly homogeneous over a widespread area, prehistorians assume a large amount of cross-traffic and communication, probably via the river systems. As tribes expanded, new communities formed around regional centers. Cave art served as a kind of almanac in stone. According to Marshack, it provided a pictorial system of information about the rhythmic life cycles of plant, animal, and human necessary for a thriving tribal culture. Such information-sharing reduced the dangers of any single social group succumbing to starvation.

Magdalenian engraving of a snake on an antler from Lorthet. The snake is linked to the moon because it periodically sheds its skin and is reborn. From ancient times the snake has been a symbol of metamorphosis connected to women and their fertility. She lays moon-shaped eggs—one of the oldest symbols of creation, birth, and rebirth.

The sites of the painted caves functioned as community centers where people from different tribes could meet to perform seasonal rites. These ceremonies, which occurred during the warm seasons—possibly around the summer solstice—unified the tribes and provided an arena for sharing practical, psychological, and spiritual wisdom.

The caves chosen for decoration were obviously revered for their symbolic value. Often they harbor water—underground springs, lakes, or streams—or there are unusual water sources like thermal or mineral springs near their entrances. Most archaeologists think the wavy symbols called meander lines found in many caves were meant to represent water. As we have seen, the people of the Upper Paleolithic venerated water and its associations with the maternal womb, birth, death, and rebirth. This is one of several indications that their painted caves were more than regional social centers: They were sacred sanctuaries as well.

As Mario Ruspoli, the last photographer allowed to document the paintings in the cave of Lascaux, points out, the opening of a cave is an orifice leading into the womb of the earth—surely a powerful natural metaphor to a people who worshiped a Mother Goddess. A ritual cave, he says, "was used as a sanctuary . . . To pass from the external world with its bright light to the deep darkness within is to make the journey into the 'beyond,' where the spirits of deified animals become embodied in the rocky shapes."

Andre Leroi-Gouran, who made the study of cave art his life work, describes the caves symbolically as female entities. His analysis of the paintings themselves divides the animals into male and female imagery. He considers the horse, the most commonly depicted animal, a male symbol, and the bison or aurochs (ancient wild cattle) a female symbol. Both these animals are associated with goddesses of historical cultures. Many of the richly painted chambers of the caves were difficult to reach, and Leroi-Gouran, like Ruspoli, concludes that they were sanctuaries for initiation rites.

Detail of a black bull from the cave at Lascaux, 15,000–10,000 B.C.

Reclining relief of a woman in labor in the cave at La Magdelaine, France, circa 10,000 B.C. Marija Gimbutas describes this figure as "expressions of a woman (and symbolically the Goddess) in labor." This is the earth as mother, giving birth to all beings.

The cave at La Magdelaine, near Penne du Tarn, France, contains images of women, presumably representing a Mother Goddess, in labor. Nearby are images of a mare and bison, also pregnant. The message is clear: The goddess, the embodiment of the bountiful earth, is the original mother of all life—animals, birds, insects, as well as humankind. The goddess as Mistress of the Wild Beasts is a familiar theme in later historical mythologies. As we will see in the next chapter, the goddess began to assume the forms and powers of animals, birds, serpents, and insects even before the beginning of recorded history. The images at La Magdelaine place the origins of this association at least as far back as the Magdalenian period.

ANIMAL MAGIC

Cave paintings contain no scenes of domestic life. They depict, predominantly, animals. Meat was a staple of the Paleolithic diet. The demands of the hunt dictated the rhythms of life. Tribes followed the herd, living in a symbiotic relationship with the animals they hunted. There are indications that both horses and reindeer, the primary food supply, were partially domesticated by the Magdalenian period. Yet we don't find cave paintings glorifying the hunt. They speak of a more mystical human/animal relationship.

Animals, birds, and insects have long been a source of wisdom for humankind. Beavers building dams, spiders spinning webs, the organization of bees and ants in their hives, the group dynamics of herds, the migratory patterns and nest-building of birds imparted useful lessons in survival. This promoted a profound sense of kinship with the animal world. Yet Paleolithic hunters needed to kill animals for food.

Cave rituals may have arisen in part to resolve this contradiction. The cave, womb of the earth and symbol of the Great Mother, was the place where the relationship with animals was honored, purified, and made sacred. The image of the goddess may already have embodied some idea of rebirth. Hunters chiseled their flint spears in her shape, perhaps hoping that she might not only bless the hunters but also recall the beasts they hunted to her domain, there to await rebirth.

Cave paintings are preserved in chambers deep within the earth. Initiates would have had to make their way underground to experience the underworld—the subconscious realms of their minds. The paintings reflected ritual control of natural processes and a means of evoking the mysterious sacred powers of different animals.

Bone carving of a ceremonially dressed dancing male figure possibly playing a flute or bowed instrument, often referred to as a sorcerer, circa 15,000 B.C.

The human beings depicted in cave paintings tend to be either naked or clothed in animal skins. They usually wear masks representing various animals, and seem to be dancing. In one painting there is a male figure costumed as a bull who appears to be playing a musical instrument, possibly a sounding bow or flute. Later in Mesopotamia and Egypt, animals or humans dressed as animals are depicted playing frame drums, sistrums, harps, and other instruments. Archaeologists sometimes describe the figures in the cave paintings as sorcerers or shamans.

Animal orchestra from Mesopotamia.

The origins of shamanism are lost in the mists of prehistory, but shamanistic tribes in Siberia whose way of life is virtually unchanged since the Stone Age provide archaeologists with a model for interpreting signs and symbols found in Paleolithic art. Eliade draws many parallels between some of the Paleolithic images found in caves and forms of shamanism that have survived into the present. He concludes that "the existence of certain types of shamanism during the Paleolithic period seems to be certain." McNeill concurs: "The fact that animism —to give the idea a modern label—is familiar among all peoples despite the enormous variety of their cultures implies that the notion arose very early."

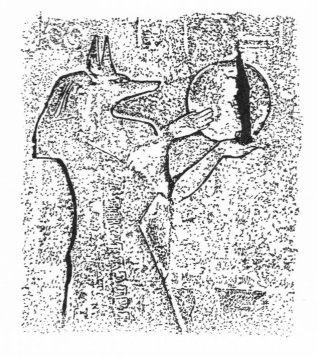

Anubis, the Egyptian jackal-headed god of the underworld, playing a frame drum. Ptolemaic period.

THE SHAMAN'S DRUM

The defining quality of shamanism is the ecstatic experience derived from self-induced trance states, most often reached through drumming. During trance states, shamans enter a world of disembodied spirits existing parallel to the world of the living to ask the spirits to intervene in human events.

Mystics have traditionally sought connection with a primordial vision in caves. By the Eleventh Dynasty in pharaonic Egypt, the necropolis at Thebes included a cave shrine dedicated to the goddess Hathor. Many other Hathor shrines were cut into rock to resemble caves. In Crete, sacred caves were the sites of rituals and initiations, a tradition that carried over into the mystery cults of Greece and Rome. The ancient Cretan goddess Rhea sat in her cave and played her frame drum. Both Dionysos and Zeus were born in caves and nurtured there by dancing priestesses and priests who played the frame drum.

A celebrated and much-discussed scene in the cave at Lascaux depicts what appears to be a wounded bison, a naked man lying on the ground, and a bird mounted on a pole. Many scholars—Campbell, Thompson, Kirchner, Buffie Johnson, and Steven Larson, to name just a few—interpret this scene as a shamanistic trance-induced vision. Kirchner sees the man lying in a deep trance in front of a ritually sacrificed bison, with the bird as his power animal.

In most historical forms of shamanism, the sound of the frame drum generates the trance state in which the shaman travels back and forth among the three realms—the heavens, the earth, and the underworld. The interconnectedness of these realms is universally represented by the Tree of Life, which is rooted in the underworld, bears fruit on earth, and reaches with its topmost branches into the heavens. This central image of shamanism figures prominently in the myths of Inanna, great Mother Goddess of Sumer; in the early cultures of the Indus Valley and Egypt, it also represented the spinal column, the channel through which divine energy traveled in consciousness-raising techniques. The continuing beat of the shaman's drum maintains the link with

In a remote part of the Lascaux cave is a scene interpreted as a bird-headed shaman in a trance experiencing a power vision. A bird perched on a staff next to his body symbolizes the shaman's ability to fly through various dimensions of reality. Circa 20,000–15,000 B.C.

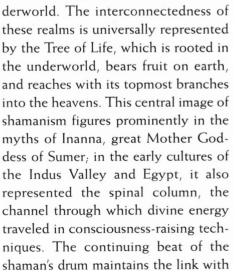

everyday reality so the shaman can safely return to the earth realm of the living.

The drum's beat also beckons and invokes the energies of the spirits. The animal whose skin provides the shaman's drumhead is ritually asked to release its earthly existence and to work with the shaman in the spirit world, to benefit plant and animal communities as well as humans. Thus the drum is not only the voice of the earth but also the voice of the shaman's power animal.

According to Campbell, the inspiration for the design of the drum and the special symbols painted or carved on it traditionally comes to the shaman in an oracular dream or vision. The shape of the shaman's frame drum and the materials from which it is made are highly symbolic. The drum is moon-shaped; its beat represents the inner pulse of all life. The wood of the frame represents the Tree of Life. The wood ideally should come from a lightning-struck tree, symbolizing the energy of the pure self striking through the constructions of the ego into the inner structure of the psyche.

In their travels to other realms to seek healing for their patients, shamans often used the power of the drum to bring back souls from the realm of the dead. Campbell recounts an ancient story of the Buriat people of Siberia in which the Lord of the Dead becomes angry at this continual theft. Observing that the two-headed frame drum gives the shaman this power of resurrection, the Lord of the Dead casts a thunderbolt that strikes and splits the drum in two. For the Buriats, this explains why most shamans' drums are now single-headed.

The Tree of Life—seven branches with birds opening out of the seven chakras. On the central stem is a five-headed cobra sitting on a lotus/sun/wheel symbol. Bulls flank the base. Bronze, India, circa A.D. 1336–1546.

BEHIND THE MASKS

Given the ritual nature of cave paintings and the historical association of shamans with power animals, it is very likely that Magdalenian cave artists were shamans or other prominent religious figures. In a religion steeped in the feminine mysteries of blood and childbirth, we might expect religious activity to be largely the province of women, as was the case in later goddess-centered cultures, yet most research takes for granted that the word *shaman* usually indicates a male.

In *Dawn Behind the Dawn,* Geoffrey Ashe cites evidence from Russian anthropologists and linguists suggesting that, in some parts of the world, the original shamans were women. The clues are hidden in tribal languages. Among the Siberian and Altaic tribal peoples with a long tradition of shamanism, the words for a female shaman are very similar, showing that they derive from the same root. But the words for a male shaman are unrelated. Ashe concludes, "We can infer that these tribes are descended from groups that were . . . in close touch, and then all shamans were women, known by a single term." Later, when men insinuated themselves into the sacred rituals, each tribe had to invent its own word to describe them. Male shamans to this day often dress in the clothing of women.

Handprints found in more than twenty caves throughout Italy, France, and Spain may offer more evidence that women functioned as shamans during the Paleolithic. Often these prints are negative impressions, created by placing the hand on the wall and blowing paint around it, though sometimes a hand is drawn as a positive image. They are very colorful—red or brownish black or violet, even yellow or white. Many scholars have noted that the size of the hands indicates they belonged to women or children. Buffie Johnson, for example, points out that "the hand- and footprints found in the Paleolithic cave of Peche Merle fit the skeletal remains of women." A number of scholars have suggested that the handprints may be the signatures of individual artists. If women painted at least some of the shamanistic scenes and symbols in Magdalenian caves, then we may surmise that the spiritual life of Paleolithic clans was at least partly in the hands of women.

In a religion based on veneration of the female power of creation, the idea of female shamans or spiritual leaders makes sense. Yet the orthodox archaeological community has never seriously entertained that possibility. Their bias is indicative of the almost complete burial of women's spiritual legacy.

I experienced a powerful sense of women's spiritual losses when I attended a performance of traditional songs and chants by a trio of Siberian women. They were tribal people, belonging to a culture that remains in many ways largely unchanged since the Paleolithic. Two of the women looked to be in their twenties or thirties; the third was in her seventies or eighties. Dressed simply in her handmade ceremonial robe, she seemed unremarkable until she picked up her frame drum and led the group in a heartbreakingly beautiful dance and chant. Tears streamed down my face as the incredible power of her drumming and singing flowed through me. This woman, traveling for the first time from her native steppes to midtown Manhattan, conveyed a sure sense of her place and power in the world. I could not help contrasting her with my own grandmother, who spent the last years of her life watching television, afraid to venture out even into her own suburban backyard. I felt sorrow for my grandmother—and also for myself, that she had nothing like this singing and drumming to teach me.

After the performance, I slipped backstage to try to thank the woman for her gift of joy. Dressed in nondescript Soviet clothing, she again seemed unremarkable. Her eyes burned bright in a face that had never known makeup. I doubt she understood how profoundly I had been affected by something that, to her, was so ordinary—singing and playing the drum just as her grandmother had.

The female drummers of Siberia are an important clue that women played drums in earlier shamanistic societies. In their isolated homelands, some Siberian tribes have preserved an ancient way of life that has long vanished in other parts of the world. Studying these tribes has helped archaeologists understand the significance of discoveries like the Magdalenian cave paintings.

It is almost certain that the people of the late Paleolithic had already developed an animistic worldview and practiced shamanism. The rituals and magic of Paleolithic shamans may be the original source of music and art. The Mother Goddesses they sculpted in stone ruled over a spirit realm as well as the physical world.

Excavations have turned up fish-shaped bullroarers, bone and ivory flutes and whistles, and rattles made of strung beads or bone scrapers, but no wooden drums have survived from the Paleolithic. An instrument made of skin and wood would have disintegrated long ago. Yet researchers suspect that drums made their appearance very early in human prehistory. Shamanic and other tribal cultures seem to indicate that percussive sound accompanying chanting or dancing is the oldest form of music. McNeill speculates that drumming may be almost as old as bipedalism, "allowing the first dancers to keep together in time . . . by listening to the tap of a drum—even if, at first, there was only a stick hitting the ground at regular intervals."

Shaman's dress, decorated with brass mirrors, cowries, and bells. Headdress, with horns and bird, and drum had belonged to the elder daughter of the ex-chief of the Numinchen of Mongolia, A.D. 1932. These symbols were associated with women of power from ancient Europe and the Mediterranean cultures from Paleolithic times to the fourth century A.D.

CHAPTER FOUR
··

MOTHER
OF THE
FRUITED GRAIN

MY SEARCH FOR the first appearance of the frame drum led me to one of the earliest known urban cultures, located in a region of what is now Turkey. In these early Neolithic cities, shrine rooms devoted to a Mother Goddess testify to a continuity of religious expression. Frescoes on shrine walls depict scenes of birth and transformation reminiscent of the Magdalenian cave paintings. In these painted visions the energy of the Great Goddess was merging with the mythological powers of animals, birds, and insects. One of these paintings includes the earliest known depiction of a frame drum.

A dramatic climate change that began around 10,000 B.C. put an end to the peaceful, nomadic lifestyle of the Upper Paleolithic. As the warming trends that began during the Magdalenian intensified, the glaciers retreated and melted. The climate turned rainy. Sea levels rose about three hundred feet—the height of a twenty-story skyscraper. Dense, dark forests spread across the grassy plains of Europe, drastically changing the landscape, vegetation, and animal life. The great herds of larger animals so essential to Paleolithic life disappeared. Some species became extinct; others, like the once-plentiful reindeer, migrated farther north. A way of life that had remained viable for thousands and thousands of years was forever altered.

The Mesolithic era, lasting from about 10,000 to 8,000 B.C., was a time of great confusion and upheaval. After at least fifteen thousand years of continuous use, the painted caves were abandoned. There followed a dark age in which the quality of art deteriorated sharply. For several thousand years, people had to adapt constantly to the shifting climate and seek out new food supplies. They fished and domesticated animals, a practice many scholars now believe began during the Paleolithic. Women turned from foraging and gathering to gardening. With this new way of maintaining the food supply, they set the scene for the next great social revolution.

Scene of a drummer, musicians, spirits, and the Great Goddess surrounding a bull, Çatal Hüyük, circa 6000 B.C.

As the traditional sources of meat became more scarce, the grains collected by women became an increasingly important alternate food source. William Irwin Thompson tells us, "Experts agree that in the foothills of the mountains of Southwest Asia, certain forms of wild cereals grew . . . women and children could collect enough grain in three weeks to feed a family for an entire year."

By learning how to cultivate grains, Neolithic women could ensure a reasonably predictable food supply, year in and year out. Unlike meat, grain could be stored against leaner times. Surpluses led to the almost universal practice of animal husbandry. When animals could be corralled in one place and fed with grain, it was no longer necessary to follow the herd. The quest for food had made nomads of human beings for millennia. Now people could settle down in permanent villages.

To store the accumulation of grain from farming, women developed the art of ceramics. (Women's fingerprints on ancient pottery bear testimony to the sex of the potters.) Clay figurines of the goddess and of animals had been fired during the Paleolithic, but it wasn't until the grain revolution that women put this ancient craft to practical use, creating cooking and storage vessels of fired clay.

As their traditional role as hunters became less and less necessary, men turned to trading. Tame, grain-fed cattle could carry enough food to feed groups of traders on long journeys, and excess grain was easily traded. A cross-cultural trade in obsidian, a much-prized volcanic glass, sprang up.

Craft work revived, and there was a vast increase in sculptures—mostly figurines of the goddess, in the tradition of the Paleolithic Venuses. Larger and larger grain surpluses called for more capacious storage facilities, leading to the invention of domestic architecture and the rise of large, permanent communities.

Çatal Hüyük vulva symbol, baked clay stamp seal.

Çatal Hüyük spiral, clay seal.

Çatal Hüyük womb symbol, clay seal.

These great cultural centers of the Neolithic, the first cities, spawned a brilliant renaissance of the religious thought and art of the Magdalenian period.

ÇATAL HÜYÜK

In ancient Anatolia, now the peninsula of Asia Minor in Turkey, two of these early cities—Çatal Hüyük and Hacilar—flourished for at least several thousand years. Çatal Hüyük, inhabited continuously from 7200 to 5500 B.C., is one of the largest known Neolithic sites. It supported at least six thousand people in its heyday. Nestled along the banks of a river that cuts through a wide prairie, it was a homogeneous culture that did not appear to engage in warfare. These people raised domestic sheep, goats, cattle, and dogs. They made high-quality vessels of wood and clay and wove garments of wool. They probably brewed beer and wine, and possibly also mead. Skeletal remains reveal that at least three distinct racial types appeared to coexist harmoniously.

In the early 1960s, archaeologist James Mellaart spent four seasons excavating the remains at Çatal Hüyük. What he found there revolutionized the way archaeologists look at prehistory.

Mellaart uncovered wall paintings, reliefs, and sculptures that disclosed astounding evidence of a peaceful, multiracial, highly developed society whose art and architecture centered around religious rituals and concepts harking back to the ancient Mother Goddesses of the Paleolithic. Previously it had been assumed that the great Paleolithic artistic tradition had disappeared in the cataclysms of the Mesolithic, but Mellaart was able to demonstrate its survival in the art of Çatal Hüyük. He deduced that some of the population of Anatolia must have been descendants of the Magdalenian cave artists.

Mellaart believes that Çatal Hüyük was an extremely important religious center whose religion was created and conducted by priestesses. He describes the hierarchical order of importance in the divine family as "mother, daughter, son and father." Women also seemed to hold the most prominent positions in the social and religious structure of the community. The sleeping platforms of the women of the household were always built into the east wall of the living quarters and were raised slightly higher than the men's, whose quarters seem to shift in location from household to household. A number of women's skeletons have been found painted with red ocher, while only one of the men's burials showed traces of red ocher. Only women were buried with the tools of the artist (often referred to as "cosmetic palettes"), although in a re-creation of everyday life in Çatal Hüyük mounted in a contemporary museum in Berlin, men are depicted painting the shrine panels.

HOLY BREAD

The development of agriculture enriched the worship of the Great Mother. The moon, already her ancient symbol, became increasingly important. Planting and harvesting had to be synchronized to a lunar calendar. As another largely female undertaking, farming also added a new dimension to the ancient Paleolithic religious mysteries. The mythic transformation of water into blood, blood into milk was now extended to include grain, particularly as bread.

Grain bins are found in nearly every household in Çatal Hüyük, indicating that grain had become the main food supply. The germination of grain seeds in dark storage containers apparently generated a new metaphor for rebirth. Ceramic pots used for germination were sometimes fashioned in the form of the goddess, and statues of birthing goddesses have been found in grain bins. Burial within earth pits that had once been used to store grain was common. These associations evoke archetypal images of the Great Mother as vessel, expressing the qualities of giving life, nourishing, containing, protecting.

The women of Çatal Hüyük had learned to bake bread, and no doubt the traditional recipe was passed from woman to woman. But the preponderance of bread ovens in shrines indicates there may have been a sacred bread tradition as well. The baking of bread generated a new metaphor of transformation: grain to flour to dough to bread. The bread oven represented the womb of the goddess, the baked loaf her body. Sacred bread or cakes figure prominently in later religions of the region. The temple complexes of Sumer contained kitchens for the baking of sacred loaves. Ceramic bread molds in the form of the goddess offering her sacred breasts have

Goddess from Hacilar holding her breasts, circa 6000 B.C.

Goddess from Çatal Hüyük shrine wall with concentric circles over womb, circa 6000 B.C.

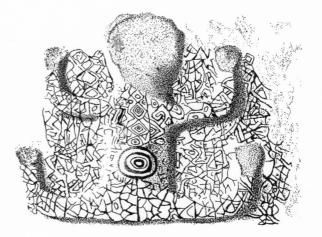

Frame drum from Roman period with concentric circles—the ancient symbol for "omphalos," the Greek word for navel. Many frame drums have womb symbols painted on the head.

been found in later Mesopotamian cultures. During the Thesmophoria, the Greek festival of the grain goddess Demeter, the participants carried cakes of honey and sesame baked in the shape of the vulva. The Christian communion rite preserves this emblem of union with divinity.

Pre-Christian rituals of consuming the body and blood of the goddess made symbolic use of the frame drum, which functioned as the sacred container of grain or food. Since ancient times the grain sieve and the frame drum have been thought to share a common origin. One of the oldest names for the frame drum in the ancient Sumerian language also means grain sieve.

In Egypt, the hieroglyph for a cycle of time or a drum is also part of the hieroglyph that represents grain. A skin tray or sieve used in rites associated with the Celtic grain goddess Brigid is identical to the bodhran, an Irish frame drum. The bodhran is thought to have been used originally in religious processions. To this day in Sicily, the people who make grain sieves also make frame drums.

Grain sieve from gallery exhibit of tambourines in Sicily. One of the origins of the frame drum is thought to be the grain sieve.

THE FIRST DRUM

On the wall of a shrine room at Çatal Hüyük, a band of human figures, clad in leopard skins and playing various percussion instruments, dance ecstatically around a large stag. A second group of dancers ritually sur-

Shrine painting at Çatal Hüyük of dancers clothed in leopard skins with some of the oldest percussion instruments: frame drum, rattle, and struck bow instrument, circa 5800 B.C. This is the earliest known depiction of any drum.

round a gigantic bull. Among this second group is a figure holding a horn-shaped instrument in one hand and a frame drum in the other. These are two of the oldest known instruments in history. Other figures carry bowed instruments similar to the Brazilian berimbau and shakers or rattles. Many scholars have suggested that this scene, dated around 5600 B.C., depicts a shamanic ritual.

The frame drum is central to historical forms of shamanism, as the shaman's voice and tool. Its presence in this scene suggests a similar function in prehistoric times.

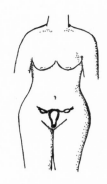

THE GODDESS AND THE BULL

The murals at Çatal Hüyük, like Magdalenian cave art, include no representations of killing animals, only what appears to be their capture. The dominant figure in the art of Çatal Hüyük is a powerful goddess. She is a majestic figure, shown with arms uplifted and legs spread, more often than not pregnant or in the primordial act of giving birth. She is linked with four animal powers associated with shamanism: the bull, the vulture, the bee, and the leopard or lion.

"This figure provides the key to understanding why the bull is linked with regeneration: it is not a bull's head but the female reproductive organs."
—Marija Gimbutas

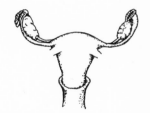

Woman's reproductive system.

The goddess and her bull were at the center of Çatal Hüyük's religious practices. The same image reappears in the mythologies of Sumer, Egypt, and Crete, but it is always clear that, although the bull embodies the fertilizing power of the divine consort, his power derives from the goddess.

It is easy to see how the cow could become associated with the Great

Sumerian cow's head (copper) from Mesopotamia, showing pearl triangular symbol of womb on forehead.

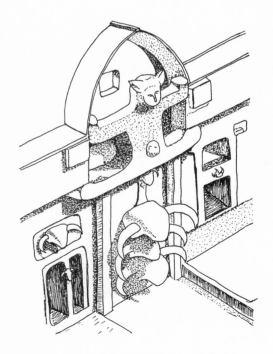

Shrine painting of feline goddess giving birth to bull heads, circa 6000 B.C. Earlier at Lascaux we assumed the cave represented the body of the Great Mother and the painted images of animals were beings within her womb. Here there is a clear depiction of the Great Mother giving birth to the horned animals.

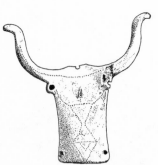

Neolithic drawing of bee goddess on a bull's head carved of bone plate. Ukraine, 3700–3500 B.C.

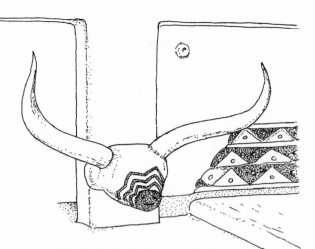

Shrine room at Çatal Hüyük. Bull's head with lotus symbol on mouth, circa 6000 B.C.

Gold bull-head earring in womb or vulva shape. Cypriot design found in Cretan grave, 1300–1200 B.C.

Silver Mycenaean bull-head rhyton with gold lotus symbol of womb on forehead, circa 1450 B.C.

Mother, because she also participates in the miracle of birth and the related mystery of transforming water to blood to milk. Once she was domesticated, her milk also sustained the human community and could even be stored as yogurt and cheese. The ancient association between goddess and bull, though, is more puzzling. Most scholars focus on the bull's role as a symbol of procreation. No animal in ancient Anatolia would have possessed a more impressive phallus. Neolithic efforts to raise domestic herds would have cast paternity in a new light. For breeding purposes, only one stud is needed per herd of cows, goats, or sheep. In fact, to have more than one dominant male in a herd causes violence and chaos, so only the most powerful bull would be kept for breeding. The rest would be slaughtered or castrated. We can well imagine the psychological effects of this practice on the Neolithic male psyche. The idea of the dominant male ruling the entire herd is thought to have given rise to the concepts of kingship and rule by force. Mellaart points out, however, that the religious art of Çatal Hüyük includes no sacred symbols of the phallus, animal or human, that would become common later in India, Egypt, Greece, and Rome.

In a shrine room at Çatal Hüyük is a graphic image of the Great Goddess in the act of giving birth to the horns of great bulls. This is interpreted by some scholars as an extension of the imagery of the Mistress of the Beasts found in the cave paintings of the Magdalenian period. But Mellaart suggests that, to the Anatolians, the horned bull's head may have had a more specific connotation. He bases his theory on his observations of Anatolian burial customs.

The Neolithic people of Çatal Hüyük practiced excarnation: The bones of their dead were left above ground at specific sites until vultures had picked them clean of flesh. Then the bones were buried in the fetal position beneath the bed that the living person had occupied. (This is how archaeologists know who slept where.) Because of this custom, the people of Çatal Hüyük probably had a much better grasp of human anatomy than most people do today. They could not have failed to notice that the shape of a bull's head resembles a woman's uterus and fallopian tubes.

Linked with the ancient association of bull's horns with lunar and menstrual cycles, this would make the bull's head a vivid symbol of the female power of birth. It also explains why mythology is replete with images of goddesses giving birth to bulls and cows nursing human beings. The emphasis is not the bull itself but the female reproductive system it invokes.

It has been suggested that the sacred shrine rooms at Çatal Hüyük were used for childbirth as well as initiatory rites of rebirth.

Terra-cotta Apulian bull-head rhyton, circa 360 B.C.

THE VULTURE GODDESS

As later chapters will demonstrate, the first historical cultures worshiped many female deities, representing the Paleolithic goddess's fundamental aspects of creation, preservation, and regeneration. At Çatal Hüyük, the goddess makes her earliest appearance in the archetypal form of the vulture. The Anatolian vulture goddess partakes of all these

Vulture shrine, Çatal Hüyük, circa 6000 B.C.

functions: She gives birth, she protects, she consumes and resurrects. Later, the vulture goddess Nekhbet, who ruled Upper Egypt, was one of the primary goddesses of the Nile River Valley. A shrine fresco at Çatal Hüyük shows a pack of vultures swooping down on headless corpses. They are not painted black, the natural color of vultures, but red, the color of life.

The vulture goddess represents one of the oldest mythologies of death and resurrection—one that lies at the heart of initiation rites. As vulture, the goddess does not kill. She consumes the dead in order to transmute the soul once again to life, in the form of an egg. The sacredness of the egg as a symbol of regeneration goes back further in time than we can trace. Birds are twice-born. First the mother lays the egg. Then the chick breaks out of its shell, in effect giving birth to itself. This second birth enables it to soar into the higher realms as a winged being.

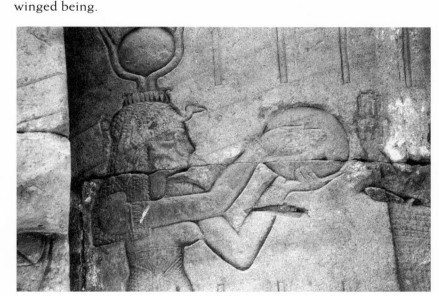

The Egyptian goddess Hathor with her vulture headdress playing a frame drum. The oldest hieroglyph for the goddess of Upper Egypt is a vulture.

The bird goddess, freed from the gravity of earth, moves through the vastness of heaven—the magical realm where weather originates. The behavior of birds was studied for indications of changes in the weather. Eventually birds were thought to be the messengers of deities able to control the weather, and the bird goddess was often consulted for weather omens. People probably learned to sing by copying the melodies of birds, and traditionally it is always a goddess associated with birds who brings the gift of music.

The ancient mythological path of the bird goddess is a process of breaking forth from outgrown structures of personality and behavior, just as the chick breaks out of the outgrown shell. This is the basic metaphor of initiation. Until that shell is broken, what lies outside must remain unknown.

Once broken, the shell can never be put together again. It is the wisdom of no return, the womb cracked open, lost forever in the initiate's rebirth as a winged being whose spirit can fly through the shaman's three realms of heaven, earth, and underworld. And music, particularly drumming, is always present in the rituals of initiation.

Because the bird goddess has dominion over all these realms, giving her knowledge of the past and future, she is the source of prophecy. Later, in Mesopotamia, Egypt, Cyprus, Crete, Anatolia, Greece, and Rome, priestesses of bird goddesses used the frame drum to enter the trance state from which they could divine the future.

In time, the frame drum of the bird goddess will be recognized as the symbol of the egg of beginning, the ultimate symbol of creation. She strikes her drum, and the egg breaks open. Her drumbeats measure the first heartbeat; the sustaining rhythms of life; the fading away of the pulse.

Ultimately, the wings of this vulture goddess will become the wings of angels.

Bird goddess from Cyprus playing a frame drum, circa 1000 B.C. Women learned to sing by turning the bird's songs into lullabies, laments, and chants.

QUEEN BEE

The Anatolian goddess is often shown wearing a beehive as a tiara, most frequently at Hacilar. This is the introduction of a motif that would flourish in historical times. Of all the insects represented in the ancient world, bees are foremost in ritual and symbolic meaning. They, too, represent birth, death, and reincarnation.

Bees have an acute sense of time. They appear to use their internal circadian clocks in conjunction with the sun's position in the sky to navigate. Because their time memory is so advanced, they can be trained to appear at certain times of the day for feedings. An individual bee within the hive can communicate the location and richness of a newly discovered food source by dancing and drumming with its wings. The queen bee, deep in the hive, lays up to two thousand eggs a day, but only a few male drones mate with the queen—and just once, since the sexual act ends in his death. All these properties are echoed in historical rituals and mythologies, and will be explored further in the next section.

A panel at one of the shrines at Çatal Hüyük shows a honeycomb filled with eggs or chrysalises and with bees that transmute to butter-

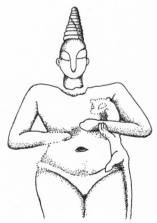

Goddess holding her young feline wearing a beehive as a tiara. Hacilar, ancient Turkey, circa 6000 B.C.

IN THE BEGINNING

flies. This painting appears to illustrate the concept of metamorphosis as a religious metaphor. If this analysis is accurate, it would suggest that the religious aims of the community may have included transformation of consciousness through initiation rituals—a common goal of pre-Christian religions.

The goddess's tiara announces her status as queen bee and suggests that she streams with honey, a much-revered substance in ancient times. At the Arana Cave near Valencia, Spain, a Paleolithic painting survives of two men taking honey from a rock wall. In later cultures, honey was poured over thresholds and temple foundations, offered to goddesses and gods, and used in medicines and burials.

The priestesses of historical descendants of this ancient bee goddess —Demeter, Rhea, Cybele—were called *melissae*, the ancient Latin word for bees. The Bible mentions a ruler and prophetess of ancient Israel called Deborah, the "Queen Bee"; her priestesses were known as Deborahs as well. Erich Neumann, in *The Great Mother*, says the priestesses of the moon goddess were called bees because "it was believed that all honey came from the moon, the hive whose bees were the stars." Mastery of the frame drum was a primary spiritual duty of these priestesses.

DIVINE FELINES

The leopard or lion is also associated with the Anatolian goddess. At Hacilar, goddesses are shown holding young felines like infants. A small statue of a goddess enthroned on a pair of lions was found in a grain bin at Çatal Hüyük.

Traditionally, lions are guardians of the passageway to the realm of power and wisdom. They guard the gate that separates the sacred from the profane, the sanctuary from the outer world, the living from the dead.

Some of the dancers in the shrine painting depicting a frame drum are cloaked in leopard skins. In shamanic traditions, lions and leopards are spiritual beings called to this realm by the shaman's drum. Initiates in a trance state are symbolically ripped to pieces and devoured by these divine beings, or by leopard-clothed initiators: That is, their personalities are ripped to shreds. When resurrected, initiates are also dressed in the skin of the animal, signifying passage to a new life. In a metaphorical sense, they now possess the feline power to stalk their character flaws ruthlessly, obliterating the limitations of past selves. In time they may mature into masters of initiation—who are very often also masters of the drum.

ANIMAL POWERS

The people of Çatal Hüyük did not necessarily believe that cows, vultures, bees, and lions were literally goddesses, but these animals were not simply metaphors either. The ancients thought that birds and animals were manifestations of a natural power stronger and wiser than human beings. The swallow doesn't just herald the spring; it is the spring. Vultures are death waiting to swallow us, simply to transform us once again into eggs.

Neolithic religions arose from intent observation of the natural world. People learned by identifying with other creatures, studying their rhythms and adaptations to the environment. From watching the bees, they learned how to organize a group, and to build the beehive shelters found in many parts of the world. From birds they learned to sing, and to yearn for flight. Fish gave human beings the idea of navigation through water.

The mystical relationship between humans and animals was expressed in the social order. Clans were identified by their power animals, or totems. Classical scholar Jane Harrison pointed out that

LEFT: Terra-cotta enthroned goddess flanked by sacred felines, found in a grain bin, circa 6000 B.C. The earliest representation of the Anatolian goddess who would be known as Cybele.

RIGHT: Roman Cybele with lions and frame drum from Ostia, circa A.D. 250–280.

totemism stands for fusion, for nondifferentiation. It is based on a recognition of a common nature and a collective participation in the energy of nature—a sense of oneness that embraces the nonhuman world.

There were many ways to partake of the power of animals and birds —by eating their bodies, by wearing their skins and feathers—but a more powerful way was by modeling their behavior or imitating their sounds. This emulation of other creatures is what researchers believe is the origin of human dance and music.

The remnants of religious life found in the cities of Anatolia represent a bridge between what can be deduced from the cave paintings of the Upper Paleolithic and what is known about early historical religions. The primordial Mother Goddess is clearly merging with the cow and bull, the vulture, the queen bee, and the lion. This marks the beginning of her evolution into the many goddesses of classical times. Each attribute of the goddess represents a means of understanding the natural world and how our consciousness is structured by this world. Like the endless reflections in a hall of mirrors, these images lead back to the primordial image of the psyche—the original energy complex behind all thought.

The many symbols of the goddess are signposts along a path of wisdom much older than recorded history. It is a path of comprehending the nature of reality and of coordinating the self with the sacred order. If these ancient archetypes of natural power seem strange to us now, it is an indication of how far removed we have become from the universal rhythms and images of nature. Just as the drum reminded our ancestors to observe and respect and rejoice in the power of nature, so it can help us today to remember and celebrate our origins.

Beehive-shaped houses in the Neolithic village of Khirokitia in Cyprus.

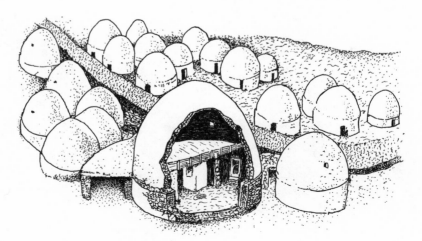

FOLLOWING PAGE: Illustration of Raga Bhramarananda, circa A.D. 1750.

PART III

İn History

My Singer, from that earthen drum,
What sweet music you bring
From the earthen drum of my body.

FROM A FOLKSONG OF THE PARDHANS OF THE
UPPER NARMADA VALLEY

They strike the sacred drum for her,
*   the sacred timbrel—*
Stand forth before holy Inanna.

FROM "THE HOLY ONE," A SUMERIAN PRAISE POEM

I am the Soul, the creation of the primeval Waters . . .
*   my nest was unseen, my egg was unbroken.*

FROM THE EGYPTIAN BOOK OF THE DEAD

CHAPTER FIVE

THE LOTUS GODDESS

Egyptian goddess Sekhmet with a frame drum in a procession of deities holding musical instruments as offerings. Egypt, Ptolemaic period.

BETWEEN 4000 AND 3000 B.C., three civilizations sprang up on the banks of powerful rivers that wound through dry desert lands. Near the Indus River and its tributaries, in modern-day Pakistan, the Harappan culture appeared. Between the Tigris and Euphrates rivers in southwest Asia Minor, an area the ancient Greeks called Mesopotamia, the Sumerians built their cities. Along the Nile the unified kingdom of Upper and Lower Egypt emerged.

The written texts and art forms describe in detail the continuing evolution of the goddess. The frame drum emerged from the women's religions of prehistory to become the symbol of the goddess as creatress of the universe. The frame drum is clearly depicted in the hands of various goddesses and her priestesses. The sacred technology for synchronizing mind and body through the power of drumming and rhythm is at the root of her oldest religions.

Excavations have unearthed a multitude of goddess figurines dated from 7500 to 3500 B.C. in the Neolithic villages that were developing in all three river basins. Between 3500 B.C. and 2000 B.C., this Great Mother emerged as the goddess of the temples of early religions. In Sumer, she was worshiped as Inanna. In Egypt, she was known as Hathor. In the Indus Valley, she was the inspiration for the early Hindu goddesses.

In earlier times, the mouths of rivers, caves, and mines were likened to the womb of the Great Mother. This ancient link is preserved in the languages of the river cultures. In Sumerian, *buru* means both "vagina" and "river." The Egyptian word *bi* means "vagina" and "gallery of a mine." The Babylonian word *pu* signifies both "vagina" and "source of a river."

As noted in the last chapter, Çatal Hüyük society was multiracial. Some of these same racial types are to be found among the four races of the Indus River Valley, as well as in Mesopotamia and predynastic Egypt. James Mellaart, the archaeologist who excavated Çatal Hüyük, feels that the evidence of early Egyptian religious attitudes, as expressed in texts and archaeological remains, suggests the

Harappan sculpture, circa 2500 B.C.

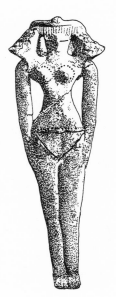

Egyptian votive offering for the goddess Hathor, circa 2000–1500 B.C.

Egyptians could have been descendants of the Çatal Hüyük people. I have traced a continuity of symbols from Çatal Hüyük into all three river valley cultures.

Peter Crossley-Holland, writing about the excavations at Mohenjo-Daro and Harappa, states, "During the Chalcolithic age (c. 2500–1500 B.C.) a people related to the Sumerians flourished in the North and formed the so-called Indus Valley Civilization. . . . Among their remains are figurines of dancers and women drumming and an ideograph of an arched harp of early Mesopotamian type."

There is substantial evidence of a brisk trade in goods between Anatolia, Mesopotamia, Egypt, the Aegean, and the Indus Valley during the third millennium B.C. Artifacts made in Mohenjo-Daro around 2300 B.C. were found at Troy, at Tel Asmar in the Mesopotamian city-state of Eshnunna, and in a tomb in the Sumerian city of Ur. Mesopotamian weapons turned up in Mohenjo-Daro. Seals from the Indus Valley have been unearthed at Tel Asmar and at Susa, capital of Elam, in present-day Iran. Steatite necklaces painted with identical designs appeared at Knossos on Crete and at Harappa; Egyptian beads turned up in the Indus Valley. Records show that two Mesopotamian kings of the period were in contact with Mohenjo-Daro. With all this cross-cultural interaction, it's reasonable to speculate that trade had commenced at a somewhat earlier period, and these ancient civilizations had long-established lines of communication.

The similarity in religious symbolism and mythology among Indus Valley, Mesopotamian, and Egyptian peoples is striking. It suggests a shared spiritual and psychological belief system that points to a common origin in the Paleolithic.

Cycladic sculpture, marble, circa 3200–2700 B.C.

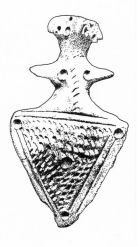

Terra-cotta figure, India, second century A.D.

THE HARAPPANS

The Indus River Valley was the cradle of a vast and highly developed civilization. Several thousand sites have been excavated to date. Five of them are large enough to be designated cities. They were founded sometime before 3800 B.C. and flourished for thousands of years without apparent change or innovation. Such continuity suggests the existence of a strong, unchanging religious/administrative organization—one that was firmly in place before these cities evolved.

Harappan culture extended far beyond the Indus Valley, covering an area roughly the size of western Europe, making it by far the most extensive of the river cultures. Its two main cities—Harappa, on the Ravi River, a tributary of the Indus, and Mohenjo-Daro, on the Indus itself—were culturally identical; they were even laid out according to

Terra-cotta figurines from ancient Syria, middle of third and beginning of second millennium B.C.

the same ground plan. By 2500 B.C., Indus Valley civic and domestic architecture was as advanced as anything to be found in contemporary Mesopotamia or Egypt. Many of the houses had bathrooms, and the intricate sewer and sanitation systems appear very modern in character. Historian Gordon Childe considers Harappan technology equal to the accomplishments of both Mesopotamia and Egypt.

So many figurines of Neolithic goddesses have been unearthed from the Indus River Valley that it's likely every household had one. Some of these figures carry drums. A bird-headed figure holds what looks like a *kanjira*, the present-day South Indian frame drum that is about five inches in diameter. Another sculpture is clearly a woman playing a small barrel-shaped drum.

More than two thousand surviving seals and seal impressions depict Harappan customs and beliefs. Some scenes show a goddess associated

Bird-headed frame drummer from Mohenjo-Daro.

with wild animals, plant life, and the fertility of crops, reminiscent of the Magdalenian Mistress of the Beasts.

Harappan art already has an "Indian" look. Many of the elements that later formed the content of Hinduism are already present in the images of sacred animals, trees, water, and symbolic representations of the sexual organs of goddesses and gods. Archaeologist Sir John Marshall finds the religious imagery so characteristically Indian that it is difficult to distinguish from Hinduism. Eliade, writing about the statuary of Harappa, notes, "The cult of the Mother Goddess is particularly prevalent . . . the latest types [of goddess figurines] resemble Kali-Durga, of whom they are probably the model."

GODDESSES OF THE VEDAS

The Harappan civilization was not, strictly speaking, a literate culture. Archaeologists are uncertain whether markings found on some seals represent counting systems or some early form of language. Until they are deciphered, we must look for information about Harappan religion in the scriptures of its direct descendant, Hinduism.

Archaeologists agree that the roots of Hinduism are very old. According to Kinsley, the Hindu tradition is the "richest source of mythology, theology, and worship available to students interested in the goddess." Danielou says, "In India it is still possible to relive and understand the rites and beliefs of the Mediterranean world and the Middle East in ancient times."

In India, despite centuries of cultural upheaval, Hinduism has preserved an unbroken history of goddess worship, music, art, and techniques for the development of consciousness. Drumming and rhythmic chanting are a fundamental aspect of these techniques. This ancient culture provides a useful context for interpreting the remnants of goddess traditions and the role of drumming in her worship throughout the Mediterranean world.

During the second millennium B.C., Harappan cities were virtually destroyed by the repeated attacks of Aryan or Indo-European invaders who swept across Europe and the Indian subcontinent. The impact of these incursions on indigenous cultures will be discussed in Chapter 10. Refugees from the cities of the Indus Valley fled to remote villages throughout rural India, bringing their goddess with them. Despite attempts by the invaders to impose their own patriarchal religion, the aboriginal religion based on a Mother Goddess dominated the synthesis of the two religious systems that came to be known as Hinduism. The Vedas, Hindu religious texts compiled after the invasions, circa 1500 to 800 B.C., describe how the goddesses were perceived.

The Hindu goddesses of the Vedas embody many qualities of the older Paleolithic and Neolithic goddesses—qualities they share with their Mesopotamian and Egyptian counterparts. In all three river cultures, cow goddesses wear horned headpieces or crowns, representing the crescent moon—symbol of the natural principle of rhythm, connected with the menstrual cycle and the regenerative power of the goddess.

Usas, the Vedic cow goddess, is called the light of dawn that illuminates the world. Like the Paleolithic Venuses, she is the mother of all animate beings, and nourishes them on the milk of divine wisdom.

Laksmi, goddess of fertility and abundance, shares many qualities with the Egyptian Hathor. Both are often depicted sitting on a lotus; both represent the primal waters and the maternal, procreative aspect of reality. The scholar Heinrich Zimmer compared Laksmi with Sumerian Inanna, calling her "the Mother Earth of old . . . she is a sister, or double, of the well known goddess of early Sumero-Semitic Mesopotamia."

Vac is the power of ritual speech, and also the capacity for speech. She is called the mother who gives birth to beings by naming them. She sometimes manifests as a sacred cow. Through the repetition of mystic sounds, she maintains the world's order.

Sarasvati was originally a mighty river goddess who blessed, cleansed, and purified, washing away all defilements. In this form she recalled the Venus of Willendorf, floating on her back, who represented the fertilizing and life-inducing energy of water. From earliest times, religious rituals have been performed on the riverbanks of India. As the "stream of grace," Sarasvati was also associated with clouds, rain, thunder.

Later, Sarasvati lost her early association with water and absorbed the qualities of Vac. She now embodies the principles of art, music, poetry, literature, sacred rituals, and communication. Radiant, floating in her lotus, she enriches the natural world with civilization—a func-

Indian goddess with damaru, A.D. 1680–1698.

tion also assumed by Hathor in Egypt, Inanna in Mesopotamia, Cybele in Anatolia, and the Muses in Greece.

Durga, the warrior goddess, rides on a lion and carries a *damaru*, a small double-headed, hourglass-shaped drum used in meditation practices. Zimmer describes the damaru as "Sound, the vehicle of speech, the conveyer of revelation, tradition, incantation, magic, and divine truth." He associates this sound with the element "ether" or space. "Out of it unfold, in the evolution of the universe, all the other elements, Air, Fire, Water and Earth." Sound together with its medium of space gives rise to the universe. Durga riding on her lion drums the world into being.

Damaru.

Lions are associated with the goddess in many cultures. Inanna is often depicted standing on the back of a lion. Hathor sometimes manifests as Sekhmet, the lion-headed war-goddess; Cybele is typically depicted either flanked by lions or in a lion-drawn chariot. The lion was among the power animals depicted with the goddess at Çatal Hüyük, and as we have seen, lions and other felines have been represented in ritual contexts dating back to the Paleolithic. All of these lion goddesses are associated with the drum that leads the initiate deep into the labyrinth of the mind in search of expanded states of awareness. At the threshold of the descent stand the great feline guardians.

YOGA

The fundamental goal of all forms of Hinduism is the reintegration of the individual with the universal through the expansion and development of consciousness. The ancient discipline of Yoga, which means "communion, becoming one with the object in mind," is the means to this end. There are a number of Yogic techniques—some meditational, some ritual, some physical. They include rhythmic breathing, rhythmic chanting of sacred sounds, and the practice of physical postures that enhance the energy systems of the body. Their origins are ancient: Deities pictured on seals excavated in the Indus Valley are found in characteristic Hatha Yoga postures.

Female marble figurine in Yoga posture, early Aegean Neolithic, circa 5000–3500 B.C.

Metaphorically, the practice of Yoga recalls much older rituals of initiation. It entails a rejection of the conventional concerns of life and of the social personality. This death of the profane self facilitates transcendence, or rebirth into the divine.

Among the most ancient principles of Yoga is ritualized, rhythmic speech. Through the repetition of certain sounds, the practitioner creates vibratory rhythms within the body that energize the brain and the nervous system. The sequence of syllables or sound frequencies used is called a *mantra*. The mantra of a specific goddess or god is equivalent to the energy of the deity itself. To repeat a mantra ritually is to invoke and enter into the consciousness of the goddess. Hindu mantras, often chanted to the rhythms of a drum, have been passed from student to teacher for thousands of years.

The sacred mantra *OM* is considered the seed syllable of created existence. If intoned correctly, it vibrates the cranium and the cerebral cortex of the brain, causing a sound similar to the humming of bees. This mantra and its sound are linked to the omphalos, the great beehive—the place of sacred utterance and the buzzing vibration of life. The concept of the omphalos will be explored in detail in later chapters.

The bee, already associated with the goddess at Çatal Hüyük, is an important element of Hindu cosmology. The Maha Devi—literally, "Great Goddess"—manifests as a queen bee or as a divine being surrounded by bees. In this form she is known as *Bhramaridevi*. Kinsley points out that in Sanskrit literature the bee symbolized erotic desire, and Bhramaridevi may also carry this association.

The traditional Yogic cleansing practice called *Bhramari*, in which the practitioner vibrates the entire nervous system, brain, and body by buzzing the vocal chords, imitates the buzzing of bees. Its aim is purification through realignment of the brain's functioning. I studied this practice with a South Indian Yogi, Swami Bua, years before I unearthed its connection to the ancient goddesses.

Later I experienced a similar state of consciousness while wandering through the ruins of Ostia, the ancient seaport of Rome. The mazelike ruins stretch on and on for acres. I began to feel very much alone. I stood at a junction of a number of paths, uncertain which to take, when a small snake darted past me into one of the enclosures. I followed it and found the remnants of a mosaic floor patterned in the form of a circular mandala, an ancient Yogic symbol. I sat in the center of the mandala and started to follow my breath, letting the slow rhythm settle my mind. A passing bee hovered directly in front of my face. The gentle rise and fall of

Female Neolithic sculpture from Crete in traditional Yoga posture.

A relief from Sanchi, India, with an omphalos, also called a stupa, decorated with lotuses under a sacred tree.

its buzzing led me to deeper and deeper levels of nonthought, until I entered into a realm of pure sound.

TANTRIC YOGA

In the fourth and fifth centuries A.D., a form of Yoga now referred to as *Tantra* became popular in India. It centered around Shakti, the feminine aspect of cosmic energy. According to Eliade, Shakti is the resurrected Great Goddess of aboriginal India—the channel through which the spirituality of the ancient religion of prehistory flowed into Hinduism. Her return signaled a triumph of indigenous religious thought over the suppressions of the Aryan invaders.

With the revival of Tantric practices came a recovery of the sacred mysteries of womanhood. Shakti is the active principle of energy and creativity residing in every woman. She is balanced by the static masculine principle of Shiva. As Universal Mother, Shakti powers the continual process of creation, preservation, and destruction. The force driving this process is desire. Desire constantly pushes, pulls, and attracts the world into being. Tantric disciplines, practiced in Hindu and Tibetan Buddhist cultures to this day, seek union with the divine through the primal force of desire.

Like all forms of Yoga, Tantra seeks to expand awareness. The initiate must become conscious of the cultural conditioning and programming that has shaped her awareness. Through meditation and other Tantric practices, the subconscious patterns that color thoughts and feelings, define perceptions, and propel behavior become clear. From knowing her inner self, the practitioner attains a sense of inner peace, harmony, and order that is reflected in a harmonious relationship with the world.

One of the fundamental premises of Tantra is that the body and its desires are not to be rejected but recognized as sacred. Although not widely practiced today, Tantric disciplines include sexual techniques and practices. Through these practices, the body and its sexual energies become a vehicle for transforming and expanding consciousness.

Initiated priestesses who performed the sacred Tantric rites in the temples of the goddess were known as *Veshyas*. "Rites were centered around the physical worship of woman, and the organs of sex in the woman's body became the *kestra*, the enclosed field of power, itself the instrument of magic and transformation," says Pupul Jayakar, a specialist in Indian cosmology.

The bindu, a black dot, represents the seed, the omphalos, the pulse, the supreme consciousness from which the entire universe springs.

The bindu expands through the radius of desire, the power that brings the world out of its sleeping seed state. As expansion into material form occurs, an individual consciousness condenses out of the cosmic consciousness.

Paleolithic moon vulva.

Greek frame drums, circa fifth century B.C. In the language of yantra the circle also represents the primordial water (blood) out of which everything arises.

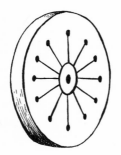

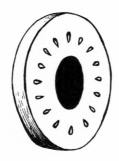

In Tantric meditation, the traditional chanting of mantras is enhanced with visual concentration on geometric forms called *yantras*—literally, instruments to hold the mind's attention. Chanting a mantra and focusing on a yantra at the same time is a means of aspiring to the desireless state of mind free from thought. Released for a time from familial and cultural ties, freed from the constraints of personality, the practitioner seeks a return to the origins of consciousness.

One of the oldest yantras is a circle with a dot in the center. The dot, or *bindu*, represents the unmanifested energy of the universe, out of which the world is created. The *nada-bindu* is the primal sound from which creation begins. This is the concept symbolized by the sacred egg of creation and the frame drum of the goddess.

The symbol of a circle with a dot in the center can be traced back to the Paleolithic. In Madhya Pradesh, a state in the central interior of modern-day India, archaeologists discovered a circular platform supporting a stone in the center of a triangular form, dating from around 10,000 to 8000 B.C. (In the language of the yantra, the downward-pointing triangle retains its ancient meaning of the vulva of the goddess, whose womb gives life to all creation.) This is the oldest shrine of the Great Mother excavated as yet.

More complex yantras, called *mandalas*, are labyrinthian. To enter one is to begin a process of initiation. The mandala serves as a receptacle for the energy of the deity. It is a point of communication between the three cosmic zones of heaven, earth, and the underworld.

The goddess Kali's yantra, Rajasthan, eighteenth century A.D. A yantra is a symbolic representation of the energy pattern of a deity, in this case the cosmic vulva of the goddess. When the deity is invoked through a mantra, rhythmic repetitions of sound syllables, it becomes the residing place for the essence of the deity.

THE SEVEN CHAKRAS

The energy of the goddess—the *kundalini*—sleeps coiled, snakelike, at the base of the spine. In the Sat-Cakra-Nirupana (a sixteenth-century A.D. text), she is said to be creation, existence, and dissolution, the consciousness behind the universe: "She is beautiful like a chain of lightning and fine like a lotus fibre, and shines in the minds of the sages. She is extremely subtle; the awakener of pure knowledge; the embodiment of all bliss, whose true nature is pure Consciousness." At times she is described as riding on a lion and holding a damaru drum; at other times she is symbolized by a downward-pointing triangle radiating the light of ten million flashes of lightning.

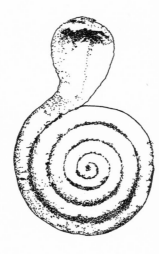

Coiled serpent shrine from India, fifteenth century A.D.

LEFT: Kundalini serpent goddess, Indian limestone relief, pre–sixth century A.D.

BELOW: Diagram of the chakras.

When the energy of the kundalini is awakened through Yogic practices, it travels up the spine in a rush of fire, heat, and light, through seven spiritual or psychic centers called *chakras*. The chakras are located along the path of the autonomic nervous system, which governs the body's involuntary or subconscious actions. Eliade, in discussing the heat kindled by the rise of the kundalini through the chakras adds, "It is well known that the production of 'inner heat' is a very old 'magical' technique, which reached its fullest development in shamanism."

Each chakra represents a higher level of spiritual development. The first chakra, *Muladhara*, is connected to the energy of the element earth; the second, *Svadisthana*, to water; the third, *Manipura*, to fire; the fourth, *Anahata*, to air; the fifth, *Visuddha*, to ether; the sixth, *Ajna*, to the unified field of pure light. The seventh chakra, *Sahasrara*, is the realm of pure light, and represents the enlightened consciousness of ultimate reality that is the goal of all Yogic practices. The Sahasrara is the altar where the goddess and god unite in a powerful orgasm of healing, expanding, and uplifting energy.

RIGHT: **Design from the handle of a predynastic Egyptian flint knife.**

BELOW: **Sumerian steatite vase with entwined snakes, circa 2130 B.C.**

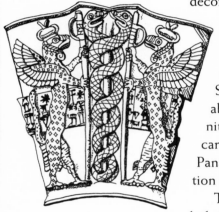

RIGHT: **Symbol of the Kundalini Shakti from an illuminated manuscript, Rajasthan, circa eighteenth century.**

BELOW: **Greek frame drum with lotus design, circa 400–300 B.C.**

The ancient symbol of this process is a pair of intertwined serpents coiled around a staff. The staff is the spinal cord; the points where the serpents' bodies cross are chakras.

The cobra as the serpent form of the goddess is a shared motif in Egyptian and Indian religious imagery. Intertwined pairs of serpents are found in the art of early Mesopotamia and predynastic Egypt as well as the Indus Valley. A Mesopotamian goblet belonging to King Gudea of Lagash, dated about 2600 B.C., is decorated with this symbol.

In the ancient world, the symbol of entwined serpents stood for the power of sexuality as a healing experience. It evoked the ritual marriage of the female and male principles—Shakti and Shiva—in a union that ensured fertility, abundance, and well-being for the whole community. The Greeks, who named the symbol the *caduceus*, carved it on the temples of the healing deities Hygeia, Panacea, and Asclepius. Today, the American Medical Association displays the caduceus as its logo.

The chakras are symbolically represented as lotuses, another symbol shared among the river cultures of the third millennium B.C. The lotus is an ancient image of the womb or vulva, and it retains this meaning in Hinduism. The flowering of the lotus symbolizes the birth and unfolding of the self and the expansion of pure consciousness. The vulva represents ecstatic pleasure as a means of union with the divine state of the Great Mother. In this sense, transcendent sexual ecstasy becomes a deeply religious experience. It reveals the mysteries of sexuality in which Neolithic religion was rooted.

In Buddhism, a religion that also drew on the aboriginal traditions of pre-Aryan India, the vulva, or *yoni*, of the goddess represents a "matrix of knowledge" that leads to wisdom. From the yoni, the undifferentiated stuff of creation emerges as something differentiated, fully developed, and evolved.

The matrix of creation and becoming is also represented by the swastika, an ancient symbol of the goddess. These wheel-like figures are first seen in the Paleolithic, and appear in all three of the early river valley cultures. They have also been found decorating archaic pottery in Cyprus, Rhodes, and Athens.

Swastika is a Sanskrit word meaning "so be it," or "well it is." In ancient times the symbol represented safety, security, and protection. It stood for the wheel of life—the eternal cycle of birth, growth, fruition, death, symbolizing the continuity of the soul through many incarnations—and was the point of intersection between the living and the dead. Swastikas combined motion and direction, representing the four points of the compass and the constantly turning cycles of the natural world. (Unfortunately, Adolf Hitler turned this ancient rhythmic symbol of life and creation into one of murder and horror for many people of the twentieth century.)

A drum from a Greek red-figured vase, circa fifth century B.C.

The lotus, swastika, bindu, and downward-pointing triangle, all representations of the womb of the goddess, are often found painted on ancient frame drums. They mirror the symbolic meaning of the frame drum—a circle of vibrations that give rise to the world.

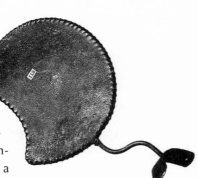

Goddess with swastika over her womb found at Troy, Anatolia, third millennium B.C.

SACRED SOUND

In India the influence of rhythm and tuning on consciousness has been explored for thousands of years. Music began and developed as a spiritual technology. It was considered another form of Yoga—Nada Yoga, which is based on the belief that ultimate reality resides in vibration. The physical world is a manifestation of different frequencies of this root vibrational energy. Human beings, as part of that world, are also essentially vibration, and subject to the same laws of sound. In Tantrism, a tiny sliver of a crescent moon represents this first vibration. The nada is the State of Power that the Yogi experiences in deep internal meditation that manifests in the human heartbeat. When this Sound of Power is heard, one is hearing the resounding echo of the universal power of life manifesting within the sound of one's own heart. The goal of Nada Yoga is communion with this pulsing vibration behind all sound—the bindu—the point out of which everything arises. The heartbeat behind all heartbeats. This communion aligns individual resonance with the resonance of undifferentiated reality.

Chandrapirai frame drum, symbol of the crescent moon, worn on the player's forehead, A.D. 1889, southeast India. It was used in the temples of the goddess Mariamman.

Music created from the study of Nada Yoga principles harmonizes everything in its presence. In humans, it achieves this by vibrating the matrix of the brain and nervous system. The most powerful and developed musicians can virtually open the inner psychic centers of the listener and create a spiritual awakening.

Indian classical music is based on ancient traditional rhythmic patterns that reflect the relationship of sound to time—not clock time, but the eternal cycles of birth, growth, fruition, dissolution, and death. India's rhythmic system is considered to be the most highly developed in the world, in particular for its extensive and logical treatment of the various principles of movement in time, known as *tala*. The tala refers to a recurring dynamic rhythmic sequence that comes to an end by finishing on the first beat of its cycle. The tala moves one into a timeless rhythmic awareness of cyclical existence.

LEFT: Women playing barrel drum and small frame drum (kanjira), India, sixteenth century A.D.

RIGHT: Raga Bhramarananda, circa A.D. 1750. Woman playing frame drum to man with buffalo horn, surrounded by bees dancing under a sacred tree.

Raga is an equally ancient concept of musical modes. Each raga is a group of sounds, a musical scale, that evokes a particular emotional state. The word *raga* means "passion," and each raga is believed to color and penetrate the mood of the listener. According to Danielou, "[Their] influence can be strong enough to bring about physical and psychological transformations."

Each raga is complemented by an archetypal visual image. The visual counterpart to the *Raga Bhramarananda*, for example, shows a

woman playing a tambourine to a man under a sacred tree, while bees buzz around him. The man has a buffalo's horn slung over his shoulder. The root word, *bhrama*, of this raga (also the root of the goddess *Bhramaridevi*, and the Yogic cleansing practice *Bhramari*), refers to "the sound of the absolute, of undifferentiated reality . . . which is reminiscent of the sounds of bees buzzing." The woman playing the tambourine and the man's buffalo horn are ancient symbols of the primordial sound at the heart of existence.

Contemporary festival for the goddess Durga surrounded by lotus symbols.

Contemporary ritual in India honoring the goddess.

The use of frame drums in Indian music is very old. Music historian Peter Michael Hamel says that "the significance of the drum, even in the earliest beginnings of Indian culture, is made clear by a comparison of Buddha's in which he likens the eternal laws of the universe to the rhythm of the drum."

In ancient India, music and drumming were at the center of the world's oldest continuing religion. Although the wisdom traditions from ancient Egypt and Mesopotamia have been lost, I believe that these cultures shared a spiritual and psychological science of mind/body consciousness with India.

These three river valley cultures sprang from the shared root religion centered around the old goddess of the Paleolithic. In India, despite repeated invasions, Hinduism has preserved an unbroken and continuous history of goddess worship, music, art, and the Yogic practices for the development of consciousness. This preserved wisdom provides a means for interpreting the goddess traditions and the role of music in her worship throughout the ancient Mediterranean world.

CHAPTER SIX

THE QUEEN
OF HEAVEN

THE SUMERIAN CITY of Uruk, sacred to the goddess Inanna, was the site of the earliest known written language—the place where "history" begins. Ancient Sumerian texts describe rituals involving drumming and the making of sacred drums. They give us the first named drummer in history—Lipushiau, the highest ranking priestess in the city-state of Ur.

Sumerian urban culture arose sometime between 4000 and 3000 B.C. on the alluvial plains between the Tigris and Euphrates rivers (the area the Greeks called Mesopotamia, "the land between the rivers"). Its people developed all the hallmarks of civilization: writing, literature, educational and legal systems, the technology of the wheel, specialized crafts, elaborately engineered irrigation systems, calendrical astronomy. Yet until the end of the last century, when the first evidence of this ancient culture was unearthed, the accomplishments of the Sumerians were erased from our memories.

The cities of Sumer housed twenty to fifty thousand inhabitants. The people raised donkeys, cattle, goats, sheep, and pigs. Donkeys and cattle were used for plowing the fields to cultivate the main crops of wheat, barley, and date palm. During the harsh summers, all vegetation died away, so it was essential to store fodder and grain to feed both human and animal populations. The Tigris and Euphrates were wild and unpredictable rivers, with recurrent flash floods and radical shiftings in their course. The culture was therefore somewhat precarious, experiencing continual water shortages at the beginning of the growing season and periodic flooding at harvest time. Such large populations could exist in this inhospitable landscape only in an artificial environment sustained by irrigation, agriculture, and animal husbandry, yet the archaeological record shows that the cities grew up around monumental temple complexes built before the development of irrigation.

Historian Robert M. Adams speculates that the impetus for urbanization may have come from "new patterns of thought and social organization crystallizing within the temples." The temple complexes were erected on holy ground, at "power spots" where people had converged to feel the presence of divine energies since Neolithic times. They were centers of pilgrimage where communication between the heavens, the earth, and the underworld took place; where priestesses and priests—technicians of the sacred—could, through the power of ritual, drumming, and song, act as conduits for the divine.

TEMPLE GROUNDS

Conceptually, the temple was an extension of the Paleolithic cave. Through the gate of the outer walls one entered into the womblike interior of the divine. The inner temple was a replica of the original shrine, a simple reed hut, though later it was constructed of more lasting materials. It was built on a raised platform that later became the pyramidlike ziggurat.

Mesopotamian terra-cotta figure of a woman with frame drum. Second millennium B.C.

Joseph Campbell describes the ziggurat as the central point in the center of the sacred circle of space, where the powers of earth and heaven join, a concept similar to the Hindu symbol of the bindu. It was a tower of stepped platforms, its corners oriented to the four directions of the compass. In the sacred inner temple at its summit the *hieros gamos*, the most important religious ceremony of the year, took place. By night, the high priestess received the prophecy and revelations of the deity in this chapel. (We don't know what ritual she used to call down the voice of the deity, but it's very likely that it involved drumming. As we will see, the high priestesses of Sumer were proficient drummers, and the prophetesses of later cultures borrowing from Sumerian traditions used drums.)

Drummer from Nippur, circa 2000 B.C.

The inner temple was surrounded by many chambers where ritual offerings were prepared. A complex of workshops, medical facilities, storerooms, and administrative offices grew up around them. Rectangular or, in a few examples, oval walls enclosed the main building of the complex. (Campbell felt that the oval walls constructed in some temples were meant to suggest the goddess's vulva.) Within this walled enclosure were the homes of the priestesses and priests, the kitchens where ritual cakes were prepared, granaries, wine stores, wells, and the barns for the sacred cattle.

Initially, the ground plans of the cities that evolved around this core were an earthly reflection of the divine order. They were laid out around the temple in a circular plan, divided into four quarters, with the ziggurat, the symbol of creative power, at the center. Temple and city were thought of as one unit, named "The Link Between Heaven and Earth." No other architecture compared in size or complexity to these compounds until the rise of the palace cultures of the later Sumerian kings.

With the advent of cities the priesthood developed into a complex hierarchy that controlled and administered the economy based on the storage, exchange, and redistribution of communal goods. This temple priesthood governed early Sumerian society and it appears that women held a high and respected place within the hierarchy. A group of priestesses called the *naditu* owned real estate and served as scribes, temple accountants, and money lenders. The earliest known example of writing is an account of payment for land rental discovered in the temple of Inanna at Uruk. It has been dated at around 3200 B.C.

The invention of writing is attributed to Nisaba, goddess of "writing, accounting and scribal knowledge," as well as a grain goddess. Similarly, the Egyptian goddess of writing, Sheshat, is called "she who is foremost in the house of books." Another name for Sheshat is Sefhet, meaning seven, and her symbol is a flower of seven petals. At the founding of a new temple, Sheshat's priest established the ground plan with a measuring cord. In both Egypt and Sumer, temples of the goddesses were centers of learning. Inanna's great temple in Uruk was called the House of Knowledge. It's been hypothesized that priestesses developed written language as an extension of the lunar calendars they used for marking menstrual periods and months of pregnancy.

The spiritual head of the temple was the *en* and could be either a woman or a man. The en of Inanna's main temple at Uruk was a man; the en of the Ekishnugal, the moon god Nanna's temple at Ur, was a woman. In 2380 B.C., the en of the Ekishnugal was Lipushiau, the granddaughter of King Naramsin. She was also designated the player of the *balag-di*, which Curt Sachs, the eminent musicologist, identified as a small frame drum used in liturgical chanting. That makes Lipushiau the first named drummer in history.

Terra-cotta of Astarte from
Gezer, Syria-Palestine
1200–900 B.C.

FACES OF THE GODDESS

Ancient Sumerian texts describe many deities both female and male, but one goddess was revered above all others for thousands of years.

This is Inanna, the Great Goddess worshiped from the beginning of Sumerian culture. She is transformed into Ishtar in later Mesopotamian periods; Anat and Atagatis in ancient Syria; Ashtoreth and Astarte in Canaan and Israel; Aphrodite in Cyprus; Athena and Aphrodite in Greece. In Mesopotamia, she splinters into many goddesses, but there is always an overlapping of qualities and attributes that lets us know this is the One with Many Names.

Nammu is the Mother Goddess who gives birth to the sky and the earth, the great ancestress who brought forth the gods from her womb. Her name is signified by the pictograph representing the primordial sea. She resembles the nurturing mother represented in the Paleolithic Venus of Willendorf. Ninhursaga is the Earth Mother, titled the Mother of All Children, the one who creates and gives birth—not only to all people but to all wildlife as well. She is also referred to in written texts as the mother of all the gods, an overlapping of functions with Nammu.

As the cow goddess of the early dairy temple, Ninhursaga nourished the Sumerian kings with her divine milk, probably produced by the sacred temple cows who were her manifestations. Her temple was called Kesh, meaning "protection" or "sanctuary."

In her role as the goddess of childbirth, the goddess is sometimes called Nintur, a name which has been translated as Lady Birth Hut. This name includes a sign that appears to be a drawing of the birthing hut in a cattle pen. The Sumerian word for sheepfold represents the birth house inside the sheepfold, the womb, and the vulva. According to Thorkild Jacobsen, her emblem, which was "shaped like the Greek letter omega, has been convincingly interpreted from Egyptian parallels as a representation of the uterus of a cow." Nintur's epithets include Lady of the Womb, Lady of Form-Giving, Lady Potter, Carpenter of the Insides, and Lady of the Embryo. She is the awesome power of the womb, which makes the embryo grow, giving a unique form to each being.

As Inanna, the divine female is represented as the beautiful, aristocratic young goddess of erotic love and fertility, and later of war. She shares characteristics with Ninhursaga in that she manifests in the corral, the sheepfold, and the cattle barn, shelters that became the first temples of the ancient cow goddess.

Inanna as rain goddess floating and offering her breasts, illustrating the mystery of water into blood into milk.

Vulva symbol, Middle Assyrian votive offering from the temple of Inanna/Ishtar at Ashur.

Inanna is also a rain goddess, and her power in this respect is shamanistic. She can bring or withhold rain. She controls the thunder. "I step onto the heavens, and the rain rains down; I step onto the earth, and grass and herbs sprout up," she sings. Clouds were called the "breasts of the sky." Thunderstorms were manifestations of Inanna's wrath, loud with the roars of her animal allies, the lion and the bull—power animals associated with the goddess at Çatal Hüyük. Traditionally, the frame drum was used to invoke rain by mimicking thunder.

Cylinder seal of Inanna on lion, circa 2334–2154 B.C.

Like the Hindu goddess Sarasvati, Inanna is credited with endowing humankind with civilization—a reflection of women's primary role in creating culture. Her gift is called the *me*, or mother-wisdom. These are the principles that control and set in motion cultural patterns that give rise to civilization.

Ereshkigal, goddess of death, is Inanna's mirror opposite, her dark shadow. She embodies the hidden, raging, and destructive aspects of the goddess, which Inanna, like all women, must learn to respect and acknowledge as part of herself.

SYMBOLS OF THE GODDESS

Inanna preserved many of the ancient symbols of the Paleolithic and Neolithic goddesses. She was titled the First Daughter of the Moon and she wore the lunar horned crown, often formed with seven superimposed pairs of horns. These horns show her as the ancient cow goddess. She often stood with one foot on her lion or rode upon the lion, the ancient guardians of the thresholds of consciousness. She was also identified with Venus, the morning and evening star.

Rosette from the temple of Inanna/Ishtar at Ashur, Middle Assyrian period.

Inanna was known as the goddess of the date palm. There was always a living tree growing within her temple compound that was cared for as the Tree of Life. Inanna appears with the dove and the serpent. Since ancient times the bird and snake were connected with the gift of prophecy, the power of rebirth, and the Tree of Life.

The rosette, one of the oldest symbols connected to Inanna, appears in Uruk before 3000 B.C. Many rosettes were found at her temple in the city of Ashur, from the Middle Assyrian period (1350–1000 B.C.).

Older representations of rosettes were composed of seven dots, with six arranged around one in the center.

These seven dots or stars, which often appear with depictions of Inanna, date back to the earliest periods of Sumerian culture. Later the seven dots are arranged in two rows of three dots, with the seventh dot placed between the rows at one end. These dots are thought to represent the Pleiades, but also the seven gates Inanna passed through into the underworld and possibly the concept of the seven chakras. Another star symbol with eight points was known from the prehistoric period through the Neo-Babylonian period as the symbol of Inanna.

Inanna also appears standing on the back of her lion holding lotuses. These flower symbols along with the rosette represent the vulva or womb of the goddess, out of which pours the waters of creation. In later cultures we repeatedly see these types of symbols painted on the heads of frame drums. (Only one representation of a frame drum with a symbol painted on it has survived from Mesopotamia. This drum was painted with the symbol of a swastika and played by a woman.)

Star symbol of Inanna/Ishtar.

RITUAL MUSIC

The cyclic energies of the seasons and the year were comprehended, remembered, and preserved in the rhythm of the temple rituals. Keeping the urban population in close touch with the processes of nature was one of the primary purposes of the rituals performed by the priestesses and priests of Sumer. Inanna's temple at Uruk was acoustically designed to enhance the effectiveness of the rituals that took place within its walls. The temple itself acted as a transformer, amplifying the sacred music and chanting.

Mesopotamian plaque, circa 2100 B.C.

Music played an essential role in temple rituals and also in daily life. The primary instruments that were used included frame drums, larger drums, lyres, harps, cymbals, sistrums, and flutes of metal and reed. The drum is particularly prominent in religious texts.

"Small hand drums, played by women, we know of from the earliest

Drummer from Megiddo
(present-day Israel), circa
1000–800 B.C.

Yemenite musician bringing his
drum on the pilgrimage to
Mecca, photo taken between
A.D. 1867–1885.

periods of Sumerian culture," says music historian Walter Wiora, "and they surely derive from a Neolithic tradition."

Scholar Joan Rimmer describes a large number of figurines and plaques of women holding "flat circular objects." She interprets these as frame drums. "These figures have generally been interpreted as being connected with the cult of the Mother Goddess, and the circular objects as being either votive disks or tambours [frame drums], which were almost exclusively women's instruments even in Greek and Roman times. There are a few examples in which an indisputable tambour is realistically represented, held to one side and actually beaten. It seems probable that the tambour, whether used to mark the rhythm of chanting or dancing or both, would have been played by skilled, professional priestesses or cult leaders."

These sculptures of women with frame drums have been identified as "woman with votive disk" or most often "woman with cake." There is a traditional position of holding and playing the frame drum still practiced today in Morocco, throughout the Middle East, and into Turkey that looks identical to the position labeled "woman with cake." Furthermore, anyone who has actually baked a cake would only attempt to carry it in this position once.

Sumerian frame drums are referred to as painted red, the sacred color of blood. There is also a linguistic connection with the word for copper. This may imply that the drums had jingles or a metal-covered frame. We can't say with certainty that frame drums had jingles attached, making them tambourines, until the Roman era, but sistrums —rattles with metal jingles—appear in close relation to the frame drum in the earliest representations of musical instruments.

Harps found in the tomb of Queen Pu-abi (or Shub-ad) at Ur are the earliest complex instruments so far recovered. Queen Pu-abi and her consort, King A-bar-gi, were buried in ornate tombs around 2700 B.C., along with their attendants—about sixty-five for the king and twenty-five for the queen. Both parties included a number of female musicians with their instruments. The attendants are richly dressed in courtly attire. There are no signs of violence and it is almost certain that they went to their deaths voluntarily. Scholars conjecture that, after performing some ritual, they drank a poisonous drug and simply went to sleep. The harpists were found

Lotus bowl, gold, from the
tomb of Queen Pu-abi, circa
2700 B.C.

sitting or lying beside their harps, as if they had continued to play to the end. One of these harps is decorated with a carved scene of an animal orchestra, in which a *jerboa* (a doglike animal) is playing a sistrum. In her lap is a frame drum. There is also a cylinder seal which depicts Queen Pu-abi with the women of her court or priestesses who are playing harp and frame drum.

Inlay from the sound box of a bull-headed harp from a tomb of the Royal Cemetery at Ur, circa 2700 B.C.

The *balag-di*, the small frame drum played by Lipushiau in the temple of the moon god, was used as accompaniment to liturgical chanting, in ceremonies to ward off calamity, and at religious celebrations. The *balag*, a larger drum, was set up in front of the temple of the goddess Babba (or Bau) on New Year's Day. This drum was named *Nin-an-da-gal-ki*, the Mistress of Wide Heaven and Earth. Babba's symbol is the winnowing fan used for cleaning grain.

In a song describing how Inanna should be received in her sacred city of Uruk, the goddess sings:

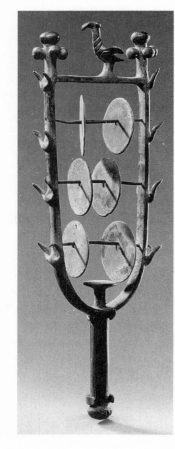

> *Let the drum and tambourine resound.*
> *Let the sweet* tigi-*music be played.*
> *Let all the lands proclaim my noble name.*
> *Let my people sing my praises.*

She goes on to enumerate her gifts, over a hundred in number, including the gift of music and specifically of drums:

> *She brought the* tigi- *and* lilis-*drums.*
> *She brought the* ub-, *the* meze-, *and the*
>   ala-*tambourines . . .*

In the hands of a skilled drummer, the beat of ritual drums could heighten dramatically the emotions behind the words. Ancient texts describing temple music seem to consider the drum and voice the music's completion. The sound of the drum and voice could "assuage the tears" and "soften the sighing." In processionals on ceremonial occasions, the drum's sound "calmed and uplifted the men of the city."

LEFT: **Sistrum from the ancient Near East or central Anatolia, circa 2300–2000 B.C.**

The drum was also a means of attracting divine attention. A Hittite inscription describes a ritual in which a female cymbal player takes the drum to summon the gods. (The Hittites were a second-millennium B.C. Anatolian culture heavily influenced by the Sumerians.) The drum's voice summoned and then became the voice of the deity.

From about 2500 B.C., offerings to Inanna were placed on an altar shaped like an hourglass drum, suggesting that in earlier times they were actually placed on a drum. This practice also implies that the drum was central to the overall well-being of the temple-based society.

Kalu priestesses and priests were the musicians and singers of the temples. Their function was to invoke the benevolence of the deity by the chanting of hymns or liturgies to the accompaniment of musical instruments, including the harp, the lyre, the flute, and the drum. An inscription on a tablet dedicated to Ishtar translates, "the *Kalu*-priests, all of them stand around with flute and drum [*lub-dub-ta*]." In a lamentation over the destruction of Nippur, the psalmist is directed to "sing to the drum [*balag*]." A worshiper says, "To the little drum [*ub*] and to the large drum [*a-la*] I sing."

Singers and musicians underwent a three-year course of training, and it's likely that high priestesses and priests studied for a much longer period.

Babylonian drummer, circa 2000–1594 B.C.

THE DARK OF THE MOON

Texts from Uruk record an occasion when the sound of frame drums calmed and reassured the population during an eclipse. Their effectiveness was probably related to the familiar use of drums in monthly rituals. In the Third Dynasty of Ur, the reigning queen was responsible for ritual offerings to the moon during the three days it goes dark at the end of its cycle. This was a time of lament, when the moon was believed to be in the underworld. Its resurrection was initiated by the sound of drumming.

This monthly ritual drumming may also have facilitated the flow of menstrual blood. Menstrual cycles and lunar cycles retained their

Terra-cotta figurine of woman with frame drum, from Ur, early second millennium B.C.

ancient association; references from the ancient world suggest that women normally menstruated en masse at the dark of the moon. Since the Paleolithic, menstrual blood had been considered a powerful magical substance for invoking resurrection or rebirth. It was believed that the concentrated bleeding and drumming of the priestesses had the power to draw the moon back, and simultaneously make the earth fertile. Describing contemporary folk traditions in India, Pupul Jayakar states, "Blood fecundates the earth and through a magical process of alchemy transforms it into rain and food."

THE SACRED GRAIN

We've seen how the rise of agriculture extended the central Paleolithic transformation miracle—water into blood into milk—to include bread. Just as in Çatal Hüyük bread ovens were installed in the shrines, in Sumer the confectioners' bakeries were attached to the temples. There, cakes used in temple rituals were prepared. According to historian George Contenau, these bakers also "made the sacred cakes which the worshipers of the goddess Ishtar [Babylonian Inanna] crumbled and left for her doves."

Grain was considered the embodiment of Inanna and flour was a sacred substance ground from her body. It was used extensively in magical or religious rituals. Healing rites took place within the protection of a sacred circle of flour sprinkled on the ground. The circle symbolized the protective power of the goddess and prevented evil from entering. Flour was also scattered on the ground in divination and exorcism rites. Cone-shaped heaps of flour, sometimes mixed with whole grains, were offered to the deities, or used as symbols of the goddess during ritual invocations. Dough made from flour and herbs symbolized the goddess during ritual invocations, and ceremonial figurines baked from this dough and placed in the magic circle of flour invoked her protection.

Incantation rituals to ward off negative energy also began with the drawing of a magic circle of flour. Next came the purification of the patient by bathing, smudging, or fumigating with incense. Then the circle was swept clean. Negative influences were driven away by the beating of a drum and the ringing of bells. (The drum's ritual connection with flour and grain is reflected in one of the Sumerian words for the frame drum, which also means "grain-measure.") Food and incense were offered to the deities. Finally, rites specific to the patient's needs were enacted, followed by closing rites returning her to everyday reality.

The first documented use of barley-based beer is found in Sumer, although it's hypothesized it was known to the people of Çatal Hüyük. The effort needed to collect wild barley or cultivate it has led some archaeologists to propose that beer rather than bread was the motivation for the development of agriculture. A praise poem to the grain goddess almost seems to substantiate this. It says, "Nisaba, you are the beer—far more than the bread."

Another poem from about 1800 B.C. dedicated to the goddess of beer, Ninkase (her name means "you who fill my mouth so full"), gives us the ancient recipe for brewing beer. The Sumerians baked a pungent, sweet barley bread called *bappir* and made beer from it.

Beer was probably originally used as a divine intoxicant, imbibed ritually. The combination of an intoxicating beverage and the trance-inducing effect of drumming and chanting was used for thousands of years as a means of attaining an ecstatic, euphoric state. Inanna is linked to the beer tavern. Hathor is the Golden Goddess of Intoxication. In Crete and Greece, the *maenads*, female worshipers of Dionysos, used wine as a sacred intoxicant equivalent to the blood of the god, as they danced to the sound of the flute and frame drum. Today, in Christian rites, wine still represents the blood of Christ.

HIEROS GAMOS

On New Year's Day, the Sumerians celebrated the *hieros gamos*, or sacred marriage rite—the most important event on the religious calendar. The bride was the goddess Inanna, who manifested in the person of her high priestess; her consort was the vegetation god Dumuzi, represented by the local king. To the resounding beat of frame drums played by temple musicians, heaven met earth within the bodies of the priestess and king. Together, through a reenactment of the original sexual act that brought the universe into existence, they regenerated the world.

The ancient Sumerians called this festival *a-ki-til*, "the power to make the world live again." Essentially, it celebrated the law of eternal return, exemplified by the cycles of the moon—Inanna's father—and echoed in the rhythms of sacred drums. Inanna, as the Lady of the Granary, the Power in the Storehouse, was the active principle of birth and fertility. Dumuzi was the life potential within the crops and produce. Their union ensured abundance and plenty for the community throughout the year to come.

Sacred marriage plaque, circa 2000 B.C., Elam, southern Mesopotamia.

Before the marriage rite was celebrated, however, the community had to be purified of the negative actions, ritual faults, and transgressions of the old year. Also, the goddesses and gods responsible for the destiny of the new year had to be honored. Only then could the new year be ritually celebrated.

The sacred consummation took place in the golden wedding bed in the primeval hut atop the ziggurat. Through the sexuality of the goddess, the world was once again brought into being. The divine energy engendered by the ecstatic act of sexual union and orgasm flowed directly into the community. It ensured the fecundity of crops; it filled the rivers with fish and the marshes with birds; it promised fertility and happiness for the population.

The ritual marriage of Inanna and Dumuzi recalls the Tantric union of Shakti and Shiva, whose ecstatic coupling, a metaphor for the merging of the Yogi's psychic energy with the energy of the cosmos, took place at the crown of the seven chakras. The Sumerian marriage hut where Inanna and Dumuzi consummated their sacred union sat atop the seven-stepped ziggurat. In both cultures, sexual union with the goddess was a metaphor for the release of healing spiritual, psychological, and physical energy. As we have seen, this concept was at the heart of primeval sexual mysteries. Later the *hieros gamos*, the yearly marriage between a grain goddess and her consort, became a familiar rite among Mediterranean cultures.

SACRED SEXUAL PRIESTESSES

The divine experience of sexual ecstasy was not solely the province of goddesses and gods. In the temples, sacred sexual priestesses could initiate any man into this experience. The priestess's body, as vessel of the goddess and dwelling place of her power, was a sacred means of initiation. Many female singers and dancers served in the temple in this capacity. Mastery of the frame drum was among their accomplishments. It symbolized their ability to incarnate the creative power of the goddess.

Julius Evola, an Italian scholar, says that the fundamentally physical act of sexual intercourse was transformed by ritual and ceremony into a powerful religious event. The priestess maintained her affiliation with the goddess, transferring her virtues to the initiate. It was a rite of communion with the deity, not unlike the Christian sacrament of the Eucharist.

Terra-cotta figurine of nude woman with frame drum, from Ur, early second millennium B.C.

The tradition of sacred intercourse endured as Inanna became Ishtar, Anat, Ashtoreth, Aphrodite. It had its counterpart in the temples of Hathor and Isis in Egypt. Sexual priestesses called *devidase* practiced in India until quite recently.

"In early history the body as a whole, as well as each separate aspect, was sacred," says Maria-Gabriele Wosien. "Food, drink, breath and copulation were regarded as sacred channels for the power to enter man."

To serve as a sexual priestess was an honor, and those chosen were sometimes called "holy virgins." In pre-Christian goddess cultures, the term meant that they were unmarried; their sexuality was dedicated to the service of the goddess. Many of the priestesses were from aristocratic families. The current view of morality, however, makes it difficult for many historians to understand sexuality as an expression of divinity. As a result, sexual priestesses are commonly labeled prostitutes, concubines, or courtesans—insulting words that misrepresent the sanctity of a widespread ancient rite. To dismiss sacred sexual initiation as prostitution is untenable.

INANNA'S DESCENT

An ancient poem from Nippur, a spiritual and cultural center in Sumer, recounts the story of Inanna's descent into the underworld. Recorded in written language around 1750 B.C., it was recovered and translated early in the twentieth century. It preserves a very old version of an initiation myth.

In the middle of her reign as Queen of Heaven and Earth, Inanna decides to descend into the underworld, the realm of death ruled by her dark sister, Ereshkigal. In preparation, she instructs her minister, the goddess Ninshubar, to watch for her return in three days. If she doesn't come back, Ninshubar is to lament and beat the drum for her.

Woman with frame drum, from Nippur, circa 2000 B.C.

Inanna must pass through seven gates in her descent. At each gate she is forced to surrender elements of the *me*, the constructions of cultural and social identity. By the time she reaches the throne room of Ereshkigal in the cavelike underworld, she has been stripped naked and brought low.

Ereshkigal and the seven judges of the underworld surround the now-powerless goddess and pass judgment against her. Because she has trespassed in the realm of the dead, she, too, must die. She is killed and left a rotting corpse, hanging on a meat hook.

After three days and nights, Ninshubar sets up a lament, beating the drum to petition the gods for Inanna's return. Enki, the water god of wisdom, sends two asexual spirits to free Inanna by sprinkling on her the food and water of life. When Inanna is resurrected, she is allowed to leave—on one condition: She must send a replacement for herself to the underworld.

Inanna's consort, Dumuzi, has taken advantage of her absence to consolidate his own power. In retribution, Inanna sends him to the underworld in her place. But Dumuzi's sister, Gestinanna, bargains with Inanna and is granted the boon of taking his place for six months out of the year.

The religious symbolism of *Inanna's Descent* mixes the archaic traditions of shamanism with elements that recall Yogic techniques and symbols. In the words of the ancient poem, Inanna turns her ear (which, in the Sumerian language, also means her mind) from "the Above to the Below"—from the conscious to the unconscious. Her midlife passage into her deepest, innermost self entails the shamanistic sacrifice of her persona—the storehouse of personal history—in order to gain further knowledge and wisdom.

The essence of shamanistic initiation rites is the experience of death and rebirth. Siberian shamans, whose practices have remained virtually unchanged since the Stone Age, undergo an initiatory illness and dissolution of personality culminating in a "death" during which they lie in an inanimate state in a lodge or isolated place for three to seven days. They are restored to ordinary consciousness only after an experience of initiation.

The Hindu Yogini also experiences a rebirth into the eternal present only after she has sacrificed her personal consciousness. Her journey is to the self beyond conceptions, where the "below" of the unconscious and the "above" of the conscious are united in a new identity.

The seven gates through which Inanna descends into the underworld mirror the seven levels of the ziggurat, the seat of Inanna's power and accomplishments in the outer world.

Like the seven chakras of the Hindu psychic body, the seven steps of the ziggurat represent seven levels of consciousness. Inanna must descend from the highest level of divinity back to the most primitive state of consciousness. At each gate she must surrender aspects of the *me*—the mental trappings of cultural identity that are useless in death—until the dissolution of her personality structure is complete.

Inanna remains dead for three days and three nights—the same length of time that the moon "dies" at the end of its cycle. (This aspect of ancient initiation myths is reflected in the Christian tradition of Christ being dead for three days.) While she is dead, all fertility ceases. Nothing grows or mates.

When Ninshubar beats the drum to petition for Inanna's release, she is enacting a very old shamanistic rite. Drumming is the traditional means used by shamans to descend to the underworld and to return. Often during a shamanic trance the shaman's assistant takes over the playing of the drum to maintain the link between worlds. Without the sound of the drum to lead the way, the shaman would be lost forever in the underworld.

The ancient water god revives Inanna with the food and water of life. To quote Sylvia Brinton Perera, Inanna emerges "restructured, reborn in an inner process and connected to the full range of feminine instinctual patterns."

Her revival prefigures the resurrection rites of the mystery cults that flourished in the classical world, in which initiates received new life through the body and blood of the deity. It is symbolically reenacted to this day in Christian communion rites.

All of the female figures in this myth are aspects of the one Great Goddess, the Divine Feminine. Inanna is the compelling, seductive goddess of love and sexuality; Ereshkigal is her opposite, a manifestation of the dark forces of dissolution and death. Nin-

Syrian or Phoenician pyxis showing musicians in procession toward a goddess. (See illustration on page 11.) From Nimrud, circa ninth century B.C.

shubar is the conscious aspect of Inanna, responsible for providing the thread of rhythm for her return through the labyrinth of consciousness. Gestinanna represents her aspect as caregiver who sacrifices herself for her loved ones.

Dumuzi's position as Inanna's consort is interesting. His attempt to usurp Inanna's throne is dealt with swiftly. Inanna is obviously the greater power here, and can easily sanction the sacrifice of her husband to maintain her own autonomy.

In other versions of this myth, Dumuzi is killed by evil forces, and his wife, mother, and sister are left to mourn his descent into the underworld. Dumuzi is the god of vegetation, and his death was commemorated ceremonially in Sumer during the brutal summer months. The chief mourners—then, as always, women—would grieve dramatically, dressing in rags, covering themselves with ashes, and tearing at themselves as they chanted ritual lamentations to the sound of their frame drums and reed flutes. These ceremonies of ritual grief, which brought about the joyful resurrection of the vegetation deity, served as a powerful catharsis for the community.

The drum and flute were also used in funeral rites for ordinary citizens, and female, drum-playing figurines were often interred with the body to facilitate rebirth.

Religious texts from Sumer help scholars trace the evolution of the goddess of later cultures back through the river cultures to Çatal Hüyük, to their roots in the Paleolithic. Initiation myths very like *Inanna's Descent* were central to many of the mystery schools that sprang up a little later around the Mediterranean. They are found in the rites of Isis and Osiris, Cybele and Attis, Aphrodite and Adonis, Demeter and Persephone, Ariadne and Dionysos. The alternating presence and absence of the goddess or god became a means of understanding the process of life and death. In all of these traditions, the frame drum was the primary instrument that invoked the trance states necessary for transformation.

CHAPTER SEVEN

THE GOLDEN ONE

WOMEN HELD HIGH and important positions in ancient Egypt. There were great woman pharaohs, and great priestesses who wielded enormous political and economic power. Their civilization endured for many thousands of years, much longer than the early Harappan or Sumerian civilizations. From her earliest incarnation as a Neolithic cow goddess to her final form as Isis, central figure of a popular mystery cult, the goddess pervaded Egyptian religious history.

The dry desert climate has preserved a wealth of architecture, art, and artifacts that speak to us of Egyptian life, including numerous representations of goddesses and priestesses using frame drums in a variety of ceremonial contexts. The pictorial record also suggests similarities between Egyptian religious life and the symbols and spiritual practices of India and Sumer.

In Egypt, all life revolved around the Nile River. There was no other source of water—almost no rain and few oases. While the rivers of Mesopotamia were wild and unpredictable, the great Nile flooded every year in an orderly way, rising from twenty-five to fifty feet. "Egypt," Herodotus remarked, "is the gift of the Nile."

To this day, only about 5 percent of Egypt is inhabited. The rest is desert. The 766 miles of the Nile afford about a mile of fertile valley on either bank. Even the delta, the wetlands at the intersection of the Nile and the Mediterranean Sea, is only 130 miles across at its widest point. Essentially, Egypt is a country two miles wide.

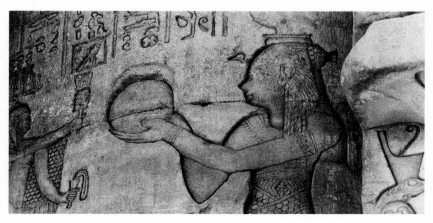

Hathor offering the drum to her son, who offers her a sistrum and menit. From the outside of the birthing chapel at Hathor's temple at Dendera, Ptolemaic period.

For many thousands of years, the strip of land that became Egypt was protected from the rest of the world by its geography. To the west was desert; to the east were impenetrable mountains. This made possible a peace and continuity of civilization unimaginable to the Sumerians, who were open to invasion from every direction. The Nile's gentle current made of the river a superhighway between organized rural areas. As a result, the Egyptians achieved their high culture while maintaining a small-town population pattern that did not tax the natural environment. The Egyptian paced her life to the rhythm of the Nile, and it was good.

BEFORE THE PHARAOHS

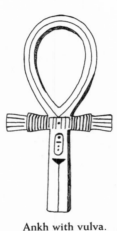

Ankh with vulva.

Traditional Egyptian history begins with the military unification of the Upper and Lower Kingdoms —one in the fertile delta, the other along the Upper Nile's banks—sometime between 4000 and 3000 B.C. The next five hundred years saw the rise of the first dynasties. Their pharaohs were worshiped as embodiments of the gods, a belief that was to endure until the last pharaoh, Cleopatra, met defeat at the hands of the Romans in 30 B.C.

An astounding cultural flowering during the Old Kingdom, circa 2900–2400 B.C., produced the most majestic painted reliefs, sculpture, and architecture Egypt has ever known. The symbols and mythology that permeated Egyptian civilization throughout its long reign were already in place. It is as if Egyptian culture appeared at its peak and slowly declined. Some scholars now believe that the culture that gave rise to historical Egypt had its roots thousands and thousands of years further into the past.

Ankh with arms, from terra-cotta vase, circa 1290–1252 B.C.

A clue to the antiquity of Egyptian culture is provided by one of its most popular and enduring symbols, the *ankh*. The ankh resembles a cross with a loop at the top and has been ubiquitous in Egypt from earliest Neolithic times. All the ancient deities hold ankhs, and all the temples are inscribed with row upon row of them. In modern-day Cairo, the ankh is still made and sold by the thousands to tourists as the preeminent symbol of ancient Egypt.

Scholars usually translate *ankh* as life, health, prosperity, contentment. But it encompasses many meanings. It sometimes stands for the ear, a symbol used in temples to denote receptivity of the mind to divine inspiration. In Egyptian, as in Sumerian, *ear* and *mind* are synonymous, perhaps an acknowledgment that the mind gives meaning to information received as sound vibrations. *Ankh* has also been translated as strength, wheat, grain, corn, food, flowers; a mirror, an unguent; a vessel, a house or dwelling place; the land of life, the other world; living fire or the imperishable, eternal divine existence. Nearly all of these interpretations recall attributes of the primeval Great Goddess.

In the Egyptian Museum at Cairo, I came across a whole case of ankhs inscribed with the ancient pubic triangle—a symbol linking Egyptian civilization to the oldest goddess cultures and clarifying that the ankh represents the goddess herself.

LADY OF THE HORNS

Hathor, the Lady of the Horns, is the oldest depicted Egyptian deity. She was said to be the "mother of every god and goddess," from primeval time, she herself "never having been created." She appears sometimes in human form, sometimes as a cow, sometimes as a woman with a cow's head or cow's ears and horns. When appropriate she takes the forms of a cobra, a vulture, a hippopotamus, a lioness, the sun, or the sycamore fig tree—to Egyptians, the Tree of Life. The dimensions of meaning she embodies are too vast and complex to be held in one thought or image, and her essence can only be described as fluid, capable of endless differentiation. As time passes, she splinters into many different goddesses symbolizing her various aspects, but, like Inanna, she can always be recognized as the power behind her many manifestations. The famous Cleopatra, last of the Ptolemies, dressed for ceremonial occasions in Hathor's headdress and functioned as her high priestess.

Hathor is a descendant of the ancient sacred cattle of Çatal Hüyük and a sister of the cow goddesses of Sumer and the Indus Valley. The Lady of the Horns is fecund and beautiful, the tender nursing mother whose milk is the redemptive, magical ambrosia of life. Her face appeared on the palette of Narmer, one of the earliest examples of Egyptian art, dated around 3100 B.C. Amulets of her head were placed in graves before the rise of dynastic Egypt.

Herodotus reported that cows were greatly revered in Egypt. The wild cattle that lived in the marshes of the delta were thought to be incarnations of Hathor. The *tjentet* cows, sacred cattle of Hathor, were kept in her temples, and at least some of them were buried within the temple compound. Scenes in some temples show priests making offer-

Predynastic funerary bird goddess, whose arms are raised to invoke the horns of the cow goddess, circa 4000 B.C.

ings to cows and temple statues, suggesting that both were considered divine.

The milk of Hathor's cows was a sacred fluid, imparting life and power. In a text at the Hathor shrine at Djeser-Djeseru, a divine cow says, "I am your mother, sweet milk. (I) have suckled your person with (my) breast(s), they enter you as life and power." Geraldine Pinch and other Egyptologists have suggested that the ritual drinking of divine cow's milk was an important part of the coronation of pharaohs. It may even have been the magical substance that changed their status from human to divine.

Birthing stool depicting Hathor in her human form giving birth accompanied by two divine Hathors in human form with cow heads. Egyptian women used these small stools to sit on while in labor. They invoked the power of Hathor, who gives birth to the universe, to support their personal process of giving birth.

In cow form, Hathor was also the goddess of death. She stood at the threshold of the door to the Mountain of the Dead, beckoning to arriving souls, whom she took into her womb for rebirth. Her vulva was the gateway between worlds. Kings who stood beneath her chin or suckled her milk were often painted black. Black, the color of the rich mud deposited every year by the Nile, symbolized revitalization and rebirth.

Hathor caves were typically carved into cliff sides to represent an entrance to the other world. Like the Magdalenian caves of Europe, these caves functioned as sacred sites or chapels in which rituals of transition were enacted.

In the Coffin Texts, a collection of ritual incantations from the Middle Kingdoms, the deceased is instructed to recite ritual spells identifying him- or herself with Hathor's sacred cattle in order to enter the afterlife under her protection. In the Eleventh Dynasty temple of Nebhepetre Mentuhotpewere, Hathor's royal priestesses were laid to rest in shrines and sarcophagi embellished with scenes of cows being milked. There are similar scenes at other shrines dedicated to Hathor.

HATHOR'S HEADDRESS

Hathor is often shown wearing an elaborate headdress on which the round, golden disk of the sun is cradled between cow horns. The wings of a vulture shelter her face; a cobra rears up on her forehead. These symbols represent key aspects of her power, and also emphasize similarities she shares with the goddesses of other early civilizations.

Cow horns, so prevalent at Çatal Hüyük, were familiar symbols of the moon and its cycles in all the early river valley cultures and recall the Venus of Laussel. On Hathor's headdress, the unification of the sun and moon stands for the union of the everlasting and the ever-changing that permeates Egyptian thought. The sun is constant, always taking the same form. The moon is constantly changing, growing from the crescent to the roundness of the full moon, then fading into nothingness. The sun brings light into darkness, illuminating and uncovering. It is the light of conscious reality. The moon, visible only in the absence of the sun, is the shadowy unconscious rising to the surface.

The sun's daily journey reminded the Egyptians of their limited time on earth. Each evening the sun dissolved into the dark, healing womb of night and sleep. Each morning it rose in the same state of perfection as the first dawn. This metaphor was enacted every day in temple rituals. The motif of completion and release found its echo in the cycles of other celestial bodies and the seasons of the Nile.

The cycles of the moon control the sacred fluids of life—the water that feeds the grass, which is transformed by the cow into milk, which is transformed into the blood of life. In Egypt as elsewhere, the transformation mystery of the Paleolithic retains its association with the goddess.

The vulture and the cobra were the symbols of the earlier kingdoms of Upper and Lower Egypt, respectively, and on a political level represent their unification. Both produce the sacred egg that symbolizes rebirth.

Hathor/Isis with her headdress holding sistrum and menit, circa 1300 B.C.

Tomb of Neferhotep at Thebes. Women with round and rectangular frame drums, circa 1320 B.C.

GODDESS OF CULTURE

As the goddess Maat, Hathor embodies law, truth, and order. Egyptologist Manfred Lurker says that in Egyptian mythology "the heart of the deceased was placed on the scales of justice and balanced against the feather of Maat, symbol of truth."

Maat's Rules of Behavior are benevolent, particularly when compared with the harsh commandments of the gods of patriarchal religions, who threatened savage retaliation to those who transgressed their laws.

From Hathor comes language and the ability to communicate, both human to human and human to divine. Each hieroglyph was a sacred expression of her mind. As language evolves, she becomes the gifts of poetry and prophecy. Like Sarasvati and Inanna, she is the source of the cultural arts. Chief among these was music.

Music was an indispensable part of religious life. Egyptian rites were based on the conjunction of ritual chanting with rhythmic sound and, like Inanna's temple at Uruk, temples were acoustically designed to amplify the sound of this sacred music. The frame drum and two types of rattles—the *menit* and the *sistrum*—were customarily used to create the rhythmic foundation of temple rituals.

EGYPTIAN FRAME DRUMS

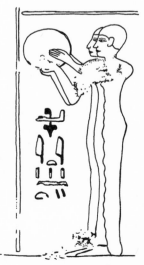

Frame drummers at the erection of the djed pillar at the Sed festival of Amenhotep III.

The round frame drum first appears in Egypt in a religious context. Two women, probably priestesses, played them as a *djed* pillar was ritually erected at a festival during the reign of Pharaoh Amenhotep III, circa 1417–1379 B.C. The celebration was commemorated on the tomb of Kheruef, an official in the pharaoh's service.

As a symbol of the energy in the grain, the *djed* pillar had played a role in fertility rites from predynastic times. It became a symbol of the stability and vitality of the pharaoh, and also of the spine of Osiris, the god of resurrection and rebirth. (Male pharaohs were considered incarnations of Osiris.) The ceremonial raising of the *djed* pillar may have represented the rise of divine energy up the spine.

The skin heads of some of these round frame drums, painted with symbolic scenes, have survived. Two from the New Kingdom (c. 1600–1100 B.C.), found at Thebes, depict Isis giving life to Osiris. Hathor and

Bes, both connected with childbirth, attend her, appearing among a group of women playing frame drums. These scenes illustrate the drum's power of invoking creation and resurrection and its use in related rituals. Two skin drums from the Ptolemaic period show priestesses playing the frame drum before Isis, who sits on her throne. An inscription reads, "Isis, Lady of the Sky, Mistress of [all] the Goddesses." A very similar scene appears on a Nineteenth Dynasty stone relief from Medamud: Four women identified as priestesses in the accompanying text play frame drums before Hathor and Mut.

The djed pillar represents stability, endurance.

The beat of the drum was used to coordinate the rhythms of oarsmen on the boats that sailed the Nile, and this function had its divine counterpart. Priestesses are often depicted playing the frame drum accompanying the sacred boats of the deities in ritual processions. Every day, the sun god, accompanied by Thoth, god of wisdom, and his daughter Maat, embodiment of truth and order, sails across the celestial waters of the sky. In the sun god's boat a woman plays the frame drum, ordering the natural rhythms of the universe.

In the Ptolemaic and Roman periods, the frame drum continues to appear frequently in religious contexts. It is played by priestesses in the temple of Hathor at Dendera, the temple of Mut at Karnak, Horus's temple at Edfu, Isis's temple at Philae, the temples of Athribis and Armant, and a temple at the oasis of Kharga. A block of red sandstone depicts a group of women playing frame drums painted red, a color associated with blood and life as far back as the Paleolithic.

Though women are most often the drummers, there are exceptions. The dwarfish, lion-headed god Bes, clothed in a leopard skin, often plays a frame drum while dancing ritually. Bes is the ancient, shamanistic protector of women at the critical moment of conception and the

Sarcophagus of Nespanetjerenpare, with the djed pillar, circa 945–718 B.C.

Women in boat. Egyptian silver bowl found on Cyprus, circa seventh century B.C.

dangerous moment of birth. His dancing and drumming ward off all evil influences.

Anubis, the jackal god, is shown playing a frame drum at the temple at Deir el-Medina at Edfu and in the birthing chapel at Dendera. Before the rise of Osiris, Anubis ruled the underworld with Hathor. The connection between the frame drum and the underworld is very old in Egypt. It was used in funeral rites to protect the deceased from negative influences and to hasten rebirth. At rituals and feasts in the home of the deceased, women played the drum, lyre, and flute to invoke the presence and protection of the goddess. As the corpse was ferried across the Nile, two priestesses in the roles of Isis and Nephthys, one stationed at the head and one at the feet, would lament the death of Isis (if the deceased was female) or Osiris (if male). The funeral boat was accompanied by boatloads of female singers and musicians who lamented in classic manner, ripping their clothes and exposing their breasts. This symbolic passage over the water is a dominant theme in Egyptian mythology.

The funeral rites were based on the *Songs of Isis and Nephthys*, a mythological account of Isis's search for her dead husband, Osiris, the

Women musicians from the necropolis at Thebes, circa sixteenth century B.C.

Fourteenth-century B.C. tomb scene from the necropolis at Thebes. Egyptian dance was of sacred origin and purpose and expressed the secrets of the structure of consciousness. To the goddess Hathor, dance was the "food of the heart."

Hathor-headed percussion clapper, circa 1480 B.C. Clappers date back to prehistoric times. Made of ivory or bone, they were common in tombs of Eleventh and Twelfth dynasties.

Hathor-headed faience naos sistrum, circa 300 B.C.

archetypal vegetation deity. At death, he is ripped into pieces and scattered over the earth. Isis searches out the pieces and restores him to a mystical life in the underworld. The song cycle of this ceremony was sung for five days almost entirely by two priestesses manifesting as Isis and Nephthys who accompanied themselves on frame drums. In Roman times, this myth became the basis of a popular mystery cult.

Images of women playing frame drums as they receive the deceased frequently decorated the walls of tombs, and frame drums have been found among the deceased's burial goods. Hatnofer, the mother of Queen Hatshepsut's architect, was buried with her frame drum.

As in Sumer, rattles often appear with drums in religious art. The *menit*, commonly carried by Hathor's priestesses, dancers, and singers, was a percussion instrument composed of a number of strands of beads gathered into a counterpoint. It was used in the rites of Hathor as early as the Sixth Dynasty. When it was not being used as an instrument rattle, it was worn around the neck as the "life-giving necklace" of Hathor. Its sound when shaken was an aspect of Hathor, and was thought to be healing.

Scholars have pointed out that the counterpoise of the menit resembles wooden fertility figures and probably represents the body of Hathor. It is often inscribed with a lotus, a vulval symbol, and P. Barguet feels the menit was therefore a symbol of birth and rebirth.

There are pictures of Egyptian queens functioning as priestesses of Hathor and of Hathor herself offering menit necklaces to kings. These are thought to represent the sexual union from which Hathor, through the queen, gives birth to the king as her son. Pinch points out that the menit is often present in suckling scenes, when the king is rejuvenated by drinking the divine milk, and concludes, "This probably means that a kind of divine energy emanated from the menit."

The *sistrum* was a descendant of the ancient shaman's rattle. In Egypt, it evolved from an archaic ritual of cutting papyrus stems and rattling them rhythmically to open one's heart to Hathor (the words *mind,*

soul, and *heart* were used interchangeably to indicate human consciousness; "to wash the heart" meant "to cool, to gratify and appease the mind").

Egyptian sistrums took two forms. The *naos*-shaped sistrum (*ssst*), the older of the two, is first depicted in the Old Kingdom. It is fashioned of faience (cast ceramic), with a papyrus-shaped handle that recalls its origins. Its frame takes the form of a small chapel, or *naos*, representing the "image of heaven," the inner chamber of sound in which the goddess resides. The chapel is pierced by metal bars from which small jingles hang.

The naos sistrum is bifrontal, and Hathor is represented on opposing sides as Isis, goddess of life, and Nephthys, goddess of death. The inscription "Hathor Nebet-Hetepet"—Lady of the Vulva or Lady of the Uterus—is commonly present. According to Pinch, this suggests that the instrument embodies the female creative principle.

Hathor holding two sistrums from Horus's temple at Edfu, circa 300–100 B.C.

The *shm*, a loop sistrum in the shape of an ankh, evolved during the Middle Kingdom. It was made of metal and would have made more noise than the naos sistrum. It hangs from Hathor's neck when she is depicted at the threshold to the underworld and is found occasionally among burial goods.

Sistrums were used in the most sacred rituals of all Egyptian gods and goddesses. Their rhythmic rattling was a means of aligning one's consciousness with the consciousness of the deity. Texts describe Hathor shaking the sistrum in order to bestow the blessings of spiritual development. The word for *sistrum* also meant "to shine, to give out

---

HIEROGLYPHS

hieroglyph for "joy" and "to beat a frame drum"

"to rejoice, to praise, to beat a drum or tambourine"

"to play the tambourine"

djed pillar, the Tree of Life

"something beaten, drum, cycle of time"

"a kind of grain"

"to revolve, circuit, cycle, circle, drum, tambourine"

"to beat a tambourine"

"women players of tambourines"

light." In her hands, its movement symbolized the movement of the world into existence through the medium of sound.

The sistrum also had a powerful protective function. The ringing of the metal drove away harmful spirits, enemies, or the effects of the evil eye. From the most ancient times to the present day, the shaking of jingles, the ringing of bells, the clash of cymbals, and the striking of gongs have retained this shamanistic function. Dancers since the Paleolithic have attached rattles and bells to their feet or clothing, or worn them as necklaces. Jingles and bells have been found in tombs in Egypt, Mesopotamia, and Greece. Hebrew rabbis used them to protect against death when entering the most sacrosanct areas of the temple. In Rome, bronze gongs drove away wandering ghosts. In medieval Europe, church bells rang out protectively against the dangers of lightning, plague, and death. In the Eifel Mountains of Germany, the tolling of small hand bells kept evil spirits away from a dying person. The ringing of metal still invokes the deity, and protects the sanctuary and attendants in the religious traditions of Africa, China, Indonesia, Tibet, Japan, and the Roman Catholic Church.

A spoon or holder for offering aromatics in rituals in which music and dance also formed a part of the offering, circa 1350 B.C.

ETERNAL RETURN

The sacred waters of the Nile flowed from Hathor's udders. Its annual flooding was the central fact of Egyptian life. Each year when the waters receded, new seeds were planted, destined to ripen and be harvested and wither away in the unrelenting heat of the sun. Then, once again, the water would rise and irresistibly sweep everything away. The impermanence of the physical world was undeniable.

The seasons of the Nile provoked an understanding of the permanence of change within the symbolic thought process. Flood time was a transitional period in which the past was washed away and the world purified by celestial grace. The power that gave rise to creation returned the world to its original state of nonbeing. Yet this descent into nonexistence was always followed by a fresh rebirth.

The Egyptian mind learned to balance on this boundary between the transitory and the everlasting, between order and nothingness, time and timelessness. The understanding that life is a constant process of cessation, renewal, and resurrection inundated religious thought. Life blossomed and withered, and death was a temporary state, a necessary means to renewed life.

MY HOUSE IS THE SKY

Just as they mapped the seasons of the Nile, the Egyptians charted the course of the heavens. They kept separate calendars for the cycles of the moon, the sun, Sirius, and the fixed stars, since they understood that the effects of these celestial bodies were different from one another. They timed their religious festivals to make the most of these rhythmic influences.

Hathor is sometimes called My House Is the Sky, or The House or Womb Above. She is the infinite void that contained all celestial phenomena—thunder, lightning, rainbows, the sun, moon, stars, clouds, and the flight of birds. As the night sky, Hathor rules the realm of the dead. The Egyptians saw the stars as the souls of their ancestors, held in the vastness of the goddess.

As the goddess Nut, she arches her body over the earth, sometimes as a woman and sometimes as a cow. Nut swallows the sun at evening and gives birth to it every morning. The red rays of dawn are the blood of Hathor giving birth to the sun.

Hathor's star was Sirius, the brightest star in the night sky. To the Egyptians, Sirius was known as Sothis, the Great Provider. Sothis was thought to be the womb of Hathor, which contained and gave birth to the vegetation god Osiris, who was recalled to life annually by the flooding of the Nile. Her temple at Dendera was aligned to face the rising of this star at the beginning of the New Year. As Sothis rose heralding the coming of the Nile's floodwaters, the starlight reached deep into the inner sacred precincts of the temple to shine on the altar of Hathor.

TEMPLES OF LEARNING

The temples were the universities of the ancient world. In both Mesopotamia and Egypt, tradition has it that written language developed within the temple culture.

At Dendera, near the banks of the Nile, stand the remains of Hathor's temple. In Egypt—as in Mesopotamia and other parts of the ancient world—temples were built on "power spots" that had attracted worshipers for thousands of years. According to inscriptions, this site

Hathor's temple at Dendera, Ptolemaic period.

had been sacred to Hathor for ten thousand years. The original temple was a mud hut on a mound revealed by the receding Nile. This became the primordial mound on which the later temples were built. It was considered the site of the first sunrise, the seat of creation, death, rebirth, and resurrection—the navel of the world.

The legendary Followers of Horus, warriors who were involved in the conquering and unification of Upper and Lower Egypt, built one of the most ancient temples to Hathor at Dendera. During the Fourth Dynasty, around 2600 B.C., Cheops, the pharaoh who is identified with the great Pyramid, built a new temple to Hathor on the same spot. Throughout the long course of Egyptian civilization, the buildings on this site were continually renovated or rebuilt. The ruins we see there today date from construction toward the end of the Ptolemaic period in the first century.

The temple at Dendera was famous for its papyrus library. Papyrus, the parchmentlike paper made from the plant of the same name, was first

The remains of a Hathor-headed column at Dendera.

used to record sacred rituals and ceremonial rites. Later, information about metallurgy, medicine, art, music, sculpture, architecture, and astronomy was also stored on temple papyri. As historian Robert Lawlor points out, the study of science was an integral part of religion. The temple was a learning center "whose purpose was to reveal and develop symbolic, intellectual and physical techniques which might effect perceptual, behavioral and physiological changes in the human organism." It was

Procession of thirty-two priestesses from the birthing chapel, Dendera.

Hathor from the birthing chapel at Edfu, circa 300–100 B.C.

the place where sacred techniques were developed and taught for the conscious and spiritual evolution of the Egyptian people.

The remains of Hathor's temple at Dendera constitute one of the most profound sources of spiritual information still available to us from ancient Mediterranean cultures. The architecture and the images on the walls form a repository of the accumulated experience and wisdom of thousands of years of human endeavor. They give us a symbolic map of the origin and development of human consciousness.

The outer court of the main temple was supported by six gigantic columns. Inside were eighteen massive Hathor-headed columns that were symbolic as well as functional. They represented the sustaining energy of earth supporting the creative energy of heaven. The Hathor heads of each column faced the four cardinal directions. In the ancient world, the cardinal points were used to chart spiritual as well as physical orientation. They provided a meaningful system for organizing physical, psychological, and spiritual information.

The four faces of Hathor also represented the four elements that make up the physical world—earth, air, fire, water. The Egyptian priestess took her strength from the earth, embodying the four elements. Her energy rose through her spinal column, radiating throughout the four directions of the heavenly realms.

As in Sumer, a complex of buildings serving the spiritual and physical needs of the community evolved around the central temple. Within the temple complex at Dendera was a *mammisi*, or birthing chapel. On its outer walls, large frescoes show Hathor making offerings of the frame drum and also playing it herself. The protector god Bes adorns the capitals of the outside columns. Inside, thirty-two priestesses dressed as Hathor play the frame drum as they march down the left wall toward the main shrine relief. Twenty-nine priestesses with scepters and sistrums advance along the opposite wall, creating a procession of frame drums and sistrums. It seems clear that the rhythms of these ritual instruments were used to guide women through the sacrosanct—and physically dangerous—time of childbirth, and it is reasonable to suggest that the Egyptians were familiar with certain rhythms of the drum used to strengthen labor contractions, facilitating childbirth.

A sanitarium next to the birthing chapel seems to have functioned as the local hospital as well as the site of specific healing rituals connected with water therapy.

FESTIVAL OF THE REUNION

On the temple walls at Dendera, texts and reliefs describe the Festival of the Reunion, celebrated from at least 2000 B.C. at the beginning of the Nile's annual flooding. This event marked the beginning of the New Year and was the most important event of the year. It was a time to let go of the past. Its rituals helped to refocus mental, physical, and spiritual energies. The ceremonies required elaborate preparations. For weeks, people from outlying regions poured in, setting up festive camps along the riverbanks. Priestesses performed purification rituals with frame drums and sistrums.

Before dawn on New Year's Day, the sacred image of Hathor was taken from her inner sanctuary and carried in procession to the temple roof. As she faced the Nile, where she was beginning to rise in her form as the mighty river, the first rays of dawn would illuminate her golden face.

Shortly after, at the rising of Hathor's star, Sirius, four days before the rising of the new moon, a procession known as the Beautiful Journey of Hathor began. Priests carried altars of flame and burning incense; priestesses beat out rhythms on their frame drums and shook their sistrums as the sacred image of the goddess was borne to her barge on the Nile. For three days, the barge made its stately way upriver, to the rhythms of chanting, singing, and drumming, stopping at various temples for rituals and offerings. On the day of the new moon, to the clamor of euphoric crowds chanting "Joy forever, joy forever," Hathor arrived at the temple

Procession of the sacred bark with drummers, Tomb of Amenmosis, circa 1225 B.C., Nineteenth Dynasty, Abydos.

Hathor, with cow ears, playing to Horus in his hawk form. Hathor's temple, Dendera.

of Horus, her consort and son, at Edfu.

For thirteen days, while the people celebrated with feasting, dancing, and song, Horus and Hathor joined in the sacred marriage ritual. Their union ensured the rising of the Nile and the fertility of the land, crops, and humans for the ensuing year. At dawn on the fourteenth day—the day of the full moon—Hathor was carried out of Horus's temple and, with great ceremony, towed down the Nile to Dendera.

Hathor offering drum to Horus in his hawk form.

The similarities between the Sumerian and Egyptian New Year's observances have been noted by many historians. Both were rituals of renewal. Both were an important means for invoking, channeling, and harmonizing the energies of divine and human communities. They formalized the sacred link between humankind and the rhythms of the natural world. Both recall the ecstatic union of Shakti and Shiva.

For the Egyptians, thought was a vibrational energy that pervaded

Hathor playing to Horus in his human form while he offers her an ankh.

the physical world. They believed that mind, body, and spirit could be aligned with the ultimate divine intelligence by meditative practices coupled with the sacred sounds created by voice and musical instruments. According to Lawlor, the Egyptians believed that the purpose of humankind was "to embody and express the vibratory, rhythmic life of cosmic Humanity, which was felt to exist abstractly, like an inaudible music."

THE GOLDEN ONE

The Greeks named the system of mind/body techniques the Egyptians practiced in pursuit of expanded consciousness "gymnosophism." The disciplines they described—rhythmic breathing, visualization, chanting to rhythmic accompaniment—appear to be similar to many of the Yogic practices of Hinduism.

Hathor embodies a number of concepts that identify her as the Egyptian version of the lotus goddess. She holds a mirror that reflects the vastness of nonbeing and also all that exists. Reality is constantly in flux, but she herself remains unchanged. To the rhythms of frame drums and sistrums, her priestesses performed the ritual Dance of the Mirrors, reflecting her glory. She is too bright, too dazzling to behold directly—the Gold, the Golden One, the Beautiful, the Lovely One. Even the gods must avoid looking directly at the blinding radiance of pure consciousness.

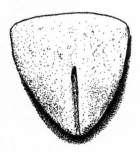

Hathor kneeling in lotus, playing the frame drum at her temple in Dendera.

Offering to the goddess found at Medinet Habu, circa 1100–700 B.C.

In this form of radiant light, Hathor rises from the lotus. The lotus is the ancient image of the womb or vulva, creating life from the power of the waters and the mud of earth. The symbol is the same in Egypt and India; the concept is as old as the Venus of Willendorf.

Symbolic of the human psyche, the lotus illustrates the unfolding and blossoming of higher consciousness. Its roots are in the mud of the earth—the undeveloped mind, or unconscious. Its slender stem (like a spinal column) grows upward through the waters of the physical plane —ordinary consciousness. Drawing on the powers of the five elements —earth, air, fire, water, and space—the lotus presses upward toward the light. It bursts into the air to receive the fire of the sun—the royal symbol of elevated consciousness. Hathor, floating in the center of the lotus, rules over all dimensions, connecting the unconscious with the conscious. She symbolizes authentic spiritual perfection and authority.

Like the goddess of Çatal Hüyük, like Shakti, like Inanna, Hathor inspires love in all its forms: motherly love, familial love, erotic love. Her presence is revealed in sexual desire. She is the attracting hormonal scent of woman and the radiant glow of sexual satisfaction. She is the Mistress of the Vulva, and the Sacred Vulva is the Queen's Altar, the receptacle of offerings of love and semen. From her altar pours the celebratory, erotic energy of love, the original mystery of birth, the cry of new life.

In Egypt, the physical ideal of an erotically beautiful woman was one blessed with the heavy thighs of Hathor. Prayers have been found in which women beseech Hathor to bestow large hips and thighs upon them. Burial rituals included a prayer chanted by the embalmer that the deceased's face be made the most perfect among the gods, and her thighs the heaviest among the goddesses.

As the Tree of Life, Hathor connects the three realms she oversees—the underworld of death, ruled by the serpent, the world of daily life, ruled by the cow, and the universal heavens, the realm of the vulture. The Egyptians identified the sycamore fig tree as the Tree of Life. Eating its fruits, the fruits of Hathor's blood and body, was a rite of sacred communion.

As a metaphor for birth, the cosmic tree represents the treelike placenta that nurtures life in the womb. As a symbol of rebirth, it recalls the human nervous system. Its trunk is the base of the spine, where the cobra of earth energy lies coiled—very like the energy Hindu philosophers call the *kundalini*. It is also the ancient shamanistic Tree of Life that unites the three worlds.

Hathor in the Tree of Life, bringing forth the food and drink of eternal life, circa thirteenth century B.C.

Drummers playing at a sacred tree with birds. Relief, located in a building of Akhenaten in el-Amarna.

COBRAS AND CHAKRAS

Hathor sometimes manifests as the Seven Hathors, or the seven Celestial Cows. These seven birth goddesses set the fate of a newborn child by giving it seven souls.

The *ab* was the most important of these souls "because it was the central blood-soul emanating from the essence of the mother." The Egyptians believed that the mother's menstrual blood descended from her heart to her womb to create the new child's life. The mother's heartbeat was the power behind the child's new life as the goddess's heartbeat was the power behind creation. This was why her frame drum was often painted red—it represented the pulse of creation.

The hieroglyphic sign for *ab* was a figure dancing, conveying the concept of the heartbeat as the mystical dance of life. "The same mystic symbol in India was the dance of Shiva, who was supposed to dwell at the beating heart of the cosmos within the world-body of [the goddess] Kali."

The Seven Hathors who bestow seven souls is a concept also reflected in Hindu philosophy, where personality and physiognomy are thought to be determined by the vibrations of psychic energy in the seven chakras. The parallel between the seven chakras and the seven steps of the Babylonian ziggurat has already been noted. The number seven appears in similar contexts in Egypt as well. A passage in the Pyramid Texts, Egypt's oldest religious funeral texts, tells us that the king "absorbed the seven frontal cobras, which then became the seven cervical vertebrae, which commanded the entire dorsal spine."

Uraeus located in the heart and head.

The *uraeus*—the divine cobra on Hathor's forehead—corresponds to the location of the sixth chakra. The rearing cobra was one of the hieroglyphs for the word *goddess*. Tail in mouth, the snake encircles the world. It exists at the boundary that separates the transitory and the eternal, order from chaos, life from death. In Egypt, a pair of snakes intertwined —the caduceus, classical symbol of health—represented a balance of these opposites.

Among Hindus, the sixth chakra is sometimes referred to as the third eye, and the eye is a key symbol in Egyptian religious thought as well. The right eye was called the solar eye; the left, the lunar eye. While on one level this expresses the classic Egyptian balance between the sun and moon, permanence and impermanence, it may also indicate an awareness of the role of both hemispheres of the brain in perception.

According to Egyptologist R. T. Rundle Clark, "Complex meshes of eye symbolism are woven all around the Egyptian Mother Goddess," and the eye is "always a symbol for the Great Goddess." The opening of this eye when the flame and rushing heat of the cobra goddess rise up the spine is a recurring theme in Egyptian literature. "I am this one who escaped from the coiled serpent, I have ascended in a blast of fire, having turned myself about." It heralds a new birth into an expanded state of consciousness, guided by the rhythmic sounds of chanting, drums, sistrums, bells.

The religious symbolism in the river valley cultures of the Harappans, the Mesopotamians, and the Egyptians is similar in too many respects to be dismissed as coincidental. Their sacred rituals and traditions, insofar as they can be pieced together from the evidence of texts and archaeological artifacts, appear to differ mostly in particulars that can be traced to environmental influences. In the broad perspective, however, all three civilizations seem to pulse to the rhythms of the primordial Mother Goddess. As the strands of these cultures meet and diverge over the course of centuries, she will continue to appear throughout the Mediterranean worlds, assuming new names, reflecting new cultural nuances.

Egyptian eye. The vulture is the goddess Nekhbit, the ruler of the south, and the serpent is the goddess Wadjet of the north. From the tomb of Tutankhamen, circa 1350 B.C.

Priestesses pouring a libation to female musicians, circa 1185–1070 B.C. Inscribed with a hymn that sings of a goddess who is the "uraeus cobra of gold." The Latin word "uraeus" is derived from the ancient Egyptian name "Iaret," which means "the risen one."

CHAPTER EIGHT

THE MOTHER OF THE GODS

AS PEOPLE FROM different parts of the Mediterranean world were thrown together by war or trade or immigration, the myths and deities of various religious traditions blended together. This constant dissemination and reabsorption created crowded pantheons of goddesses and gods. The Phrygian goddess who emerged from Anatolia to become the Mother of the Gods in Aegean cultures was essentially the old fertility goddess worshiped throughout the area in prehistoric times. Everywhere, her worship was marked by ecstatic trance states entered through ritual drumming and dancing that induced prophetic revelation.

THE GODDESS OF ÇATAL HÜYÜK

The Neolithic goddess of Çatal Hüyük survived the city's extinction to become Cybele, the major deity of ancient Anatolia. Historians next find her among the Hittites of the second millennium B.C. under the name of Kubaba. Mellaart reports a concentration of shrines to the ancient Anatolian goddess around the Hittite city of Midas in west-central Turkey and adds, "The Goddess and music is an ever-recurring combination." In these religious centers a number of representations of Hittite women playing frame drums have been found. In particular there is a representation of a sacred marriage rite in which women are drumming.

Kubaba, Cybebe, Dindymene, Rhea, Dictynna, Berecynthia are all regional variations of Cybele, whose rituals traveled with the trade winds throughout the Mediterranean world. At Çatal Hüyük she was depicted seated on her throne flanked by two felines—

Cybele holding frame drum and lotus bowl, circa 350 B.C.

descendant of the Paleolithic Venus, Great Mother of gods, humans, and animals. In the classical world she was worshiped as "Cybele, the All-Begetting Mother, who beats a drum to mark the rhythm of life." Her frame drum was one of her most important symbols. It is the ancient symbol of the moon, and of the primordial egg of creation, whose beat is the pulse of life.

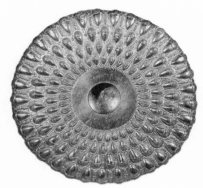

Gold omphalos libation bowl, with bees and acorns, bottom view, circa third century B.C.

Her throne was the high mountain peak where heaven meets earth; "The Lady of the Mountain" was one of her epithets. Wearing her battlement crown, shaped like a fortified tower on the city wall, she embodied the city itself, whose walls, like the natural landscape, rose from her womb to protect her children. In hundreds of statues, she is shown seated on the throne of her mountain, crowned with the tower of the city, holding a lion in her lap or flanked by two lions. In her left hand she holds her frame drum, painted red; with her right hand she pours forth a libation from her lotus bowl. Her lotus bowl, the *patera*, was the great cosmic vulva that poured forth the water of life—symbolized by honey, milk, wine, or blood. The lions symbolize that she is the mistress of wild nature and the initiator into higher levels of awareness.

Greek patera, lotus libation bowl, circa fourth century B.C. The primordial lotus is the ancient image of the womb or vagina of the goddess that gives rise to the universe. It is the fully blossomed plant that creates embodied life from the power of water and earth. It symbolizes the unfolding and blossoming of the highest spiritual development of consciousness. The goddess holds a lotus bowl filled with water, milk, or wine and pours forth creation.

Lotus drum from a cup that depicts Cybele with her attributes: the cymbal, thyrsus, drum with rosette, and a torch.

THE ISLAND QUEENS

As natural ports of call for ships crisscrossing the Mediterranean, the beautiful, fertile islands of Cyprus and Crete were centers of cultural interaction.

Cyprus has been inhabited at least since the eighth or ninth millennium B.C., and its abundant supply of copper stimulated trade and encouraged invasion from about the third millennium B.C. The culture was influenced in turn by Western Anatolians, Egyptians, Minoan Cretans, Phoenicians, and Greeks. There was a brisk trade with Ugarit, a main port of Canaan (now Syria and Lebanon). The Canaanites revered the goddess Astarte, who rode a lion, carried a lotus, and played the

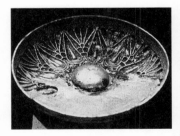

Macedonian silver patera (omphalos bowl with sacred mound in its center) gilded with gold Egyptian style lotuses, 510–500 B.C.

Kneeling Ugarit drummer, contemporary Ras Shamra, Syria, 1300–1200 B.C. Judging from the delicate shape of the body and the hair, the excavator, C. F. A. Schaeffer, suggested that this might be a depiction of the Syrian goddess Anat, described in a text found at Ugarit as a tambourine player.

frame drum. They settled Palestine around 2500 B.C., and frequent condemnations of Astarte (Ashtoreth) in the Old Testament show that the Israelites were often attracted to her. In Ugarit, where the goddess was also known as Anat, she is depicted kneeling playing her frame drum.

THE DOVE GODDESS

Recent excavations have shown that from 3800 to 2300 B.C. a very complex culture flourished on Cyprus. Many sophisticated figurines have been found, which appear to be associated with fertility, sexuality, and childbirth. As early as the Copper Age, there is evidence of a specialized dove cult devoted to a descendant of the ancient bird goddess. By the twelfth century B.C., the Mycenaeans had built a magnificent temple to this goddess, later known as Aphrodite.

Cyprus is the legendary birthplace of Aphrodite. A blend of Inanna, Ishtar, Astarte, and Cybele, she is the dove goddess of sexual attraction and the archetype of alluring beauty. Her beauty is golden, sunlike; she shines radiantly like Hathor. She is depicted as a bird goddess playing the frame drum from as early as 1000 B.C., and female figures playing frame drums, possibly representing her priestesses, are found in her temples particularly from around the sixth century B.C. Like the Mother Goddesses of the river valley cultures, she brings the gift of song and music. Her priestesses were renowned as musicians of the frame drum, lyre, and flute, as well as the voice. One of the most famous poets and lyricists of the ancient Mediterranean world, Sappho of Lesbos, is generally thought to have been a priestess of Aphrodite. Her poems invoking the goddess or her rites have a decidedly ritual character, as in this fragment quoted by Hephaestion:

Phoenician figurine found in grave, necropolis of Byrsa, contemporary Tunisia, sixth–fourth century B.C.

Cypriot sanctuary model that recalls Çatal Hüyük shrines. A figure pours a libation into a large amphora. Clay, from the necropolis of Kochati, circa 2000 B.C.

The moon rose full,
and the women stood
as though around an altar.
Thus at times with tender feet
the Cretan women dance
in measure round the fair altar,
trampling the fine soft bloom of the grass.

At the temple of Astarte/Aphrodite at Kition, on Cyprus, inscriptions describe an orchestra of musicians that was a permanent part of the temple staff. Music festivals there and at her temple at Paphos were an inseparable part of the goddess's worship, and the frame drum was the instrument most often represented. Thousands of votive figurines making offerings to the deities have been found in Cypriot shrines. The many statues of women drummers indicates that playing the frame drum was a form of offering to the goddess.

Eros playing to Aphrodite, Corinthian, circa 350 B.C.

LEFT: Cypriot priestess with tambourine, circa 700–650 B.C.

BELOW LEFT: Frame drummer from the excavations at Amathus, Cyprus, circa eighth century B.C.

Drummer from the temple of Aphrodite/Astarte at Kition, circa sixth century B.C.

Aphrodite's rituals also preserved the ancient tradition of sacred sexual practices. Pilgrims traveled to her temples at Paphos on Cyprus, at Aphaca and Heliopolis in Phoenicia, and at Corinth on the mainland of Greece to experience sexual communion with her priestesses. The priestesses not only were thought to represent the goddess but to *incarnate* the goddess. Here the physical union of female and male became a ritual sacrament. Aphrodite's dove, the "holy-spirit-bird" of ancient shamanism, symbolized possession by the goddess, in the form of orgasmic energy. After death, the initiate believed, the soul would return to the goddess in the form of a dove.

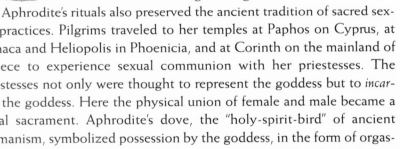

Aphrodite was the eternally radiant, youthful goddess of erotic beauty. As the mysterious power of love and desire that commands the continuity of life yet never submits to the rational mind, she mocked the custom of permanent wedlock prized in patriarchal societies. Therefore, in the patriarchal cultures of mainland Greece,

Cypriot priestess, circa 700–650 B.C.

Cretan goddess blowing triton shell, from Idaean cave.

Omphalos from Delphi with snake, Greece, circa 300 B.C.

her mythology was distorted to diminish her function and powers as much as possible. She who was the goddess of inspiration was reduced to the temptress; she who was the mother of the gods became a flirtatious, relatively powerless playmate. In the Biblical Book of Revelations, Aphrodite's number—666—became the "number of the Beast."

Aphrodite's rites also included the annual ritual bath to renew her virginity and the Sea-Birth, both ancient forms of baptism. To renew one's virginity was a means of returning to the original, pristine state of unconditioned awareness, and every spring her sacred sexual priestesses participated in this ceremony. In the pre-Christian world, virginity referred to a state of mind. Priestesses were often called virgins; in the annual ritual baths, their sexuality was rededicated to the goddess.

The Sea-Birth was a variation of the ancient agricultural rite of rebirth, which released the past and its hold on the mind, allowing the initiate to exist freely in the present moment.

As goddess of the sea, Aphrodite was depicted blowing a triton shell, an image that is as old as the ancient Venus of Laussel with her bison's horn.

THE OMPHALOS

Paphos, Cyprus, the site of Aphrodite's tomb, was known as the navel of the earth. The Greek word for navel—*omphalos*—also refers to the sacred stone found in temples or shrines. Symbolically, the omphalos brought together a number of important spiritual concepts. The heart-seat of the great Earth Mother was the very center or navel of the world. The navel cord connects the fetus with outer and inner worlds, and is the source of nourishment until it is time for birth. Similarly, Aphrodite's temple was the place where initiates were nourished and birthed into higher planes of consciousness.

BIRDS OF THE MUSES

An omphalos is typically shaped like a beehive, though some are conical or egg-shaped. Bees have an ancient reputation as the bringers of order, and their hives served as models for organizing temples in many Mediterranean cultures. Priestesses at Cybele's temples in Asia Minor, Greece, and Rome were called *Melissai* or *Melissae*, the Greek and Latin words for bees. *Deborah* was the ancient Hebrew name for the bee priestess, and

these priestesses were often prophets.

Bees, familiars of the goddess since Çatal Hüyük, appear frequently in classical mythology. They are called the "Birds of the Muses" and are attracted to the heavenly fragrances of flowers, from which they make the divine nectar, honey. Melissa, the goddess as queen bee, taught mortals how to ferment honey into mead. In the *Homeric Hymn to Hermes*, the Melissai feed on honey and are inspired "to speak the truth." These traditions made the omphalos the place of sacred utterance—the oracular power associated with the buzzing of bees and the buzzing vibration of life.

Bees create hexagons in their honeycombs. In Aphrodite's temple of Eryx in Sicily, her symbol was a golden honeycomb. The Pythagoreans believed the nature of reality could be perceived through the study of sacred geometry. They "meditated on the endless triangular lattice, all sixty-degree angles, that results from extending the sides of all hexagons in the honeycomb diagram until their lines meet in the centers of adjacent hexagons." These geometric meditations were identical in function to the yantra meditational practices of ancient India. The triangles within the hexagrams symbolized the perpetual sexual union of male and female that maintains the flowing energy of the universe. Sacred honey cakes shaped like triangular vulvas evolved from these meditations and were used in rituals to celebrate Aphrodite.

Honey is antibacterial, and its mildly laxative properties and sweet taste made it a primary ingredient in ancient medicines. It was widely believed to be a source of divine nourishment. In the myths of the ancient world, honey often nourished a divine child raised in secret by a goddess in the depths of caves.

In the *Georgics*, Virgil relates one of these stories. Cybele defied Saturn—who routinely devoured their sons at birth to protect his sovereignty—by hiding the infant Jupiter (Greek Zeus) in a cave. She instructed her Corybantes (young warriors who danced for her) to clash their cymbals and beat their drums, making as much noise as possible in order to hide the child's cries. The bees came and nourished Jupiter on their honey, enabling him to survive. When he grew to manhood, he overthrew the Titan gods. The advantages of civilization ("the

Goddess with wings, bee body, and lotus emblems, connected with the worship of Artemis Ephesia, from Camiros, Rhodes, Greece. Jane Ellen Harrison described the Melissai as "honey-priestesses, inspired by a honey intoxicant, they hum and buzz."

Symbol of the Kundalini Shakti from an illuminated manuscript, Rajasthan, circa eighteenth century A.D.

civility of law, prosperity, the grandeur of cities and delights of the countryside") are his gifts, dedicated to the bees.

Virgil also described a means to attract a swarm of bees to a new hive baited with scented herbs and flowers: When a column of bees floats by, the frame drum and cymbal of Cybele should be played to attract them.

REBIRTH

The omphalos was also egg-shaped, often with a bird perched on it and a snake wrapped around it. It represented the hive of the bees, the egg of the bird, and the egg of the sacred snake—all transformative symbols of birth and regeneration.

From Mycenaean times, omphalos was also the name of a beehive-shaped tomb. It was revered as the mound of the goddess, marking the point where the forces of the underworld, earth, and heaven intersected. Harrison called it "a grave-mound, an omphalos-sanctuary, and she who is the spirit of the earth incarnate rises up to bring and be new life." In India the omphalos tomb was called a stupa.

I saw the Paphos omphalos a few years ago, in a poorly guarded museum. Until very recently the black stone had stood in the midst of the ruins of Aphrodite's temple, and local Cypriot women still made offerings of flowers, bread, and fruit to it. Its black surface is polished smooth by the caresses of generations of women over thousands of years. Alone in the room with the ancient stone, I lit a stick of incense and offered it in honor of the beauty in life that is the gift of Aphrodite.

Cretan vase, late geometrical period from Milatos, with serpent and omphalos symbol.

Greek vase painting of Dionysos and Apollo standing at the Tree of Life at Delphi. A satyr plays flute over the omphalos. The tripod of the Delphic oracle stands to the left. A priestess plays a frame drum with the oracular symbol of a laurel wreath painted on it.

THE TREE OF LIFE

The Tree of Life was said to grow at the site of the omphalos. It represented the vertical passageway between spiritual worlds, where the dead can move from the underworld to the heavens. In many creation myths, it shoots up from the navel of the earth, often with a pure spring at its base that flows with honey or milk. At the root of the tree lives a goddess with the power to regenerate life through her gift of life-giving fluid—milk from her breasts or the honeylike sap of the tree.

In Sumerian mythology, Lilith, a variation of the Mistress of Wild Beasts, lived in the Tree of Life. Some revisionist scholars think the Biblical story of Eve is a purposeful, patriarchal distortion of this tradition. In the *Odyssey*, Homer says that Calypso lived in a cave in a sacred forest on an island at the navel of the world.

In many versions of this legend, the wise serpent dwells at the foot of the tree and in its upper branches lives the sacred bird. The image recalls the Hindu kundalini, often visualized as a serpent, coiled at the base of the spine. This correspondence is strengthened by the fact that the sign associated with the concept of the omphalos is a small circle or dot within a circle—in Hindu cosmology, the most primitive form of the yantra, ancient symbol of the bindu, lotus, or chakra. This sign was often painted on the skin heads of frame drums. The Honey Doctrine of Hinduism delineated the secret knowledge of the Yogi, and

the sound of the awakened kundalini is described in the Sat-Cakra-Nirupana (an investigation into and of the chakras) as "the indistinct hum of swarms of love-mad bees." The commentary on this text describes the kundalini as "the source from which all sound emanates."

The *bendir*, a contemporary North African frame drum, has several strings strung across its head that buzz when the drum is played. It may well be a descendant of the ancient bee priestesses' frame drums, which hummed the world into being.

The omphalos was the place where libations—sacrificial offerings of liquids like water, milk, wine, honey, and oil—were poured. They were offered in gratitude to the goddess, the source of all sustenance. In the ancient world, there was no prayer without ritual, and the simplest ritual was a libation of wine and sprinkling of frankincense in the flame. Ritual behavior was a means of focusing the mind. The process of invoking the goddess through ritual and prayer, often accompanied by the powerful music of flute and frame drum, was a means of visualizing

Altar to Cybele depicting the Tree of Life with frame drum painted with laurel wreath and cymbals hanging from it, circa second or early third century A.D.

Omphalos symbol from a coin from Delphi, circa 480 B.C.

Bendir from Morocco, twentieth century A.D.

what was hoped for. The use of creative visualization in contemporary therapeutic practices as a means of programming thought processes is very much the same technique.

THE HEAVENLY FRAGRANCE

Ritual practices often included the use of incense and perfumes. To the ancients, scent was a channel to divine experience. Aphrodite's power resided in the seductive scent of woman—and, by extension, in the evocative smells of flowers, perfumes, and incense. She was particularly associated with frankincense, myrrh, and the rose.

Frankincense and myrrh were used to preserve and protect skin from aging, to heal the lungs, and to stabilize the mind in pursuit of higher meditational practices. Myrrh was considered an aphrodisiac; Aphrodite's lover, Adonis, was said to be born from the myrrh tree. Rose oil was applied to regulate the female reproductive system. The rose represented the sacred vulva of Aphrodite, and her priestesses presided over the mysteries of the rose.

Among Hindus, roses were also associated with the goddess, and rose oil was thought to open the heart chakra to compassion and love. According to current scientific research, smell is the most direct pathway to the brain and nervous system of all our sense perceptions. The olfactory nerves activated by the hormones of fragrance directly stimulate the brain and the pituitary gland, which controls the human hormonal system. Because of this, aromatherapists believe specific fragrances of essential oils can instantaneously change one's state of consciousness.

Incense altars dedicated to Aphrodite, depicting Aphrodite and Adonis and priestesses with frame drums. South Italian (Tarentum), first quarter of the fourth century B.C.

Ointments and oils for massaging the body were used in health practices of ancient Mesopotamia, Egypt, Greece, and Rome, in particular at the temples of the goddesses. Essential oils were used for healing various physical and emotional disorders. In Egypt, burns were treated with a mixture of rose, sweet flag, and vinegar. Rose oil, chicory juice, and vinegar was recommended for headache. These treatments were often combined with hydrotherapy —bathing the body in hot or cold water, depending on the patient's condition.

Oils, unguents, and incense have also been used since the beginning of recorded history in ritual, purifications, prayers, and meditation practices. Often an offering of incense and libations of scented oils was accompanied by a simultaneous offering of music, particularly the playing of flute and frame drum. Sacred plants were thought to have special powers, and shamans used them to heal, as well as to facilitate trance states, as a means to enter the other worlds. The ritual practice of anointing someone with oil indicated an initiation into a higher level of consciousness. These disciplines for transforming consciousness were transmitted and administered by the bee priestesses of Aphrodite, Cybele, Demeter, Persephone, and the old goddesses of Crete—Rhea and Ariadne.

Greek fifth century vase painting of Ariadne, Eros, and Dionysos.

CRETE

Like Egypt, Crete was the site of a very early, very advanced society. Arthur Evans, whose excavations of the palace at Knossos uncovered the existence of the Minoans, considered their civilization "in some respects more modern in its equipments than anything produced by classical Greece." In particular their achievements in government and the peaceful arts set them apart from the rest of Mediterranean cultures. Minoan women were powerful leaders in religion and society.

The Minoan civilization was the full flowering of a culture with a sacred female presence at its center. *Crete*, a Greek word, means "strong, or ruling, goddess." Of all the ancient civilizations, the Cretan goddess ruled the longest as a goddess who was One in Herself, without losing all or part of her power to a divine husband. No comparable Cretan male deity has been identified.

Minoan culture shares many symbols with predynastic Egypt,

Phoenician crowned goddess with drum and lotuses on the front of her gown, Tunisia, circa 500–400 B.C.

including the ankh and Hathor-like images such as cows suckling calves. Evans remarks that the Minoan snake goddess and her attributes show a remarkable resemblance to Wazet, a manifestation of Hathor who sometimes appears as a serpent and carries a papyrus scepter with a snake wound around it. The orientation of the palaces on Crete was determined in relation to Sirius, as was the position of Hathor's temple on the Nile. Like the Egyptians, the Cretans celebrated the New Year at the early rising of Sirius in July. Evans speculates that during the unsettling time of the military unification of Upper and Lower Egypt, refugees from Lower Egypt may have immigrated to Crete.

But there is also an influx of West Asian imagery, possibly arriving through Cyprus. In Anatolia, Cybele is the goddess of Mount Ida; the Cretan Mount Ida is a sacred mountain. Dikte is the name of sacred places in both areas. Remarkably similar Neolithic clay figures, mostly of women, are found in Crete as in Asia Minor.

This powerful Cretan goddess, honored in dance and in the bull ring, was called Rhea or Ariadne by the later classical Greeks. Rhea sat before the sacred cave "playing on a brazen drum, and compelling man's attention to the oracles of the goddess." Her drum dispelled all evil influences and served to summon and dismiss the sacred bees. Her symbols were the bull, the dove, the serpent, the sacred tree, her double axe, and the labyrinth. From the oldest of times, her rites were celebrated with orgiastic dancing and singing.

THE LABYRINTH

The story of Ariadne and Theseus is among the better-known myths. In order to win Ariadne, Theseus must kill the Minotaur—half man, half bull—who lives at the center of a labyrinth. Ariadne gives him a ball of string so that, after accomplishing this, he can safely return to her. They marry, but later, when Theseus leaves her, Ariadne becomes the beloved of Dionysos.

The labyrinth is a widespread symbol of initiation. Ariadne is the goddess of the labyrinth; her name in Greek means "very holy." She is the daughter of the moon goddess, Parsiphae—"the all-illuminating." By offering Theseus her ball of thread, Ariadne guides him through the experience of initiation. In shamanistic ritual, the beat of the drum is the thread guiding the shaman back to the natural world, and it can hardly be coincidental that Ariadne is often pictured with a frame drum. Both her marriage with Theseus and her union with Dionysos are versions of *hieros gamos*, the sacred marriage at the heart of earlier religious traditions as well as the mystery cults of the classical world.

The classic labyrinth is a single path meant for meditative circumambulation. It was originally a spiral, but slowly evolved into the maze of angular turns familiar to us today. To enter it is to experience a ritual death; to escape from it is to be resurrected. In the ancient world, prayer was an active, trance-inducing combination of chanting, music, and dance, and it is most likely that initiates danced the sacred spiral. The danced line into the labyrinth was a sacred path into the inner realm of the goddess. The *Genaros* dance performed at Delos in Greece commemorated Theseus's initiation rites. Dancers holding a rope signifying Ariadne's thread followed a leader into the labyrinth, spiraling right to left, the direction of death. At the center they turned, dancing out in the direction of evolution and birth, all to the rhythms of the frame drums.

Cretan labyrinth from a coin from Knossos, first millennium B.C.

Ancient labyrinths are almost always associated with caves, often appearing at the cave's mouth. Caves were the first Paleolithic temples, and the association of caves with sacred ceremonies consecrated to the goddess continued in Crete and Anatolia. In Greece and Rome, the mysteries were often revealed in cavelike grottoes or structures built to resemble artificial caves.

The labyrinth also represents descent into the unconscious structure of the mind, in search of wisdom and enlightenment. The Hindu mandala, used for concentration in Yogic meditations, is labyrinthian in design. Here the beast that must be slain becomes the forces of the unconscious. At the center is the goddess in her lotus, radiating light.

Initially the early Christian fathers rejected the use of labyrinths because of their connection to the earlier goddess traditions, yet around the eleventh century A.D., labyrinths began appearing in European cathedrals dedicated to the Virgin Mary. There is one at Chartres measuring exactly 666 feet—the number sacred to Aphrodite. At its center is a six-petaled flower, the ancient symbol of the goddess. In the center of the flower, the medieval master builder of the cathedral identified himself as Daedalus—the name of the legendary creator of the Cretan labyrinth who lived at least 2,400 years earlier. But at Chartres, the devout crawled through the labyrinth on their knees—a far cry from dancing the maze to the rhythms of the drum.

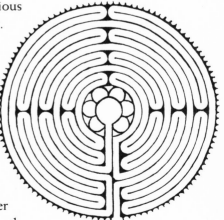

Chartres labyrinth, gothic cathedral, circa thirteenth century A.D.

PASSAGE TO GREECE

The Minoan civilization was devastated by a series of natural disasters, including major earthquakes around 1730 B.C. and the volcanic eruption that destroyed the Cretan island of Thera. By 1500 B.C. the Mycenaean culture had arisen on the Greek mainland. The Mycenaean rulers were Greek, but their culture was markedly Cretan and Near Eastern, with a warrior element that was much more prominent than anything seen on Crete. From 1400 to 1200 B.C., the entire eastern Mediterranean world from Anatolia, Ugarit, Cyprus, Crete, and Greece was inundated by waves of Kurgan or Aryan invasions. With the collapse of their social and economic systems, native populations sharply declined, and Aegean civilization sank into the dark ages for four hundred years, from about 1200 to 800 B.C.

As the classical Greek culture began to come into its own after the eighth century, they colonized the western coast of Asia Minor, including Anatolia, where they absorbed the worship of Cybele from her original sources. The city of Ephesus, one of the great trading centers of the area, had been devoted to the Great Goddess as Mistress of the Mountain and Wild Beasts at least since the tenth century B.C. The title shows her ancient Paleolithic roots. She became associated with the Great Huntress, protectress of the ancient warrior Amazons who took no consort.

Bejeweled and crowned Cybele holding a frame drum. Modern cast from terra-cotta mold from the excavations at Olynthus, Greece. Thirteen molds were found in one building which appears to have been a studio, circa fifth to fourth century B.C. At least three of the molds were of Cybele with her frame drum.

The Greeks worshiped her as Artemis and turned her into an adolescent virgin. They built a succession of temples to her. The most magnificent, erected at Ephesus, was one of the seven wonders of the ancient world. Pilgrimages to this shrine became the city's chief source of wealth. The Ephesia, a spring festival celebrated with music and ecstatic dancing, drew devotees from all over the known world. The celebrations eventually incorporated the spring rites of Cybele, and the frame drum played a primary role in the dancing. Early Christian leaders found the popularity of this shrine particularly galling, and Saint Paul demanded its destruction (Acts 19:27). But local silversmiths roused the people to riot in defense of their goddess, and her worship flourished until Artemis's temple was destroyed by Christians at the beginning of the fifth century A.D.

Colonists returning home brought the "foreign" cult of Cybele back to mainland Greece. They were actually reintroducing the ancient Great Mother of Minoan-Mycenaean tradition. For centuries, the Greeks had known her as Rhea or Gaia, the Mother of the Gods, ranked first among their deities. Rhea is of Cretan origin, and scholars agree that she and Cybele are the same goddess.

At first the introduction of Cybele's Phrygian cult to patriarchal Athens caused religious turmoil, but by the fifth century B.C. her religion had become an official state cult. Her temple shared quarters with the law archives. Athens also supervised her sanctuary at the nearby port of Piraeus, appointing its priestesses by lot each year. (There is no record of priests at this shrine until after the Roman conquest.)

Cybele began to appear in Grecian art alongside the Olympian goddesses—Athena, Hera, Aphrodite, and Artemis. She and Rhea merged again, and she was subsequently identified with Rhea's daughter Demeter and her granddaughter Persephone—the ancient trio of maiden, mother, crone. Travelers and emigrants spread her cult to the coastal towns of the Black Sea, into present-day Rumania, Bulgaria, southern Russia, and the Crimea.

Cybele with Greek gods, holding a (broken) tambourine with a lion on the head. Sarcophagus from the necropolis at Sidon, ancient Lebanon.

THE AGE OF PROPHECY

In the first millennium B.C., the priestesses of Cybele and her descendants had assumed the old shamanic function of prophecy. In the ancient world no one, not pharaoh nor queen nor emperor, senator, soldier, or slave, made decisions without consulting oracles. They were questioned about the meaning of events, portents for the future, appropriate personal conduct, the performance of religious ritual, political appointments. The early Roman practice of choosing a king by augury gave us our word *inauguration*.

The concept derives from the belief that this world is a reflection of an unseen pure realm and worldly events are shadowy manifestations of events in the ideal realm. By aligning themselves with divinity, oracular priestesses could transmit and interpret this divine order.

Methods of divination were numerous. Priestesses and priests looked for patterns in the entrails of sacrificial animals or the flight and calls of birds. They drew lots. They interpreted the prophetic dreams of petitioners who had spent the night in a temple sanctuary after ritual purification.

The most dramatic mode, favored among the priestesses of the bee goddess, was inspired utterance. In the depths of ecstatic trance, the oracle was possessed by the deity, who spoke directly through her lips. The words might not have made literal sense, but to the listeners who shared her trance state, they would be charged with significance. The Greek word for this state of transfigured consciousness is *enthusiasmos*—"within is a god"—the root of our word *enthusiasm*.

Ecstatic prophecy has many parallels with shamanism. Prophetesses sought inspiration through a number of external stimuli, including fasting, ingesting honey, inhalation of burning herbs or essential oils, and intoxication via alcohol or psychotropic plants. Cybele's priestesses relied most heavily on the trance-inducing properties of music and dance. The rhythms of frame drums, cymbals, and flutes moved them toward the consecrated, concentrated state of divine revelation.

The oracular tradition very likely reached the classical world through the Minoan civilization on Crete. There is a legend that the first of the famous Delphic oracles was Cretan. According to Robert Graves, the first shrine at Delphi "was made of bees' wax and feathers," symbols of the Great Mother as bee and dove goddess. She took the form of the Python, the archaic snake goddess, to speak through her priestesses. One of the most famous utterances of the Python was "Know thyself." After bathing in a sacred spring, the Delphic oracle sat on a tripod and inhaled the fumes of prophecy, her temple having been purified by the burning of barley meal and laurel leaves. It is even thought that she may have chewed the leaves of the laurel. Many of the same rituals took place at Didyma in Asia Minor, said to be founded by Cretans.

Oracles were almost always women past the age of childbirth. The tradition probably derived from the primordial veneration of menstrual blood as the divine fluid. When a woman passes out of the cycle of bleeding and giving birth, her blood becomes "wise blood," and its energy flows in the guise of prophecy. Oracles prophesied at temples and shrines all over the Mediterranean world, often at the site of sacred springs or caves. They served as mouthpieces for a variety of deities.

Robert Graves contends that originally the Great Mother was the source of all oracular inspiration. Later it was Apollo who spoke through the oracle at Delphi, just as other oracular sites became the domain of gods rather than goddesses. Sometimes a priest intervened between priestess and petitioner, interpreting the words of the prophecy or arranging them in hexameters. Graves sees this as an attempt by patriarchal invaders to limit the authority of the oracles. Because their utterances determined the course of public events as well as personal destinies, they would have wielded enormous political power. From about the eighth century B.C. on, the more prominent Greek oracles achieved international importance.

THE SIBYLS

The Sibyls, a group of women scattered throughout the Mediterranean world, were among the most powerful prophetesses, exercising far-reaching influence on political events. Their sayings were preserved in the Sibylline Books and used as a divination tool in much the same way that the Chinese *I Ching* is still used. A succession of Sibyls at Cumae, just above Naples, prophesied at the mouth of a cave thought to be the entrance to the underworld. They were said to be the incarnation of the same soul for over one thousand years, similar to the way the Tibetan Buddhist Dalai Lama is said to continually reincarnate as himself. Through the cave at Cumae, Aeneas, the semi-divine founder of Rome, descended into the underworld in search of his father with the Sibyl as his guide. She led him through the dangers of the underworld until he found his father and obtained his prophecies. Under the Sibyl's protection, he was able to return to the upperworld. His story is a classic illustration of a shamanic death and rebirth. According to legend, the Sibyl at Cumae sold the Sibylline Books to one of the first kings of Rome, and they were consulted by the Roman senate in times of conflict or distress.

Many prophetesses waved laurel branches or inhaled the fumes of burning laurel leaves, and the laurel wreath is painted on numerous frame drums played in their presence in ancient art. Frame drums remained a principal method to induce the prophetic trance state.

Prophecy and poetry are inspired in similar ways: Revealed truth was often uttered in rhythmic speech. The laurel wreath crowned poets favored by the Muses, the nine daughters of the goddess of memory, Mnemosyne, who inspired the fine arts.

In the melting pot of the Aegean, the ancient mysteries of the goddesses of Europe, Asia, and Africa met and strengthened one another. Out of this matrix the religious imagery of the earliest recorded civilizations passed into the mystery schools of Greece and then Rome.

The laurel wreath symbolizes the power of the frame drum to induce prophetic trances.

Greek vase, red-figured, Attic, circa 420–410 B.C. Legendary musician Mousaios, his wife and child, Deiope and Eumolpos (the legendary ancestor of the family who presided over the Eleusinian mysteries). Also depicted are the Muses and Aphrodite. One of the Muses plays the frame drum.

CHAPTER NINE

....

THE GREAT PROTECTRESS

IN THE FINAL centuries of the Roman Empire, its people embraced mystery traditions that made Rome the last great flourishing center of the goddess's spiritual practices. From the Middle East and Egypt came the mystery schools that had developed out of ancient agricultural rites; from Asia Minor and Greece came the practices of the Mother Goddess Cybele. At the heart of these traditions was the frame drum, the voice of the goddess for thousands of years.

By the third century B.C., the Romans were becoming a strong military presence. For a hundred and fifty years, Rome had been at war conquering and colonizing the rest of Italy. By 205 B.C., they had been embroiled for sixty years in a bloody conflict with the Punic city of Carthage in North Africa that was waged on the Italian peninsula. The loss of life on both sides was staggering. The Romans had lost 130,000 men in murderous hand-to-hand combat—more than twice the number of U.S. fatalities during the Vietnam conflict, and at a time when the world's population was a small fraction of what it is today. In the ravaged countryside, abandoned fields lay fallow. Countless peasants and farmers had died in the crossfire, and many of the survivors had fled to the cities, causing food shortages. These crushing military losses triggered a loss of religious faith in the traditional gods: For the Romans, the fortunes of war mirrored the fortunes of their deities.

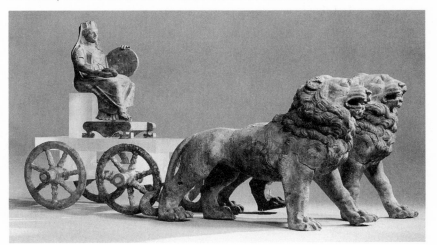

Cybele enthroned on a chariot drawn by lions, found in Rome, circa second century A.D.

In 205 B.C., the tide in the war seemed to have been turning in Rome's favor at last. But the city was too exhausted to mount the final effort necessary to drive the Carthaginians out of Italy. The government coffers were depleted. Inflation was rampant. Frequent meteorite showers rained on the city like urgent messages from the heavens.

Later Roman historians recorded how the senate turned to the Sibylline Books for answers, as had been customary in times of crisis for centuries. According to Livy, a Roman historian of the first century B.C., the books decreed that "if ever a foreign enemy should invade Italy, he could be defeated and driven out if Cybele, the Idaean Mother of the Gods, were brought from Pessinus to Rome." The oracle at Delphi was also consulted, and gave her enthusiastic endorsement to the mission of bringing the goddess Cybele to Rome.

The Romans sent a diplomatic mission to Attalus of Pergamum, their only ally in Asia Minor. Attalus thought it appropriate that Cybele's traditions take root in the capital city of the area's growing military power. He presented the delegation of Roman leaders with a sacred meteorite that was believed to embody the energy of Cybele.

The meteorite representing the goddess came to Rome by ship, sailing though the Hellespont to the Aegean Sea, around Sicily to the Roman port at Ostia, where the city had turned out to receive her with great pomp and celebration. A young man and a young woman chosen as Rome's best formally accepted the meteorite from her Phrygian priestesses and priests. As her boat was towed up the Tiber toward the gates of the city, the whole population crowded onto the riverbanks. Altars smoked with incense and the priestesses and priests accompanying her

Priestess playing frame drum, Greek vase found in Lipari, Italy, circa fourth century B.C.

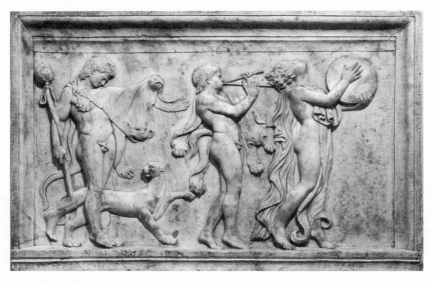

Maenad and two satyrs in a Dionysian procession. Marble relief from the Villa of the Quintilla on the Appian Way, A.D. 100.

sounded their frame drums and cymbals. The meteorite was given a ceremonial bathing in a shallow tributary and installed in the temple of Victory on the Palatine Hill until her own temple could be completed.

The choice of temporary lodgings was not accidental. Many upper-class Romans considered themselves descendants of the Trojans who founded Rome after the fall of Troy. This new deity, Cybele, was the national goddess of the Phrygians, of the same west Asian stock. They were counting on her to bring victory to their homeland. As the Sibylline Books had prophesied, the Romans defeated the Carthaginians, and the Great Protectress Cybele was to reign in the Eternal City for six hundred years, until late in the fourth century A.D.

Roman copy of fifth-century B.C. Greek relief of dancing maenads.

THE MYSTERY SCHOOLS

Cybele's flamboyant Oriental priestesses and priests, playing their frame drums and clashing their cymbals as they danced barefoot with ecstatic abandon, must have shocked and magnetized the Romans. She was the first goddess incorporated directly from Asia into the Roman pantheon. The official religions, primarily concerned with preservation of the state, were cold and remote. In the austere climate of the Republic, the people apparently yearned for a more personal spiritual experience. Cybele's cult caught the popular imagination. It opened the door for the proliferation of mystery schools that flourished when Republic gave way to Empire.

Many cults came to Rome by way of Greece, but their roots were in the older cultures of Anatolia, Mesopotamia, and Egypt. They had grown from ancient Neolithic and even earlier Paleolithic rites. The

Roman relief of a sacrifice to Mithras. A priestess offers incense and fruit as another plays the frame drum.

mystery schools were the last great flourishing of the transformation mysteries of the Great Mother.

DEMETER AT ELEUSIS

For a thousand years, Greek-speaking women and men from throughout the Mediterranean world traveled to Eleusis, outside of Athens, once a year to celebrate the mysteries of Demeter and her daughter Persephone. The Eleusinian mysteries could only be performed at this ancient sacred site. The oldest known sanctuary there dates back to Mycenaean times (circa 1500–1200 B.C.).

Cybele with Hecate and Hermes from the Piraeus, first quarter of fourth century B.C.

Herodotus said the mystery rites of Demeter came from Egypt, but they arrived by way of Crete, where Demeter was the daughter of the Minoan goddess Rhea. After the destruction of Crete, the Minoans migrated to Cyprus, Anatolia, Greece, and possibly on to Ireland. Demeter, like her ancient Sumerian counterparts, was a fertility goddess, the power in the harvest and the grain. One of her titles was "The Fruitful Barley Mother." Her mysteries were based on the symbolism of the seed. Sophocles (the fifth-century Greek poet) said, "Thrice blessed are those mortals who have seen these rites and thus enter into Hades: for them

IN HISTORY

alone there is life, for all others there is misery." From this and other allusions in classical literature we know that the Eleusinian mysteries involved initiatory death and resurrection.

One unusual feature that demonstrates the antiquity of the Eleusinian cult is that it is a goddess, Persephone, rather than a god who must be retrieved from the underworld. Persephone, Demeter's daughter, is the queen of the underworld, the goddess of death. Like Inanna and Erishkigal in the prototype Sumerian myth, they represent opposing aspects of the same Great Goddess. Persephone, like Inanna, is recalled to earth by the playing of the frame drum and the ringing of a gong: "They called Demeter (the noisy) from the noise of the cymbals and drums which was made in searching for Kore [Persephone]."

Vase painting showing Demeter seated on an altar and Persephone crowned with laurel holding torches. Dionysos is seated on an omphalos and a maenad plays a frame drum with a laurel wreath painted on it. Early fourth century B.C.

Persephone in the underworld, her frame drum hanging above her head. South Italian Apulian vase.

Persephone leads a double existence between the underworld and the upperworld. Over her throne in the underworld hangs her frame drum—her means of traveling between the worlds. The importance of the goddess's drum in the secret rites of the cult is clear from an ancient ritual based on the Eleusinian formula: "I have eaten from the drum (tympanon, tambourine); I have drunk from the cymbal (kymbalon); I have carried the sacred dish (kernos); I have stolen into the inner chamber (pastos, shrine)."

The Eleusinian mysteries are thematically linked to the Dionysian rites of the more widely known—and most frequently misinterpreted—of the mystery schools. Both depended to a large extent on music, for Campbell says, "We know . . . that in the Greek rites of the goddess—and of her dead and resurrected daughter Persephone, as well as of her dead and resurrected grandson Dionysos—the choral chant, the boom of the drum, and the hum of the bull-roarer were used."

THE LOVERS OF DIONYSOS

Dionysos's origins are something of an enigma. In Crete he is the son of Rhea or Demeter. In the Greek pantheon he is the son of Semele—yet another incarnation of the One With Many Names—and Zeus. But Dionysos is a much older god than Greek Zeus. There are parallels in the mythology of Dionysos with the Egyptian god Osiris, consort of Isis. Both are vegetation gods who are ripped to pieces and then magically resurrected every year. Some mythologists think Dionysos is the ancient, indigenous consort of the Mother Goddess, and Zeus, the god of a conquering people inserted into the original divine family. The patriarchal Greeks subsequently raised Dionysos over the goddess in importance, but Demeter/Cybele/Persephone/Ariadne remains an important goddess in the Dionysian tradition.

Priestess with wreath and frame drum.

The Dionysian mysteries have an enduring reputation as drunken sexual orgies. This is in part due to the later descriptions by Christian and other patriarchal cultures to whom the ancient sexual mysteries of the goddess along with ecstatic drumming and dancing were anathema. Our word *orgy* comes from *orgia*, derived from a root meaning "deed." The term was used for the celebrations following initiation in mysteries, which might or might not include sexual imagery or behavior. Its ancient connotation seems to have been simply "secret rites." Their aim was the ecstatic transformation of consciousness.

Priestesses officiated at the Dionysian festivals at Delphi for more than a thousand years. They raced surefooted over the mountaintops,

Maenads preparing wine for ritual use beneath an effigy of Dionysos. Red-figured Greek vase found in Italy, circa 420 B.C.

performing secret dances to the beat of their frame drums at intervals along the sacred road. Their journey was made at night in strictest secrecy.

The maenads, priestesses of Dionysos and Cybele, have been associated by historians with unbridled licentiousness and savagery. The word *maenad* means "mad women." Their erotic longing for union with Dionysos found expression in wild, barefoot dances to the primordial music of flute and drums, their unrestrained hair flying wildly about their faces, snakes wrapped around their arms. According to some reports, they drank blood and tore wild beasts limb from limb. Their entranced behavior was disturbing to the uninitiated, but examined in the context of the mystery cults and the goddess tradition they sprang from, they appear in a different light.

Wine, which was introduced to Greece probably from Crete during the Mycenaean period, was indeed an important part of the Dionysian mysteries. There is some evidence that mead, made from fermented honey, was used in Cretan rites in the earliest periods of Minoan culture, but external stimulants were always used in pursuit of higher consciousness—the divine intoxication with the spirit of the deity. References to drinking blood may actually allude to a communion rite in which the fruit of the grape represented the blood of the deity—as it does today in Christian communion rites. According to scholar Walter Burkert, "The association of red wine with blood is widespread and very ancient."

Similarly, a representation of "dismemberment" is a typical aspect of shamanic initiation. The initiate is metaphorically or spiritually torn to bits by wild beasts, often leopards or lions—a ritual dissolution of the old personality so that a new one may be "pieced together."

Roman maenad with snake, frame drum, accompanied by lion.

The Dionysos myth includes a very similar scenario, and it's likely that the maenads ritually reenacted it. They sometimes danced in leopard skins, and Dionysos is also depicted riding on a leopard in a mosaic from the island of Delos. Recall the shamanistic painting in Çatal Hüyük where we found the first frame drum. The dancers in that scene, too, wore leopard skins, which, according to archaeologists James Mellaart and Mary Settegast, indicates a link with shamanism.

Mastery of the precise musical rhythms required to align the devotees' consciousness with divinity suggests a control and sophistication of technique that contradicts the historical image of wanton, frenzied women. Creating rhythms powerful enough to move hundreds of people into ecstatic trance states required skilled and disciplined musicians who were well rehearsed.

The maenads were often depicted on vase paintings adorned with snakes as they danced to the rhythms of the frame drum. Like birds, snakes lay eggs, and the "second birth" of the embryo from the egg is an age-old natural metaphor for resurrection. Many goddesses appear in the form of a snake, and in Egypt and ancient India it was a symbol for the transformative rise of spiritual energy up the spine.

The worship of Dionysos almost certainly involved sexual imagery. The rites clearly derived from the prototypical *hieros gamos*, the sacred marriage rite, performed between the Mother Goddess and the local king or vegetation god. The maenads—mad with divine inspiration, intoxicated with the presence of the goddess—took on her role in the divine consummation.

Burkert describes the state of frenzy the maenads achieved as blessedness and refers to Euripides' Baccae in which the earth is "transformed into a paradise with milk, wine, and honey springing from the ground." These three sacred liquids are the ancient celestial nourishment of the earth goddess.

Enthroned Cybele, second century B.C. Her frame drum has traces of green pigment on it.

Devotees of the Hindu god Krishna, called the *gopis*, were women who also danced themselves into energetic trances to the music of flute, drum, and cymbal, abandoning their families and responsibilities in order to make love to the god. Their manic passion is understood as an appropriate metaphor for the longing of the devotee for the divine presence.

RITES OF THE GODDESS

The Eleusinian and Dionysian mysteries were among the most popular, judging by the frequency with which they are mentioned in contemporary literature, but they were by no means the only ones. The Great Mother's odyssey around the Mediterranean had given her many names—Rhea, Cybele, Magna Mater, Meter, Demeter, Dea Syria, Astarte, Aphrodite, Isis, Ma. The ancients used them and many others interchangeably and different mystery cults evolved around her various regional forms. Initiation into one cult did not exclude membership in others, and it was not unusual for a priestess or priest to serve in the hierarchies of different temples.

Frame drums were played in the traditional marriage rituals in Greece and Italy. Greek marriage vase found in Sicily.

Women were particularly drawn to the mystery rites, though most schools seem to have accepted initiates—called *mystai*—of either sex. In the first four centuries of the Christian era, the mysteries of the Persian god Mithra were revealed to men only. In earlier traditions, Mithra had been the dying and resurrecting consort of the goddess Anahita, who was linked to the frame drum. The wives and daughters of Mithraites celebrated the rites of Cybele.

Many rituals took place in the depths of caves, sometimes called marriage chambers. There are references to going down into caves to unite with the goddess, but because the rites of the mystery cults were performed in secret, we have very little information about their content. What we do know has been pieced together from allusions in classical literature and the distorted allegations of Christian detractors.

PURIFICATION

Initiates into the divine mysteries went through ritual purification by the four elements. At Eleusis, purification by air involved a *liknon*, or winnowing basket, which is a kind of grain sieve, associated with the frame drum in ritual contexts from Neolithic times. A Greek text calls the goddess's drums "the leathern clamorous sieves, played at Bacchic orgies." The bodhran, the large frame drum still used by traditional Irish musicians, was closely associated with folk ritual and played in religious and festival processions. It is identical to the skin sieve of the Celtic

Vase painting of priestess conducting a ritual with the sacred symbols of a bull's head and rosette, south Italian.

goddess Brigit, ritually filled with sprouting grain. Robert Graves suggests that Brigit might be a descendant of the ancient Minoan goddess.

Initiates into Cybele's mysteries were apparently actually buried in a grave or spent time sleeping in an underground pit to receive dream oracles. Upon resurrection, they received "nourishment of milk as if they were being reborn." Initiation into the cults of Osiris and Dionysos also involved lying in tombs. The symbolic experience of death ideally would free the initiate from the fear of actual death. But more important, it was a way of ending one's past conditioning, returning one to an original unconditioned state of awareness. Cult rituals may also have included instructions for the soul after death on the order of the Egyptian and Tibetan *Books of the Dead*. These books contain instructions about the alignment of consciousness in life as well as in the afterlife realms the soul must pass through.

Mythology and analogies from nature provided the metaphors for these rites. They probably evolved from the worship of grain goddesses that first arose in the Neolithic. Though the characters change, the basic outline of their story is a familiar one. A young god or hero, consort of the goddess, dies or is torn to bits. Women mourn him with weeping and beat their drums to petition for his return. The goddess restores him to life, often by giving birth to a divine male child at the winter solstice.

Roman sarcophagus with Dionysian scene, frame drum decorated with a lotus, circa A.D. 250.

In the agricultural societies of earlier times, the death-and-resurrection ritual, often marking the New Year, was a fertility rite. It focused on the power in the seed to resurrect the plant. In the mystery cults, this aim had been internalized. Initiates sought individual salvation through the elevation of consciousness.

Salvation in the pre-Christian world embraced a blessed existence in this world as well as the next. Cicero, a Roman statesman (106–43 B.C.), speaking of the Eleusinian mysteries, said they taught "how to live in joy, and how to die with better hopes."

The joyful resurrection ceremonies reenacted the ancient transformative miracle of water to grain to flour to bread, often in the form of a

Greek and Roman frame drum designs. The drum has always been the means to invoke the goddess's presence. The beat of the drum is the point of contact between the worlds of the unmanifest and the manifest, of the living and the dead, of the divine and human. The sound of the drum results in an invocation of the divine presence and also acts as the containing vessel for the manifestation of sacred energy.

communion ritual involving bread and some sacred liquid—honey or milk, beer or wine. Sexual imagery and behavior celebrated new life and communion with divinity.

Those who had been initiated into a cult could participate in dramatic rites reenacting mythological events. The deities were believed to be present in the devotees portraying them. These elaborately staged productions used music and drama to induce the intense release of emotion called catharsis in players and audience alike. Classical Greek drama developed out of this religious tradition, in particular from the rites of Dionysos.

Music was central to cult ritual throughout the classical world. Its power could protect and purify; it could drive away negative influences. It called down the goddess and aligned the consciousness of her devotee with her divinity. The rhythms of tambourine, flute, and cymbal accompanied every phase of the ritual.

The tambourine was Cybele's instrument. She brought its use to the Dionysian rites, with which she is closely linked. Basically, it is the ancient frame drum of the goddess, embellished with sistrumlike jingles. In Rome by the third century A.D., the maenads are clearly playing frame drums with insets of jingles. This combined two of the most ancient and powerful instruments for changing states of consciousness— the drum and the sistrum.

When there was dancing, says music historian Johannes Quasten, "a tambourine nearly always accompanies the flute, since the tambourine is especially suited to marking rhythm." And there was always

Roman silver platter, found in England, decorated with Dionysian scenes, circa fourth century A.D.

dancing. Lucian, writing in the second century A.D., tells us, "One cannot find a single ancient initiation in which dancing does not take place." To pray was to dance to the rhythm of the frame drum.

THE LURE OF CYBELE

Catullus has left a vivid description of Cybele's worship: "Come, follow me to the house of the Phrygian Cybele, to the grove of the Phrygian goddess! There sounds the clang of the cymbals, there echo the tambourines, there the Phrygian flutist plays upon his deep-sounding, twisted reed. There the Maenads, adorned with ivy, toss their heads wildly. There they celebrate the holy rites to the sound of shrill screams."

The scene sounds very similar to descriptions of Dionysian revels. According to Burkert, the cults of Dionysos and Demeter "show specific relations to the ancient Anatolian Mother Goddess," of whom Cybele is a direct descendant. In Rome, the rites of Dionysos and Cybele became closely intertwined.

Cybele's consort was the shepherd Attis, born to the virgin goddess Nana on December 25. He was sexually unfaithful, and to punish him Cybele drove him mad. Attis castrated himself with a stone and

Cybele shrine from Lydia, Roman period, first century A.D.

then committed suicide. His body was bound to a pine tree, which is his symbol. In commemoration, Cybele's priests, the *galli*, ritually castrated themselves on Black Friday, the anniversary of Attis's death. Thereafter they dressed as women.

The annual mourning of Attis's death was followed by a ritual reenactment of his conception. His tree-phallus was carried into his mother's sacred cave so that he could be conceived again. Cybele's devotees celebrated his resurrection ecstatically with music, dancing, and sexual abandon.

Roman historians recorded the initial shock of the conservative Roman ruling class at the introduction of Cybele's rites. They had adopted her for political reasons, but she grew so popular that her

Cybele found in Virunum, Roman period. The back of the drum is decorated with a lotus.

image, with its battlement crown, came to symbolize the city. In a distortion of her function as goddess of death, she became a goddess of war. Conquering Roman legions brought her cult to Africa, back to Asia, to western Europe, and across the Channel into Britain. It seemed that, as long as she was honored in Rome, the Empire could not fall.

In the first century A.D., Claudius I made Cybele's worship a public institution. The Megalensia, a cycle of holidays celebrating the beginning of spring, from March 15 to 27, was a Romanized version of Cybele's mysteries. It began with the mourning of Attis at the vernal equinox, which included bull sacrifices in Cybele's Palatine temple, the Phrygianum, and ended with the Hilaria, a joyful procession when Cybele's statue was taken to the river to be purified. According to contemporary accounts, enthusiastic followers tossed flowers at her all along the route. Cult members, parading in bright costumes behind her priestesses and priests, danced through the streets like whirling dervishes to the sound of her sacred drums.

Unlike many of her sister goddesses, Cybele did not lose her power to the gods of an invading people. Her vanquisher was already within the city walls. In the shadow of her temples, a new Eastern mystery cult gained strength. It stemmed from a monotheistic patriarchal tradition and rejected the notion of female deities, female prophets, female equality. Its devotees were bound to the exclusive worship of one male god.

With the ascendancy of Christianity, Cybele's great temple in Rome was destroyed. On the exact spot where the Phrygianum once stood, Christians built the basilica of the Vatican. This was the beginning of the end of the ancient tradition of spiritually powerful women drummers.

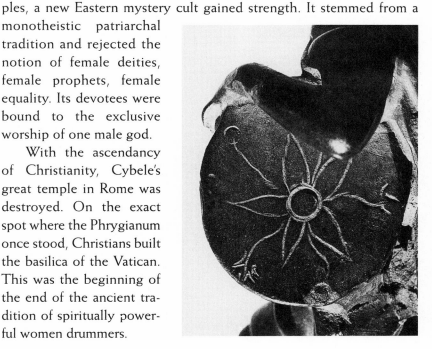

The back of the drum from the figure above.

Part IV

Dispossessed

Women are ordered not to speak in church, not even softly, nor may they sing along or take part in the responses, but they should only be silent and pray to God.

Didascalia of the Three Hundred Eighteen Fathers, circa a.d. 375

Christians are not allowed to teach their daughters singing, the playing of instruments or similar things because, according to their religion, it is neither good nor becoming.

Commandments of the Fathers, Superiors and Masters, circa a.d. 576

HOW DID THE omnipotent Great Mother, whose frame drum called both women and men to share in her divinity for so many thousands of years, vanish so completely that, a mere fifteen hundred years after the last spring festival in Cybele's temple at Rome, we hardly know of her existence?

As the Roman Empire declined, Christianity challenged the pagan religions of its citizens. But the defeat of the Great Goddess involved much more than changing religious beliefs. It was a victory in a clash of worldviews that had been waged across Europe, Asia, and the Indian subcontinent since the end of the Neolithic.

By the time barbarian hordes leveled the great cities of Harappan civilization, they had already imposed their patriarchal religion and social order upon the indigenous goddess cultures of most of Europe and western Asia. The fusion of these two traditions spawned the great body of confusing and often contradictory mythology of classical times.

Because drumming was recognized as an ancient source and symbol of the power of female technicians of the sacred, drumming was banned. Henceforth divinity was to be exclusively masculine. The suppression of women was directly linked to the suppression of the goddess.

CHAPTER TEN

THE STORM GOD

A detail of "The Effects of Good Government," Ambrogio Lorenzetti, fourteenth century A.D.

PRECEDING PAGE: Fresco by Andrea di Bonaiuto, Florence, fourteenth century.

CITY LIFE

The grain revolutions of the Neolithic allowed people to settle in one place for the first time. Large populations clustered around centers of trade, depleting the area's resources and playing havoc with its ecology. Slowly, people's perception of the natural world began to change from reverence of its sustaining power to desire to control it.

Trade stimulated the accumulation of large hoards of grain and live-stock by some groups of people, whose wealth gave them power over their less acquisitive neighbors in difficult times. The process of social stratification had begun. Jealousy, rivalry, warfare followed in inevitable succession.

These conflicts crippled the development of urban culture, particularly in Mesopotamia. As cities succumbed to chaos, nomadic bands of people were left to survive as best they could. These were not the nomads of traditional tribal culture but militaristic raiding bands that plundered one area after another, stealing cattle, murdering men, and taking women captive as part of the spoils of war. The shift from female religious authority to male military power relegated women to the status of property.

"Mesolithic society may have seen the domestication of animals, and Neolithic society may have seen the domestication of plants," says William Irwin Thompson, "but what the age after the Neolithic sees is the domestication of women by men."

What happened in Sumer is symptomatic.

THE HULUPPU TREE

In Chapter 6, the poem *Inanna's Descent* provided a glimpse into the religious traditions of early Sumer. *The Huluppu-Tree* preserves another myth about Inanna.

Inanna comes across the Tree of Creation, a huluppu tree, which has been uprooted and carried away by the erratic currents of the Euphrates. She plants it in her sacred garden in her holy city of Uruk, meaning to use its wood to make herself a bed and throne—symbols of her sovereignty and the divine mystery of sexuality.

But hidden in the tree is a host of wild creatures. A snake has built its nest in the roots. The wild woman Lilith has made her home in the lower branches. The ferocious Imdugud bird is raising its brood in the upper limbs. Inanna has unwittingly brought these unruly forces into the civilized garden of her city.

The goddess turns to the warrior-king Gilgamesh for help. Shielded by his armor, he slaughters the snake. Lilith and the Imdugud birds flee in terror. Gilgamesh makes Inanna a bed and throne from the tree. In return, she carves him a drum and drumstick: "She fashions its roots into a *pukku* for him, fashions its crown into a *mikku* for him . . . in

Relief of male military drummers from the palace of King Barrekup. Sinjirli, Neo-Hittite, eighth century B.C.

street and lane he made the drumming resound."

Gilgamesh used Inanna's gift to summon the young men to war. There followed much death and destruction. The wails of the young women caused Gilgamesh's drum to fall into the underworld. His friend Enkidu, who goes to retrieve it, dies there.

It is difficult to assign a date to this story. Although the poem we know it from was probably recorded no later than the text of *Inanna's Descent*—sometime in the second millennium B.C.—both derive from oral versions whose origins can no longer be traced. But while the story of Inanna's descent into the underworld retains the symbols and character of very old shamanistic initiation rites, *The Huluppu-Tree* introduces newer, disparate elements.

The wild creatures harboring in the Tree of Creation are all aspects of the goddess in her earliest role as Mistress of the Wild Beasts. The snake is her connection with the underworld, the bird her link to the heavens. Both are familiar motifs, appearing as symbols of the powers of the Divine Feminine in culture after culture. Lilith represents the primordial, forever untamed aspects of the female. She probably originated in Sumer; later she passed into Hebrew folklore as Adam's first wife, the demon who sent the snake to tempt Eve. In *The Huluppu-Tree*, it appears that these wilder attributes of divinity must be sacrificed to the demands of urbanization.

In *Inanna's Descent*, the goddess turned to her priestess to help her return from the underworld. The priestess showed her the way home through the beating of the drum—the traditional shamanic path between worlds. In *The Huluppu-Tree*, Inanna turns instead to the great mythological war hero, Gilgamesh. He uses the implements of war to make quick work of the wild things.

What happens next is revealing. Gilgamesh, not Inanna, builds her bed and throne—her spiritual and temporal power apparently subordinated under his protection—and she makes him a drum. In his hands the drum is not an instrument of divine guidance, but rather a military tool, drummed to incite martial rather than spiritual fervor. Gilgamesh loses the drum, but the goddess's power is compromised. In a later legend, Gilgamesh humiliates Inanna and firmly diminishes her powers.

The story mythologizes the transformation of Sumer from a temple society led by priestesses and priests to an assortment of city-states under the protection of hero-kings.

McNeill notes that "the rise of kingship in Mesopotamia . . . was also connected with the earliest known manifestation of war dances—close order drill." The drum, formerly the sacred instrument of priestesses used for spiritual transformation, took on a new, masculine function on the parade ground. As militarism increased, the progress of a battle became known as "the dance of Inanna." The ancient goddess of life and death had become a goddess of war.

FROM TEMPLE TO PALACE

The earliest Sumerians had no word for king. When a community was under threat of attack, an assembly of its male members elected a temporary war leader, but as time passed, and warlike activity increased throughout the region, some of these leaders retained their armed forces and instituted hereditary kingships.

At first these kings did not affect the authority of the temple hierarchies that governed early Sumerian society, but the maintenance of large royal retinues and military forces eventually took a heavy toll on the resources of the city-state. Shifting loyalties and the claims of rival kings kept people under constant threat of danger. They chose sides for protection. Gradually, the focus of society shifted from temple to palace.

McNeill sees this shift as the beginning of the separation of church and state, which has distinguished Western civilization from Oriental cultures for thousands of years.

This change gave rise to a different system of class stratification. Palace officials bought up small farms and created huge estates, turning landowners into tenant farmers. Metallurgists and other craftspeople who specialized in the production of goods for military markets thrived.

The increasing militarism of Sumerian culture was not only the result of skirmishes between local kings. There was also a new breed of invaders flooding the river valley.

THE PEOPLE OF THE STORM GOD

Starting in the fourth millennium B.C., a fierce warrior culture began a series of violent migratory invasions into the Middle East, Europe, and India. History has not preserved their exact origins, but they are generally believed to have come from the Caucasian Mountains in the Russian steppes. Historians refer to them as Aryans or Indo-Europeans or Kurgans.

These bearded warriors stormed across plains and valleys in horse-drawn chariots, brandishing weapons of metal. Their relentless incursions went on for several thousand years. In the third millennium B.C., more than three hundred towns and settlements in Anatolia were attacked and destroyed. Next the cities in Asia Minor, Mesopotamia, the Aegean, and Greece fell. By 1000 B.C., the Indus Valley had been subdued, and Aryan tribes occupied the Italian peninsula.

The culture of these invaders was fiercely patriarchal. They worshiped a violent storm god who resided not on earth but in the heavens. Unlike the indigenous worship of the Great Mother, tied to the natural world and the miracle of birth, their religion was firmly centered on man. The gods existed to help him establish his rightful dominion over nature, animals, and womankind.

Aryan war tactics included massacre and rape. They attempted to impose their cultural values on their victims in similar fashion, by forcibly marrying the local goddess to the storm god. This entailed usurping the powers of creation that gave the goddess her authority. The result was some new and rather startling creation myths: Eve created from Adam's rib, Athena springing from Zeus's head, male deities masturbating the world into existence.

Heroic mythology records the history of Aryan attempts to suppress the old religion. In India, Indra, the Lord of the Mountain, slays the serpent goddess Vrta. In Babylon, Marduk kills his own mother, the old dragon goddess Tiamat. Yahweh, the Hebrew storm god, destroys the serpent monster Leviathan. Perseus slays the serpent-haired Medusa. Typhon and Python, the sons of the earth goddess Gaia, are killed by Zeus and Apollo. And so on.

Serpents, ancient symbols of the goddess, were turned into representations of evil. Horned and hoofed deities, celebrating shamanic unity with the natural world, became demons. Darkness had always been the realm of the Great Mother—the darkness of the womb, of caves, of night. The new gods styled themselves lords of light.

The allure of the old goddess was strong. Across Asia and Europe, her worship continued to animate the great cultures of the Mediterranean world for thousands of years. Invading patriarchal cults were not very successful in eradicating goddess worship, as many examples in the Old Testament make clear. The books of Kings and Chronicles, which relate the migratory history of the Israelites, are full of references to the destruction of altars to Asherah, the name the Phoenician Canaanites gave to the Mother Goddess. Apparently the people simply rebuilt them. The unknown author of 2 Kings 17:41, writing of events at the end of the eighth century B.C., complains, "Even while these people were worshiping the Lord, they were serving their idols. To this day their children and grandchildren continue to do as their fathers did."

The *Dictionary of the Bible* says that Asherah (Ashtoreth) is mistakenly rendered in the Authorized Version of the Bible as the Hebrew word for *grove*. In 2 Kings, 23:4-8, "And the king commanded Hilkiah the high priest . . . to bring forth out of the temple of the Lord all the vessels that were made for Baal [the consort of Asherah], and for the *grove* [Asherah], and for all the host of heaven: and he burned them . . . And he brought out the *grove* from the house of the Lord . . . and burned it at the brook Kidron, and stamped it small to powder . . . And he brake down the houses of the Sodomites, that were by the house of the Lord, where the women wove hangings for the *grove*."

Open sexuality was unacceptable in patriarchal cultures, where property passed from father to son. A man could not be sure his heirs were truly his unless he was able to assert absolute sexual authority over his women. In these cultures, women were no longer reflections of the divine principle of creation, or even the sexual equals of their partners. Their purpose was to bear their husband's children—preferably males.

Priests of the storm-god cosmologies characterized their struggle to supplant goddess worship as a cosmic battle between good and evil. Rome was the setting for its final act.

CHRISTIAN COMMUNITY

While the mystery cults swept through the Roman Empire, Judaism clung to monotheism and continued to prohibit its adherents from participation in other rites. Instead, a number of messianic cults sprang up within the Hebrew community. Due to energetic proselytizing among pagans as well as Jews, the sect calling themselves Christians spread throughout the Mediterranean world during the first century A.D. There was a Christian community in Rome as early as A.D. 57. Only seven years later, Nero ordered the first persecution of Christians, whom he blamed for a great fire that destroyed much of the city. Most of his contemporaries believed the fire was set by the emperor himself. But the Christians must already have been numerous enough for Nero to consider them a political threat.

Initially in Rome, Christianity was a religion of foreigners. It appealed to the poor, and to the vast numbers of immigrants or slaves brought to the city from territories under Roman rule. The word *pagani*—pagans—used by Christians to describe worshipers of the old goddesses and gods, meant simply "people of the place."

The mystery cults were sanctioned by the state, which funded large public ceremonies like the spring Megalensia devoted to Cybele. Cultic celebrations were holidays on the official state calendar, but many of the mystery schools themselves, though in theory open to anyone, were too costly for any but the privileged classes. Membership fees were high, and cultic traditions like the sumptuous meals of the dead, laid out at graveside funerals, were prohibitively expensive.

Christian rites, which stressed faith rather than ritual, were more affordable. The Communion feast was largely symbolic; it did not entail enormous food and entertainment bills. The rite of sacrifice was replaced by "adoration of the spirit," saving the cost of sacrificial animals. Christianity was the only religion without social, racial, financial, or educational barriers.

The new religion was a refuge from the excesses of the Empire, the endless banquets and bloodthirsty entertainments, the whims of deranged emperors. Early Christians lived communally and set powerful examples of charity and brotherly love. They provided social services on a scale unparalleled in the ancient world. They took care of orphans, widows, and the aged; during epidemics they tended the sick and buried the dead; during sieges they cared for the wounded and dying.

Membership in mystery schools was a personal affair, but Christianity involved the whole family. Children were educated in the tenets of the religion and urged not to marry outside the sect. Sexual activity was limited to marital partners, for the purpose of procreation rather than ecstatic communion. And women were encouraged to bear large numbers of children to increase the ranks of Christians. Not surprisingly, the sect grew rapidly from generation to generation.

FAITH AND REASON

In time, Christianity also appealed to the educated classes. Since its great flowering in the fifth century B.C., Greek philosophy had dominated the intellectual life of the Mediterranean world. Thinkers like Plato and Aristotle expounded the rational, scientific definition of reality that modern Western civilization has inherited.

Greek religion was in no position to answer the challenge of new models of thought. There was no exclusive priesthood or sacred scriptures to provide rules and regulations. Instead, there was a body of garbled myth from the fusion of the traditions of the patriarchal invaders and the aboriginal worshipers of the goddess. These myths portrayed the behavior of the goddesses and gods as petty, childish, vindictive, and dishonest. Zeus, the supreme father god of the Greeks, raped literally hundreds of goddesses and mortal women. Inevitably, scholars began to question the existence of their gods. Perhaps the sun was not a great god driving his chariot across the horizon but a flat, incandescent stone, or possibly a mass of molten metal.

In the third century, while Christianity battled the old goddesses and gods for political control of the Empire, Plotinus popularized a synthesis of the ideas of Plato and other philosophers called Neoplatonism. It brought pagan intellectuals one step closer to Christian philosophy. Instead of a pantheon of bickering divinities, it posited an abstract power or divine energy behind all creation. The concept recalls the Egyptian idea of the primordial vibration; not coincidentally, Plotinus was born and educated in Egypt.

Christianity could answer the challenges philosophy posed to traditional religion. The Christian god was a single, universal force, active in the universe but devoid of the all-too-human faults that plagued the old gods. Christians had divinely revealed Scriptures that recounted an alternate sacred history and also laid down absolute rules of personal conduct. It was a faith amenable to reason.

THE BATTLE FOR ROME

By the third century A.D., the Christian Church in Rome was wealthy enough to attract political attention. A series of decrees between A.D. 250 and 260 made the refusal to sacrifice to the old goddesses and gods punishable by death. These were directed mainly at the clergy and prominent laypeople, and the number of victims was small compared to

the number of believers. In 284, Diocletian outlawed Christianity. Christians rapidly lost their civil rights, including the right to hold office. Their sanctuaries were destroyed, their books were burned. Persecution led the Church to develop an even stronger administrative core. By 312, under Constantine, it was granted legal status as an official state religion.

The next half-century witnessed a struggle between devotees of the old gods and Christians. Whose deity was more powerful? The Empire was in decline. To the Romans, who judged the strength of their goddesses and gods by the Empire's fortunes, the question was political. To the Christians, struggling against deeply rooted traditions, it was a holy war, and the soul of each convert was a battlefield.

My research for this book took me to the Vatican museum in search of tambourine players. I found plenty of them in pagan Roman art, particularly on sarcophagi decorated with Dionysian scenes. Bad Roman art is very bad, but the best is quite good and a few of these scenes were exquisite. The joy of being in the body, the radiant sexuality, the equality of size and grace between men and women projected a sense of the divine miracle of life itself. These containers for the dead were alive with the exuberance of union with the divine through ecstatic music and dance.

But as I wandered farther through the Vatican's vast holdings, my

Roman sarcophagus illustrating the beauty and joy of the sensual human body as depicted in the Dionysian rites, circa second–third century A.D.

Ariadne and Dionysos on a Roman sarcophagus.

mood dissolved into nagging irritation. I found myself staring at some reliefs from the early Christian period, produced a mere fifty years after the graceful Dionysian sarcophagi. The deterioration in artistic quality was shocking, but more horrifying was the depiction of the human body. Oversized heads perched atop stunted bodies. Hands covered genitals in shame. And where were the women? On their knees, sometimes with their heads at the feet of men. My irritation grew to anger. What happened in those fifty years?

STOPPING THE MUSIC

For people accustomed to the laissez-faire attitudes of pagan religions, the Christian demand to give up the worship of all other deities must have been difficult. On pagan feast days, they would often throw off the constraints of Christian piety, succumbing to the seductive beat of the drum. The Church retaliated by forbidding the use of music in Christian worship. It was replaced by the singing of psalms a cappella.

Adam and Eve standing naked and in shame at the Tree of Life, wrapped with the serpent—now the ultimate symbol of evil. The only other woman in the scene is on her knees.

Christians did not bow to this dictum without protest. They pointed out that the Old Testament contains explicit references to the use of music in worship. The tambourine, the harp, and the shofar figure prominently in ancient Hebrew traditions, which draw heavily on Mesopotamian and Egyptian sources. The timbrel (frame drum) was played by Jewish women in marriage rites and processions to honor the lord of the Old Testament: "Your procession has come into view, O God, the procession of my God and King into the sanctuary. In front are the singers, after them the musicians; with them are the maidens playing tambourines" (Psalms 68:24–25). David pleased God by dancing to the music of tambourine, the cymbal, and stringed instruments.

When the great Jewish heroine Judith killed the Assyrian military leader Holofernes, who was persecuting and killing Jews, she led her people in a song of praise: "Begin unto my God with timbrels [tambourines], Sing unto my Lord with cymbals" (Judith 16:1).

A passage in the Old Testament book of 1 Samuel, which chroni-

Frame drummer from ancient Israel, circa 1000 B.C.

Woman holding frame drum, circa eighth to sixth century B.C., ancient Israel.

cles Judaic history from the mid-eleventh century B.C., links music with the trance state of prophecy: "As you approach the town, you will meet a procession of prophets coming down from the high place with lyres, timbrels, flutes and harps being played before them, and they will be prophesying. The Spirit of the Lord will come upon you in power, and you will prophesy with them; and you will be changed into a different person." The ancient tradition of priestesses drumming and dancing themselves into an ecstatic, prophetic state was recorded in the stories of Miriam: "And Miriam the prophetess, the sister of Aaron, took a timbrel in her hand, and all the women went out after her with timbrels and with dances" (Exodus 15:20).

The Church fathers replied to members who pointed out the ancient traditions of worship with tambourine, flute, and harps, that the Old Testament Israelites were still being weaned from the greater evil of idolatry, picked up in Egypt. God, perceiving that they were too weak to give up music as well, had allowed them to use it in his worship —temporarily. But God's true feelings about instrumental music were revealed by the prophet Amos (Amos 5:21–23), who said, "Away from me with the noise of your songs: the playing of your harps I do not wish to hear." In the same invective, however, Amos railed against religious feasts, burnt offerings, and grain offerings, and it seems clear that it was not music in itself but all the trappings of pagan religion that prompted his fury.

The influence of Greek thought also militated against an understanding of music's spiritual potential. Plato had been among the last philosophers to consider music a legitimate intellectual pursuit. When Athens fell to Sparta at the end of the fifth century B.C., many philosophical ideals were turned on their heads. Musical, artistic, and literary competence had been a hallmark of Athenian culture, whereas the Spartans had foregone the arts to concentrate on warfare. In the aftermath of defeat, Athenian society turned from the study of the arts. In time only professional musicians received any musical training, and they were no longer considered cultured people.

The strength of the converts' attachment to music as worship is clear from the frequency and vehemence with which it was condemned by early Church fathers. Clement of Alexandria, writing at the end of the second century, bitterly attacked musicians, saying, "Such a man creates a din with cymbals and tambourines, he rages about with instruments of an insane cult."

More than a century later, the Egyptian monk Shenute complained, "While in the church the Eucharist is celebrated and psalms are sung, outside there is the noise of cymbals and flutes." Shenute was describing the atmosphere at a Christian Feast of the Martyrs, a ritual that developed to supplant the popular cult vigils for the dead.

NEW VIGILS

Because music seemed the most alluring aspect of pagan worship, the Christian Church would not compromise its ban. But it made other concessions. New rites were deliberately designed to replace popular pagan practices. The Commemoration of the Martyrs was modeled after the Roman *perviglia*, the all-night vigils in honor of the dead.

No other religious festivities were celebrated with more singing and dancing—performed primarily by female musicians and dancers.

Christianity attempted to answer these popular activities with all-night marathons of Communion (commemorating Christ's sacrifice), Bible readings, prayer, and the singing of psalms. Sometimes there was a feast within the Church; in other areas, worshipers apparently fasted all day, took Communion, then went home for a feast before returning for the all-night prayer vigil. The scheme had its drawbacks. The people did indeed associate Christian vigils with the *perviglia*, and continued to celebrate them with the same pagan customs they were designed to subvert. Chief among these was music. Clerics across Christendom complained that it led to debauchery in the darkest corners of the sanctuary.

The Church responded by barring women from vigils. Misogyny was never far from the surface of Church actions, as the letters of Paul attest, but the predominance of women musicians in pagan cults no doubt contributed to the tendency among Church fathers to blame women for lapses in their rules for piety. Women and their music were intimately involved with the image of the goddess and her regenerative powers. The first such ban was issued in 300; it was far from the last. A Church council in 826 prohibited the singing and dancing of women. In the thirteenth century, women who "dance in pagan fashion for their dead and go to the grave with drums, dancing the while," were not allowed to attend church services. Apparently, more than a thousand years of official proscription had not succeeded in silencing the goddess's drum.

Frame drums, sistrums, flutes, and kitharas were instruments of ritual mourning in ancient religions. Female mourners lamented with music and cathartic gestures of grief—tearing their hair out, scratching

A detail of the painting by Ambrogio Lorenzetti "The Effects of Good Government," showing that the traditions of dancing and singing to the frame drum continued despite persecutions. Siena, fourteenth century A.D.

their faces, ripping their clothes. Biblical references tell us that the Israelites also mourned their dead in this fashion. The Church took the position that such extreme behavior denied the doctrine of personal resurrection, in which the bereaved should take comfort.

Ironically, the traditional role of the frame drum in funeral rites was to facilitate resurrection. It stemmed from the shamanic power of the drum to bring about rebirth in ancient initiation rites. Christian Church fathers were no longer aware of this association; in any case, they were not interested in the content of pagan cults. They wanted only to crush them.

Again, the Church identified women as the problem. In the third century they were barred from funerals—probably without much success, since this same ban was issued in the sixth and seventh centuries. (In some parts of Spain, women are still barred from funeral processions.) In some areas Christians got around the bans by hiring pagan women as professional mourners.

THE CHRISTIAN PERSECUTIONS

Despite these internal troubles, Christianity's political power grew by leaps and bounds. In an old legend, Constantine, the first Christian emperor, transformed a statue of Cybele into a statue of Tyche, the goddess of fortune. The position of her hands was changed so that the palms faced outward in a gesture of protection. Tyche was associated with Constantinople—the old city of Byzantium, newly renamed for the emperor, who was trying to establish it as the Empire's eastern capital. Constantine placed the statue in Rome opposite the statue of Fortuna, her counterpart. Perhaps he hoped to co-opt the goddess's power for himself.

Constantine initially shared his authority with three co-emperors. Gradually, through some adroit political moves, he became sole emperor and promptly initiated legislation designed to deliver the Empire into Christian hands. In 353, he forbade sacrifices at night vigils; a year later he extended the ban to all sacrifices and closed all pagan temples. He issued decrees forbidding idolatry, sorcery, and divination.

The Christians, to whom tolerance was apostasy, were determined to eradicate every trace of pre-Christian civilization. A century earlier, Romans had burned Christian texts. Now the Christians burned entire libraries. Temples, the university systems of the ancient world, were torched. On November 8, 392, the emperor Theodosius abolished all freedom to practice pagan cults. In Egypt, murderous bands of ascetic monks terrorized the countryside, destroying sanctuaries and killing non-Christians.

The status of women sank to a new low. Paul and Timothy had preached that women should not speak out in public. Early in the fifth century in Alexandria, Hypatia, a popular university lecturer in philosophy and mathematics, was singled out by Bishop Cyril. Hypatia was a pagan and her position as a beloved elder professor of both pagans and Christians offended Cyril. When the university refused to fire her, he ordered monks to drag her from her chariot into a church, where they brutally slashed her to death with oyster shells in the name of God. Bishop Cyril was later elevated to sainthood by the Vatican.

In 529 the emperor Justinian instituted the death penalty for pagans and closed the great Academy of Athens. The traditional academies of learning were all associated with pagan traditions and were henceforth to be destroyed.

Christian ethics dominated in the public arena. Music was frowned upon in private life as well as in worship. Actors, athletes, and professional musicians could not be baptized. In the sixth century, Pope John III outlawed the tambourine. The voice of Great Goddess was officially silenced.

This wholesale assault on the ancient centers of learning and the scholars, musicians, and artists associated with pagan traditions was one of the factors that drove western Europe into the Dark Ages. Yet some men and women still clung to the old ways. Not until the persecutions of the Inquisition, which began in the thirteenth century and lasted for five hundred years, were many of the old traditions finally eradicated. It took the brutal murders of hundreds of thousands—possibly millions—of women, mostly, but also men, children, and even babies, to stamp out the pre-Christian traditions in western Europe.

A young woman drumming, from the painting by David Allan "Sir John Halkett & Family," Scotland, 1781.

CHRISTIAN DOCTRINE EVENTUALLY succeeded in robbing women of their spiritual heritage, but it could not smother the human need for a divine feminine force and presence. This need found its outlet in the worship of Mary, Christ's mother. Although official efforts were made to distance Mary from the aspects of the pagan goddesses whom Christian fathers found so troubling, she has become a repository for remnants of goddess worship down to the present day.

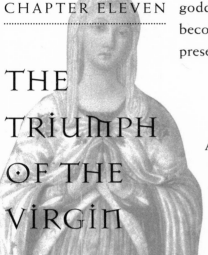

CHAPTER ELEVEN

THE TRIUMPH OF THE VIRGIN

MITHRA AND CHRIST

Although Christianity sprang from the patriarchal Hebrew tradition, its mythology borrowed heavily from indigenous religious traditions. By the time Constantine granted Christianity official status in Rome, the biography of Christ and the doctrines of his Church dovetailed with the gods and tenets of other popular cults. No doubt this had happened gradually as Christianity became dominated by converts from Roman rather than Judaic sects. The similarities between Mithra and Christ have been remarked on since the beginning of the Christian era.

Mithra, son of the Persian sun god, was born on December 25. Different myths offer several candidates for his mother. In one, she was the Mother of God, making her the sun god's consort and mother—the traditional hierogamous relationship. In another, she was a human virgin, a variant of the divine marriage myth popular in many mystery cults. In a third, Mithra sprang from a sacred female rock, fertilized by his father in the form of lightning—the sort of fantastic solution typical of patriarchal religions faced with the irksome problem of woman's powers of creation. One of Mithra's names is Petra, the Greek word for rock.

He was born in a sacred cave,
attended by shepherds and Magi
bearing gifts. Throughout his life
he performed miracles, including
healing the sick, casting out devils,
and raising the dead. He had
twelve disciples, one for each sign
of the zodiac. These twelve were
the guests at Mithra's Last Supper.
The *missa* (Latin for mass), a reenactment of this meal, was one of
the seven sacraments of the cult.
The bread at the missa was marked
with a cross.

Mithra's ascent into heaven to
rejoin his father was celebrated at
the spring equinox. He was buried
in the rock cave where he was
born, representing his mother's
womb, whence he resurrected.

Mithraic priests were celibate
men, and the high priest's title was
Pater Patrum. They taught that the
earth would end in fire after the
final conflict between the forces of
light and darkness. The good—
that is, the faithful devotees of
Mithra—would be saved. Sinners
would be cast into the darkness of
hell.

Christianity incorporated elements of all the versions of
Mithra's birth: Mary was a human
virgin, but is also called the
Mother of God. Petra, or Peter, is
the name given Christ's chief disci-
ple, his successor as head of the
Church. Saint Peter carried the
keys of heaven; so did Mithra
before him. Papa, the Latin word
for pope, is a shortened form of

Matteo di Giovanni, "Madonna with the Girdle," mid-fifteenth century.

DISPOSSESSED

Pater Patrum. The parallels between cave and manger birth scenes, Communion rites, and doctrines of heaven and hell are obvious.

Mithraism developed in Persia out of earlier storm-god religions. Interestingly, Mithra may originally have been female. According to Herodotus, the ancient Persians worshiped the sky goddess Mitra. She then merged with Anahita, identified with the Anatolian Great Goddess Ma. Later, Anahita and Mithra split again as opposing aspects of divinity—water and fire, darkness and light, female and male. By A.D. 307, however, when Mithra was proclaimed Protector of the Empire, all feminine aspects had been effectively squelched.

Early Christians were naturally questioned about the similarities between their supposedly new religion and the other cults of the day. They blamed it on the devil, who, they said, had anticipated the divine mysteries (as the sacraments were then called) in pagan cults, to confuse the unenlightened.

The hierogamous rites of Cybele and her consort Attis echo many of these same elements. Attis, a virgin's son, was also born on December 25. He died and was reborn annually at the spring equinox with rites that anticipated the Christian Holy Week. On Black Friday—March 25 —Attis's dying body was hung on a tree. After death, he descended into the underworld for three days, after which he rose from the dead. The popular Hilaria Festival celebrated his resurrection.

CHANGING TIME

Though Christianity absorbed the mythic structure of the ancient agricultural rite, it removed its central character—the life-giving goddess. This very crucial revision strips the myth of meaning by severing the important ties of religion to the rhythmic cycles of the earth. When the goddess and her consort consummated their marriage in the temple or the ziggurat, they set the New Year in motion. Their union blessed the harvest and affirmed the eternal cycle of the seasons, of life and death and rebirth. Initiatory rites gave the individual a place in this cycle, and centered her in nature and in the cosmos.

Christianity tried to change the nature of time. No longer could women see their own cycles as part of the divine wheel of life, reflected in the moon and tides and every living thing. Instead of a cyclical wheel, life became a narrow path leading to death and divine judgment. Time had become linear.

The implications of linear time in religious life are severely limiting for women and men alike. Christ's resurrection is not like the resurrection of Attis, Mithra, Osiris, or any of the other consorts of the goddess. Christ is translated one time into a divine state outside observable laws of nature by the power of the father god. The old consorts of the goddess were restored annually to natural life through communal rituals that invoked her powers of rebirth. People experienced a renewal and resurrection of their own through the grace of She who gives birth.

A WOMAN'S PLACE

The Mithraic cult was exclusive to men, yet their wives and daughters were encouraged to worship at the altar of Cybele, celebrating mysteries more closely aligned to the rites of the women's religions of the Neolithic. Judaism and Christianity denied women this alternative. Both men and women were restricted to the worship of one male god, whose outstanding characteristic in the Old Testament is his wrathful jealousy of other deities.

This male god is asexual in essence. Because the goddess is denied, there can be no sacred marriage rite. There can be no sexuality. In fact, sexuality, because it is excluded from the nature of deity, is considered wrong. The power of a woman to arouse a man sexually is no longer divine. It becomes the original sin. Eve's body became not the means to experience a sacred communion with the divine, but the source of evil released into the world. The underworld, shadowy cave and sacred womb of holy initiation, becomes hell.

When the goddess is denied, all feminine aspects of divinity become negative. Music, particularly music with a strong rhythmic element, was thought by the Christians to incite lust in the human body. Even today, some Christian sects preach against rock and roll on these grounds.

Nakedness was equated with shame and sin. In medieval paintings, Christians in heaven are covered from head to toe in sumptuous aristocratic clothing. The people in hell are in a horrid state of ugly nakedness.

A woman has no place of authority in such a religion. As Christianity developed over the first few centuries, this point was formalized in Church doctrine. It was not enough to exclude women from the priesthood and to ban their traditional instruments of worship. By the fourth century, women were forbidden in many churches to open their mouths: "They should only be silent and pray to God."

There was one exception. Women who were asexual virgins were allowed to sing in choirs. This sent an unspoken message to female converts: By denying their sexuality—their essential femininity—they might become acceptable to this god. But in general, women were not allowed to make music. *Commandments of the Fathers, Superiors and Masters,* issued by the synod of 576, decreed: "Christians are not allowed to teach their daughters singing, the playing of instruments or similar things because, according to their religion, it is neither good nor becoming." As Europe became Christianized and this policy was enforced, Western women were effectively barred from the professions of composing, teaching, or performing music. By 603, even the choirs of virgins were silenced.

THE HOLY VIRGIN

Sheela-na-Gig, from the Church of St. Mary and St. David, Kilpeck, Herefordshire, UK. As you enter the womb of the church you do so through the gates of initiation: the vulva of the goddess.

And yet the Church found it impossible to eradicate entirely the principle of the Divine Feminine. It was too deeply rooted in the soil of the human psyche.

Mary, the virgin mother of Christ, is treated respectfully in the Gospels, but none of them grant her divinity. Her history ends with Christ's resurrection. Somehow, though, she gradually took on the aspects of divinity originally denied her.

Initially the Church tried to keep Mary human and in the background. This led to doctrinal complications. How could a mere woman give birth to God's son? Females have never been well regarded in Judeo-Christian tradition. In its creation myth, woman cost humankind paradise. By expressing her sexuality, Eve brought about the separation of humankind from divinity and introduced death into the world. Eve clearly represented the Great Goddess of pagan religions. She is surrounded by shamanistic and Yogic symbols: the Tree of Life, the serpent, nakedness, nourishing fluid. As the mother of Christ, Mary had to be free of Eve's "taint" of human sexuality.

Sacred sexual priestesses were often called "holy virgins." The term meant that they were unmarried; their sexuality was dedicated to the service of the goddess. The Christian fathers extended the concept in Mary's case to include physical virginity. Some clerics still argue that she remained celibate throughout her life, though the Gospels make explicit reference to Christ's brothers.

In Christian doctrine, conception was envisioned as an ethereal affair, chastely conducted by the Holy Spirit. The dove, formerly

Aphrodite's symbol of ecstatic sexuality, became the symbol of this immaculate conception. As the Holy Spirit, it became the asexual third member of the Holy Trinity, replacing the traditional goddess and removing any trace of the feminine from the divine family.

Yet people refused to give up all aspects of a holy mother. Bowing to necessity, the Church eventually took steps to accommodate the worship of the unsexed Mary. In 431, on the site of Artemis's great temple at Ephesus, Mary was officially proclaimed Mother of God—Cybele's ancient title. The new dogma underlined her divinity by disassociating her from the human ordeal of death. Instead, she was now said to have ascended into heaven, like Christ. This Assumption was celebrated on the fifteenth of August—Artemis's feast day.

Her image became the conduit through which some of the symbols and traditions of the Mother Goddess could enter Christianity. The third-century Christian Tertullian reported that converts were baptized by drinking the milk of Paradise, also called Mary's milk, and honey. Milk and honey was the traditional meal of initiates in mystery cults; milk had symbolized woman's divine powers of creation since the dawn of history. Mary is even compared to the chaste and fecund queen bee whose buzzing generated the origin of the Divine Word. Mary was prayed to as a moon goddess; as Venus, the star of Ishtar; as a sea or sky goddess. The sacred egg of the former bird and snake goddesses, laid at the spring equinox when the earth is reborn, became the Easter egg, a symbol of Christ's resurrection.

She is the flower, the violet, the full-blown rose,
who gives out such a scent that she satisfies us all.
The mother of the lord most high is scented beyond any flower.

All over Christendom, temples formerly sacred to Aphrodite, Isis, Artemis, and Cybele were rededicated to Mary, Queen of Heaven (the title was originally Inanna's). The Church of Santa Maria Maggiore was erected over the sacred caves of the Magna Mater (Cybele) in Rome. By the seventh century, Athena's Parthenon was hers.

The Church is usually referred to as female, and the buildings themselves were identified with Mary, just as Cybele in her battlement crown embodied the city of Rome. In the Middle Ages, this metaphor found majestic expression in the Gothic cathedrals of Europe. Most are named Notre Dame (Our Lady) and are direct descendants of the sacred Magdalenian caves that were considered the body of the goddess. The *Vierge Ouvrante*, a famous style of sculpture from the Middle Ages, expresses this ancient idea graphically. It appears to be a typical statue of Virgin and Child, but it swings open to reveal God the Father, God the Son, the angels, and the saints within her body. Like the Venus of Laussel, she is the source and mother of all. Legend has it that a pagan statue of a goddess kept in the Druid Grotto beneath Chartres Cathedral was secretly worshiped as Mary.

In her cathedrals, enormous rose windows of stained glass, directly opposite Christ's cross in the apse, symbolized the presence of Mary, who was called the Holy Rose. The concept was said to have been brought from the east by Crusaders.

Ironically, in the early days of Christianity, roses had been forbidden because they were so closely associated with pagan goddesses. Rome knew the rose as the Flower of Venus (Aphrodite), and sexual priestesses wore it as a badge of their office. It also figured in initiation rituals.

"Vierge Ouvrante," German, late eighteenth or early nineteenth century.

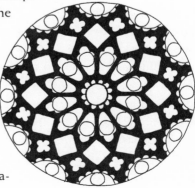

The Glorification of the Virgin, rose window from Chartres Cathedral.

Mary's rose very likely has some connection with India, where the Great Mother had been called Holy Rose for millennia. The rosary, the string of rose beads used to count prayer cycles offered to Mary, almost certainly originated in India, where the constant repetition of mantras has been a common technique to achieve union with the deity since Neolithic times. The chanting of mantras or prayers are thought to realign the devotee's consciousness. This is not a Christian concept. Matthew's Gospel reports Christ admonishing Christians, "When ye pray, use not vain repetitions, as the heathen do" (Matthew 6:7). But chanting the rosary has become an essential element of Mary worship. The Hail Mary asks the Virgin to be present at the hour of death, as does an ancient Tantric prayer to Shakti.

INSPIRED SAINTS

As the centuries passed, women played less and less of a role in the hierarchy of Christianity and in the creation of sacred music, yet there were always powerful spiritual women who drew on the ancient sources of inspiration. The twelfth-century German Hildegard of Bingen was a great spiritual leader, mystic, healer, artist, and composer. She established an independent convent for her nuns and was known as a prophetess, "the Sybil of the Rhine."

Hildegard's inspiration and visions derived from the Divine Feminine in the form of the Virgin Mary, Sapientia (the female figure of Wisdom in the Bible who "was with God from the beginning"), Ecclesia (the mother church—the bride of Christ), and Saint Ursula. Her music was devoted to glorifying these manifestations of a primordial sacred female.

She wrote that "all sacred music—instrumental as well as vocal—functions as the bridge for humanity to life before the Fall." Her compositions were extraordinarily unique in an age that followed the traditional rules of prosody, rhyme, or the Church's standard melodic modes.

Hildegard conceived the universe as a cosmic egg and she combined the image of the Tree of Life with the human body. She seemed obsessed with the imagery of blood. For Saint Ursula she wrote, "O royal redness of blood, You flowed down from a high place which divinity has touched; You are the flower that winter never damaged with the freezing blast of the serpent." In song she described Saint Ursula as "a dripping honeycomb . . . Honey and milk under her tongue. . . ."

Sibyl from the Doors of Paradise, L. Ghiberti, commissioned in 1425, depicting scenes from the Old Testament. The Sibyl survives in Christian iconography because the Christians reworked the Sibylline Oracle to predict the birth of Christ the Messiah.

Although there is no mention of Hildegard using the frame drum, the great sixteenth-century Spanish mystic Saint Teresa of Avila did play the drum. She was described as dancing before God in a chapel in Avila to the rhythms of her own tambourine. One of the greatest mystics and teachers of the Church, she mixed the strains of Jewish, Christian, and Muslim influence in her visions. She founded seventeen convents in Spain and reformed her Carmelite Order.

Saint Teresa wrote a number of books on mystical theology, the most interesting of which was *The Interior Castle*. This book describes the seven stages or steps through which the soul in its quest for perfection must pass to unite with God in a sacred marriage. In the innermost chamber—the Seventh Mansion—the soul reaches the place of complete transfiguration and communion with the divine. Saint Teresa calls it "another Heaven: the two lighted candles join and become one, the falling rain becomes merged in the river. There is complete transformation, ineffable and perfect peace." Saint Teresa's seven mansions of the interior soul completely recalls the ancient concept of seven sacred steps to spiritual illumination.

Fra Angelico angels, Museo San Marco, Florence, fourteenth century.

MUSICAL ANGELS

Angels have their origin in the bird and vulture goddesses of the Neolithic. Around the middle of the fourteenth century, angel musicians became very common in religious art, particularly in association with the Virgin Mary, who is often portrayed with angels playing harps and tambourines.

Angels are an old Judaic tradition, but angels playing music—particularly frame drums—introduce another element of goddess worship. They recall Aphrodite's *horae*, celestial nymphs who played their tambourines as they performed the Dances of the Hours to mark the passage of time throughout the night. Their tambourines symbolized the moon, and the rhythms they played were the cycles of time. Their earthly counterparts, priestesses who initiated men into the sexual mysteries, were known by the same name. The Persians

called them *houri*, the name still used by Muslims for angels who dispense sexual pleasure in Paradise. The name of the oldest Hebrew folk dance, the *hora*, comes from the same root, as does our word *hour*—as well as the word *whore*. The name of the sacred priestesses who played the frame drum now evokes the image of complete sexual degradation.

A houri or personification of the sun or moon, Ottoman Turkey. The sun and the moon in Ottoman Turkish poetry are sometimes compared to a tambourine. This image reflects the heavenly realm both by the association with the houri and with the sun. Ceramic, sixteenth century.

The frame drum traditionally facilitated progress through the three realms of the goddess—the heavens, the earth, and the underworld—or through the seven chakras or levels of the ziggurat. It can hardly be a coincidence that Mary's musical angels appear most frequently in pictures of the Assumption—the moment Mary's physical body ascended from the earth plane into heaven to unite in a sacred marriage with Christ.

VISIONS

The last century and a half has witnessed a huge increase in sightings of the Virgin by devout Catholics and even non-Catholics around the globe. She is often wearing roses and usually conveys some message through those privileged to see her. The importance of chanting the rosary is a consistent theme, along with apocalyptic prophecies. Some of her witnesses are children, and their visions are sometimes accompanied by paranormal activity.

Iranian heavenly musician of the court, sixteenth century.

The places where Mary has appeared have become modern sacred sites. Every year, millions of devotees seeking healing and divine grace visit Lourdes, where Bernadette Soubirous saw the Virgin in 1858, and Fatima, where Mary appeared to three shepherd children in 1917. The repetition of Hail Marys is the central act of devotion at both these shrines. In the last fifty years, Mary has appeared in Italy, Germany, Spain, Ireland, Yugoslavia, the United States, and the Philippines. Each new sighting brings crowds of the faithful to chant rosaries in the presence of a vision they may not personally share.

Mary's appearances to four little girls at San Sebastian de Garaban-

Renaissance frame drummer. Fresco by Andrea di Bonaiuto of Florence, fourteenth century.

dal, in the Cantabrian Mountains of Spain, from 1965 to 1971 are particularly interesting because the girls were filmed, recorded, and photographed. When communicating with Mary, the children entered into ecstatic trances in which they weighed more—so much they could not be lifted—moved with supernormal speed, and seemed to be telepathic. The Church does not officially recognize the Garabandal visions, but this seems to have little effect on the millions of believers, many of them well educated, who flock to the site.

Heavenly angel from an Indian miniature painting, circa 1595. Attributed to Manohar. Bahram Gur visits the Persian Princess in the Purple Palace in the Sixth Paradise.

The spectacle of thousands of people chanting while a medium in a trance state utters prophecy from a divine female does not evoke Christianity. It conjures the divinely inspired priestesses of ancient oracles. Obviously the need for some direct experience of divinity, the kind of experience once revealed to initiates in the mysteries of the Great Mother, is still profound.

The cult of Mary may be

Twentieth-century Italian folk tambourine.

growing in popularity largely because it offers a taste of that ancient sacred experience. The emphasis on the rosary may be the key. Chanting introduces rhythm into the religious experience, a factor that all goddess-based religions recognized as essential to entering the trance state enabling transcendence. Despite centuries of suppression and ignorance, the human spirit still yearns for the transcending power of rhythm. If chanting the rosary can have such power, we can only imagine the transforming effect of the sacred rhythms of the goddess's frame drums.

PART V

THE RETURN TO RHYTHM

When I am feeling abandoned and isolated, if I will turn to my drum, I will hold in my hands my lineage.

I have discovered an entirely new place within my rhythm . . . the simple heartbeat, the place of moving soundly from left foot to right, the place I must breathe in before flying to more complex rhythms.

So empowering! So sacred! I find drumming helps to keep me balanced.

The trust and appreciation of my drum's rhythm and that of mine and the patients I work with carries me to places of wonder.

I came for what was mine.

TESTIMONIALS FROM WOMEN WHO PLAY THE FRAME DRUM

CHAPTER TWELVE

THE TECHNOLOGY OF RHYTHM

MY RESEARCH INTO the history of the frame drum took me on a journey among women that stretched from the earliest known examples of human symbolic thought to the rise of Christianity at the beginning of the modern era. I discovered that for thousands and thousands of years people throughout the Mediterranean world worshiped forms of a nurturing Great Goddess. At the heart of her worship was the frame drum. With it she regulated the rhythmic dance of the cosmos—the progression of seasons, the cycles of the moon, the growth and fruition of crops, the lives of her people.

Ancient sources tell us that the frame drum was not just a powerful symbol of spiritual presence, it was an important tool for many spiritual experiences. Priestesses of the goddess were skilled technicians in its uses. They knew which rhythms quickened the life in freshly planted seeds; which facilitated childbirth; which induced the ecstatic trance of spiritual transcendence. Guided by drumbeats, these sacred drummers could alter their consciousness at will, traveling through the three worlds of the goddess: the heavens, the earth, and the underworld.

Scientific research from astrophysics to biology tends to support the idea that rhythm is a fundamental force. Neurological studies into the way our brains function suggest that drumming and other spiritual practices of our ancestresses could indeed bring about a transformation of ordinary consciousness. By banning her drum, the patriarchal religions that suppressed the goddess cut off our access to significant parts of our own psyches. They destroyed psychological and spiritual techniques that had been used for many thousands of years.

THE MUSIC OF THE SPHERES

Today, many people turn to science instead of religion to make sense of their world. One of our most popular origin myths is the Big Bang Theory of modern astrophysics. According to this theory, all the material of the universe was once compacted into a hot, dense ball. About 15 to 20 billion years ago, there was a tremendous explosion. The shock waves of this primordial sound flung matter across space, where it eventually coalesced into the galaxies, solar systems, and individual planets. Scientists still have no better way to describe this moment than as the "instant the universe was born."

A related concept in physics today is the Superstring Theory, which replaces the former idea of separate subatomic particles with the image of loops of vibrating strings. The frequency at which these strings vibrate and the rhythmic patterns generated by their interplay determine how they manifest.

The concentric circles in this small amount of water were generated by sound vibrations. Hans Jenny states "sound is the creative principle. It must be regarded as primordial." He found that harmonic vibrations produce symmetrical figures with mathematical regularity.

The idea that the universe is in essence a symphony of vibrations emanating out of an enormous first beat suggests the science of music, and many scientists use musical analogies to describe their theories. Princeton physicist Edward Witten says, "In the case of the superstring, the different harmonics correspond to different elementary particles— electron, graviton, proton, neutrino and all the others, are different harmonics of a fundamental string, just as the different overtones of a violin string are different harmonics of one string."

Experiments performed by Hans Jenny, founder of cymatics, the study of wave forms, lends support to the theory that vibrations give form to the material world. Jenny found that when sound waves were introduced to various material substances—water, alcohol, pastes, oils, and so forth—they created symmetrical patterns with uniform characteristics. The undifferentiated substances were organized instantly into organic forms. Put simply, Jenny's research shows that rhythm shapes matter.

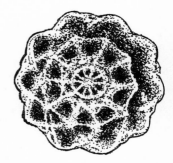

Pentagonal figure produced by transmission of high-frequency vibratory tones through a liquid medium.

THE PULSE OF LIFE

To approach creation from another perspective, let's move from astrophysics to biology, from the birth of the cosmos to the birth of a single human being.

It is often said that the first sound we hear in the womb is our mother's heartbeat. Actually, the first sound to vibrate our newly developed hearing apparatus is the pulse of our mother's blood through her veins and arteries. We vibrate to that primordial rhythm even before we have ears to hear. Before we were conceived, we existed in part as an egg in our mother's ovary. All the eggs a woman will ever carry form in her ovaries while she is a four-month-old fetus in the womb of her mother. This means our cellular life as an egg begins in the womb of our grandmother. Each of us spent five months in our grandmother's womb and she in turn formed within the womb of her grandmother. We vibrate to the rhythms of our mother's blood before she herself is born. And this pulse is the thread of blood that runs all the way back through the grandmothers to the first mother. We all share the blood of the first mother—we are truly children of one blood.

As a tiny, pulsing egg, we experienced the birth of our mother, the growth of her body, her joys, her fears, her triumphs. For fourteen to forty years we rocked as an egg to the rhythms of her body. Men cannot convey this continuity of cellular energy to their sperm. The father imparts not the imprint of a lifetime but only the fleeting energy of a few weeks. Man's nature is in many metaphorical ways a quick rise and fall—the vanishing and resurrecting energy reflected in so many of the ancient male gods.

At the fetal age of four weeks, our own heart starts to pulse. The auditory nerve begins to pick up vibrations from our environment about twenty weeks later. We begin to synchronize our movements not only to physical sounds but to the rhythms of voices, the vibrations of thoughts. Our mother's emotions create complex chemical interactions in her body, and their particular energies permeate the womb. Her dream cycles affect our sleep patterns. By the time we are born, we are already imprinted with the rhythms of the language, emotions, feelings, and interactions around us. These rhythms will always seem the most familiar and natural to us no matter how beneficial or detrimental they actually are.

Scientific studies have shown that our moods, emotions, thoughts, and bodily processes are rhythms of chemical energy. The Puerto Ricans call this fundamental rhythm that marks how we walk, talk, and interact *tumbao*. It is an expression of the totality of our personality.

THE PULSE OF AWARENESS

As the body takes shape in the womb, consciousness begins. It can be detected as brain waves—rhythmic vibrations emanating from the brain and nervous system. All through our lives, our state of consciousness is governed by the rate of these vibrations. Using electroencephalographs, scientists can measure the number of energy waves per second pulsing through the brain. They have developed a system of classification differentiating states of consciousness.

As you read these words your brain is probably vibrating at between fourteen and twenty-one cycles per second. These are called beta waves. The state of awareness characterized by beta waves is associated with active, waking attention, focused on everyday external activities. Beta waves are also in evidence during states of anxiety, tension, and fear.

Alpha waves vibrate at seven to fourteen waves per second. They indicate a relaxed internal focus and a sense of well-being.

Theta waves vibrate at about four to seven cycles per second and indicate the drowsy, semiconscious state usually experienced at the threshold of sleep.

The slowest frequency, from one to four cycles per second, is the delta level, the state of unconsciousness or deep sleep. The brains of fetuses emit delta waves.

Beta waves dominate in most humans past puberty. But the brain activity of other animals registers well within the alpha range, which also correlates to the electromagnetic field of the earth. So when the Tantric Yogi sought to bring herself into alignment with cosmic vibrations, she aspired to the alpha state, which is in fact the basic rhythm of nature. This is the process referred to by meditational adept Swami Rama as "stilling the conscious mind and bringing forth the unconscious."

RIGHT BRAIN, LEFT BRAIN

Neurological studies indicate that the brain is divided into two hemispheres that share control of mental activity. In very young children they develop as one, but at about five years of age each hemisphere begins to specialize. The right brain functions as the creative center. It is the seat of visual, aural, and emotional memory, and processes information in holistic, intuitive terms, relying on pattern recognition. The left brain is the administrator, what we sometimes call the rational mind. It proceeds in logical, analytical, verbal, and sequential fashion. Incoming information is identified, classified, and explained.

If one hemisphere is damaged, the other one is able, within limits, to take over its functions. Normally, though, the memories, mental associations, ideas, and processes of each hemisphere are somewhat inaccessible to the other. In ordinary consciousness, either the left or the right brain dominates in cycles lasting from thirty minutes to about three hours. We shift from one side to the other depending on which skills we require.

Not only do the two hemispheres of our brains operate in different modes, they also usually operate in different rhythms. The right brain may be generating alpha waves while the left brain is in a beta state. Or both hemispheres can also be generating the same type of brain waves, but remain out of sync with each other. But in states of intense creativity or deep meditation, or under the influence of rhythmic sound, both hemispheres may begin operating in the same synchronized rhythm. This state of unified whole-brain functioning is called hemispheric synchronization.

As the rhythms of the two hemispheres synchronize, there is a sense of clarity and heightened awareness. Feelings of self-consciousness and separation fall away. The individual is able to draw on both the left and the right hemispheres simultaneously. Hemispheric synchronization on the alpha level can create feelings of euphoria, expanded mental powers, and intense creativity. This may be the neurological basis of higher states of consciousness.

Many ancient religious practices seem to have originated in attempts to induce the transcendent experience of hemispheric synchronization. Chanting rhythmically while gazing at geometric figures —like the Tantric combination of mantra and yantra—facilitates synchronization by simultaneously engaging the verbal skills of one hemisphere and the visual skills of the other.

Because each hemisphere controls the motor skills of one-half of the body, rhythmic movement can also effect synchronization. Rhythmic dancing, accompanied by music and chanting, was an integral part of the pre-Christian religious experience, often bringing the dancer into a trancelike state of ecstasy.

Drumming is perhaps the most effective way to induce brain-wave synchronization. Musical comprehension has been found to be a joint function of left and right hemispheres. Andrew Neher conducted a series of well-known experiments showing that the rhythms of the drum act as an auditory driving mechanism, able to drive or entrain the subject's brain waves into alpha or theta states.

Our culture heavily values left-brain functions and has associated them with male characteristics; as a result, men have been educated to develop an asymmetrical specialization in left-brain functioning. It has labeled the functions of the right brain "inferior" female characteristics, creating a splitting-off and devaluing of half of ourselves. In the drive to develop the left brain, we've neglected the potential of the right brain and also forgotten techniques for synchronizing both hemispheres.

ENTRAINMENT

Rhythm is catching. Mothers croon soft lullabies or rock their infants to lull them to sleep. Like Gilgamesh, military drummers still pound out martial beats to rouse patriotic fervor. As we interact with other people, our personal rhythms influence one another.

This ability of one rhythm to draw another into harmonic resonance with it is called *entrainment*. The power of some people's rhythm, such as pop stars Michael Jackson or Tina Turner, Martin Luther King, Jr., or Adolf Hitler, is such that thousands and perhaps millions can entrain with them. Dr. Stephan Rechtschaffen calls it "one of the great organizing principles of the world, as inescapable as gravity."

Research by William S. Condon shows that language is structured rhythmically with body movement. To communicate successfully, people must be able to adjust the tempos of their expression to one another. When people converse, they interact in complex rhythms almost like a dance. The harmonious entrainment of their conversational rhythms allows each person to listen and respond at the right intervals, instead of overlapping or interrupting the other person or coming in too late. When a person's rhythm is continually disrupted or suppressed, the effect can be severe, leading to boredom, exhaustion, depression, anxiety, anger. Although everyone must learn to respond to the give-and-take of conversational and social rhythms to some extent, in our culture adjusting to the tempos of others is a skill particularly valued in women.

Sometimes we find ourselves naturally synchronized with another person. When a high level of effortless entrainment occurs, one's own rhythm is fully expressed. This is one of life's greatest pleasures. Falling in love is falling in rhythm with someone.

Major events like birth, marriage, pregnancy, illness, separation, or death are stressful partly because they break familiar rhythms. People who are experiencing grief or depression seem to be painfully unable to create and maintain organized patterns of behavior. They have lost their personal rhythm. The need to replace broken rhythms often drives people unconsciously to try to re-create lost relationships.

In archaic communities, the shaman used the drum to entrain the consciousness of initiates with the divine rhythms of the earth. Practitioners of Nada Yoga used the entraining capacities of music to align their minds with the vibration supporting creation. Oracular priestesses, temple priestesses, maenads were all skilled at drawing from the skin head of the drum rhythms that entrained the minds of worshipers, moving them inexorably toward a state of ecstatic union with the divine. Drumming was a necessary and respected skill among these holy women.

THE THIRD EYE

Nestled between the hemispheres of the brain, where the cerebral cortex, cerebellum, and limbic system meet, is a small organ called the pineal gland. Its function has long been a matter of scientific dispute. For a long time, scientists thought of it as a vestigial organ, perhaps used to sense light in our ancient biological past. Because its current function was unknown, it was assumed to have none.

The Indian mystic sought to raise her kundalini to her spiritual center, the third eye. This third eye, like the uraeus, Hathor's divine cobra, rested in the center of her forehead—the location of the pineal gland. The same spot is also related to the sacred Egyptian eye symbol, which stood for light in all its forms—light of the sun, the light of knowledge, the light of the spirit.

Contemporary research into the function of biological clocks suggests that the pineal gland is indeed a kind of light sensor. The sun and, to a lesser extent, the moon pour energy into the biological environment in the form of light. This penetrating energy affects our bodily rhythms through our nervous systems. The pathways and orchestration of light's influence are as yet unclear to modern scientists, but it appears that the pineal gland may be the jewel in our biological clockworks, keeping us in sync with environmental time and influencing the physiological and emotional rhythms of the body.

The study of biorhythms is a relatively new field and it is still unclear exactly how biological clocks function. What is known is that all life responds rhythmically to the cycles of nature. The twenty-four-hour solar cycle—called the *circadian rhythm*—appears to be the most basic.

OUT OF SYNC

Through an enormous expenditure of effort and resources, modern science is coming to the same conclusions the ancients knew from immediate experience: that life is inexorably rhythmic. Rhythm drives the planets in their orbits and the fetus in its growth. Rhythm prompts the cycle of the earth and the cycles of our emotions.

This hard-won knowledge seems to have little practical effect on our contemporary culture. Biological research has demonstrated that patients' receptivity to drugs and medical treatment fluctuates in twenty-four-hour cycles, and to a lesser extent in seasonal or yearly cycles. Traditional Chinese medicine has taken these cycles into account for centuries, but modern Western medicine ignores the concept of biorhythms.

It's becoming apparent that some of our major physiological and psychological ills may be a result of being out of sync with environmental time. "It is the tension between the internal clocks and the clock on the wall that causes so much of the stress in today's world," says anthropologist Edward T. Hall. "We have now constructed an entire complex system of schedules, manners, and expectations to which we are trying to adjust ourselves, when, in reality, it should be the other way around."

Shutting ourselves off within our steel, concrete, and glass prisons, insulated from rhythmic fluctuations in light and temperature, we block ourselves off from seasonally appropriate changes in physiology and behavior. We run the risk of damaging our biological cycles. Laboratory experiments in which human beings are isolated from environmental energies produce symptoms of lethargy, fatigue, irritability, and boredom in their human subjects. The physical costs may be even more deadly. Studies conducted by John D. Palmer suggest that our biological clocks affect the functioning of every cell in our bodies, and cancerous cells may be cells that have lost this vital rhythmic regulation.

OUT OF TIME

In ancient cultures, the tempo of human life was synchronized with the rhythms of the earth. The priestess's frame drum was the thread that led back through countless millennia to that first beat that vibrated the world into being. People understood life as rhythm and woman's body as a reflection of that primordial truth. Her reproductive cycle expressed her intimate connection to the environment and was the basis for the earliest time-keeping systems. The Mediterranean cultures as well as the Celts, the Germans, and others used a lunar calendar, with the new moon heralding the start of a new month.

The Romans imposed the Julian calendar we still use today on the Western world, but they were not the first to abandon the lunar model in favor of a man-made system. Lunar time caused problems for large-scale bureaucracies. First, the length of the lunar cycle is not constant. Second, the actual time of the rising of the new moon varied depending on the longitude and latitude of the observer. As early as 2500 B.C., the bureaucrats of Sumer came up with a new calendar in order to regulate tax collection. This change from calendars based on nature to calendars designed to serve the purposes of those in power was one of the earliest rejections of the truth of direct experience.

NOTHING SACRED

The ancients studied the stars and the earth with humility, motivated by a sense of awe and a desire to participate as fully as possible in the rhythms of the universe. Our division between objective and subjective truths—science and religion—didn't exist. Contemporary science, with its left-brain analytical bias, is skeptical of anything that smacks of the intuitive or mystical. The only experiences worthy of its interest are those that can be measured by machines or expressed as formulas.

Some scientific advances have greatly improved the lot of humankind, but when science attempts to define the nature of reality using only what are called objective criteria, it denies the validity of the sacred.

If scientists are the new priesthood, they minister to a religion devoid of the divine. Judaism, Christianity, and Islam have stripped divinity of feminine qualities; science goes one step further, canceling the concept of divinity entirely. Religious experience is subjective; it is not rational; therefore, it cannot be validated. In this new religion, nothing is sacred but the dry truths of statistics.

To most people, the dogmas of science are incomprehensible. They must be accepted on faith. Yet we deny the validity of personal experience in service to this "objective" truth. Those who separate themselves from the natural world in order to study it lose the vital connection that makes sense of the whole. They have forgotten that consciousness itself is subjective. When a human being subtracts herself from the equation of the universe, her results are doomed to be incomplete.

Barbara Gail teaches children drumming in Maine. Studies conducted by physicist and neuroscientist Gordon Shaw at the University of California, Irvine, demonstrated that three-year-old children showed striking intellectual improvement after participating in a musical studies program.

RECLAIMING OURSELVES

Many scientists are using new information about the natural harmonies of life to great advantage. Biorhythmic studies have breathed new life into the ancient practice of music therapy.

When the shaman's knowledge of healing through sound fell into disrepute in the West, the discipline languished. Music was felt to have a calming effect on some nervous diseases, but that was thought too vague and subjective to be worthy of serious study.

In the last few decades, however, music therapy has become respectable. This may be due in part to the fact that music's influence on pulse, blood pressure, heartbeat, and so forth can be measured on machines. These scientifically sanctioned tests reveal that music can indeed alter consciousness. Studies by the Viennese therapist Alfred Schmolz show that patients who participate actively in spontaneous music-making benefit even more than passive listeners.

At the Marino Medical Center in Boston, in an informal setting, I participated in an experiment testing the effect of drumming on brainwave activity. A volunteer was hooked up to an EEG machine. As soon as I began to play my frame drum—without any time lapse—his brain waves entrained with the sound he was hearing. When I shifted rhythms, his brain waves shifted simultaneously.

The research and hypotheses mentioned in this chapter suggest that we are locked into an interactive system of personal, cultural, and environmental rhythmic needs. Hall predicts that "rhythm will . . . soon be proved to be the ultimate dynamic building block in not only personality but also communication and health."

Yet contemporary society has forgotten this need to be in rhythm with ourselves, one another, and nature. Conventional wisdom preaches that we are entirely responsible as individuals for our own behavior.

We need to find effective ways of reconnecting with the rhythms of our environment, our bodies, and our deepest selves. For a growing number of women, drumming is once again becoming a sacred technology capable of restoring those patterns.

Brooke Medicine Eagle is a contemporary American native Earthkeeper, teacher, and ceremonial leader who uses the frame drum in her healing work.

CHAPTER THIRTEEN

GIVING BIRTH TO ·OURSELVES

IN THE LATE 1980s at the end of the concerts I did with Glen Velez and Steve Gorn, I began speaking about the frame drum's incredible history. The response was overwhelming. After each concert, women would approach me to ask if I would teach them to drum. Although most of them had never seen a frame drum before, they felt an overwhelming urge to learn its rhythms. A psychic who came to hear us perform told me that as she concentrated deeply on the music, she closed her eyes and had a vision. "Your drum opened up like a mirror or window," she said. "I saw many women through thousands of years playing the drum. I saw that your drum was red. It was twenty thousand years old. And it belongs to the lineage of the goddess Isis." This happened at a concert at which I had not spoken of the history of the drum, before I'd published any articles on the subject.

I soon found myself conducting five classes a week, teaching more than fifty women. Although some of them had studied music at some point in their lives, the majority had never played any musical instrument before. They shared a conviction that drumming could lead them back to something essential within themselves. As one student expressed it, "When I heard you play, I realized I was thirsty for something I didn't even know existed." Another woman said, "It took me back into my mother, into her womb, where I floated to the beat of the drum."

I knew these feelings from my own experience. Like many of my students, I came to the drum with no prior musical training. I only knew that I had to learn to play this drum—something within it called to me.

I discovered I had a knack for teaching other people who weren't musicians. Professional musicians spend hours alone in a room with their instrument, doing the same things over and over again. I found a way to teach nonmusicians how to practice the same strokes and rhythms repeatedly without becoming bored. I taught them to listen deeply and with concentration by synchronizing their breathing and walking to the rhythms they were playing. Drumming is an incredibly healthy and satisfying way to channel obsessive, repetitive behavior into a mindfulness practice!

A few of my students have gone on to become professional musicians, but most are not interested in music as a career. They are simply looking for a personal and communal rhythmic experience. They feel a need for meaningful ritual in their lives. And rhythm is a powerful way to experience the sacred. Learning to drum effectively has empowered these women on many levels.

During the years I played with Glen, I had considered my relative inexperience a liability. I wondered what I could possibly bring to our collaboration that could complement his expertise and virtuosity. I realized that one major thing I did have that he didn't have was feminine energy.

I made up my mind that I would discover a means of connecting to the primordial feminine energy I felt when I drummed (whatever I would discover that to be). I combined Yogic and Taoist practices of connecting to the earth and being a conduit for its energy. As I entrained with the beat of the drum—as I became the pulse itself—I felt that I was letting the force of gravity draw my essence down, down through the layers of the earth to the fire at her center. As I connected to the fire of the earth, I could feel that energy radiating up through my body and out through the sound of my drum—as if I were a radio transmitter.

These were not images I thought up consciously. They seemed to arise spontaneously out of the trancelike state my drumming engendered. Later, I realized that the concept of creative fire at the earth's core was a very old religious image. Before it became the Christians' hell, it was the fire of the goddess. As Campbell says, "Between Virgil and Dante too there was a difference, inasmuch as for the Roman the intelligence in the center of the earth was not satanic but divine."

FEMININE RHYTHMS

Teaching women to play, I felt I was really listened to for the first time in my life. I was honored for who I was and what I had accomplished. This gave me the confidence to end my professional association with Glen and strike out on my own. I had my own ideas I needed to develop, and I wanted to put some of the things I was learning about women's drumming into practice.

The most striking difference between Glen's music and mine was the tempo. Over the years, his compositions had become very complex, with extraordinarily fast tempos. My own work was much slower, at about the rate of a relaxed heartbeat. The slower pace gave the music a ceremonial character.

The frame drum has always been linked to the control of elemental powers, and I took this into account in composing. From the eminent Nubian musician Hamsa El Din I had learned the relationship of the four strokes on the drum with the four elements. *Kah*, a slap that stops the vibration of the skin head, is the sound of the earth element. *Dum*, a low, open, resonant sound, is the sound of water. *Tak*, a sharp, high-pitched rim sound, is fire. *Cha*, the sound of the tambourine's jingles, is air. On frame drums that don't have jingles, *cha* is a soft, brushing sound. Later I discovered that the Sufi mystic Hazrat Inayat Khan made the same correlations between drum strokes and elemental energies.

THE MOB OF ANGELS

Throughout my life, I have been searching for something I felt was missing. I practiced Yoga, studied Tibetan Buddhism and the Japanese Tea Ceremony with traditional teachers from those cultures. I studied Ericksonian hypnosis and the early teachings of Gnostic Christianity. As a multimedia artist, I explored mythological iconography. After studying drumming with Glen for many years, I took classes with traditional teachers from the Middle East and Brazil. Teaching women to drum provided a context for all of these practices to coalesce into something that specifically addressed my needs as an American woman of the late twentieth century. I began the process of reclaiming the authority of my own rhythm.

Originally, music, dance, and visual art served a ritual purpose. They invoked the presence of divine energy and facilitated our fusion with it. It seems to me that the purposelessness, nihilism, and self-indulgence that plague much contemporary art stem in part from the loss of its original link to the sacred. By calling the rhythm back and projecting it forward, I was learning to create sacred art.

With my students I formed a group called the Mob of Angels. We set out to revive the ancient Mediterranean tradition of women's ceremonial drumming. Although I have studied and listened to many traditions of frame drumming, I neither copied those traditions nor tried to re-create what I thought women might have played. The frame drum is the central instrument around which I compose, but I have also inte-

The Mob of Angels.

grated other ancient and modern acoustic instruments into my compositions. My aim is to create a contemporary new music that is nontraditional but pulses with the rhythms of an archaic language. The music in turn inspires rituals that celebrate the feminine.

Drawing on images from Paleolithic times to the present, we studied and absorbed the goddesses, priestesses, and laywomen who played the frame drum. We grounded ourselves in the energy of the earth and focused on the relationship of the different strokes to the elements. We learned the ancient technology for synchronizing our minds and bodies, gaining access to other levels of awareness.

Our goal is to release the primordial archetype of feminine energy. Through it our primal mind can emerge, whispering of the eternally flowing presence of the Divine Feminine—the raw force of nature, the earth herself. Freed from suffocating bondage to violent gods, she may once again be remembered and revered as the power of birth, life, death, and resurrection. Ancient emotions, thoughts, revelations pour across the barriers of time, and forgotten rites of celebration, healing, and purification can be remembered.

ANCIENT PATHWAYS

The oldest known dances were circular, ritually symbolizing the cyclical nature of existence. Circumambulation, the ritual act of walking an endless, circular path around a sacred site, was one of the most ancient religious activities. In a circle, each participant is equidistant from the still point at the center around which everything turns. I teach all my classes and workshops in a circle. I can see everyone and everyone can see me. We can really listen and hear one another.

When we began to develop ritual performances, the Mob chose to work in this archetypal tradition. We always perform in a circle—usually in circles within circles, with the audience arranged in a circle around us. This context promotes wholeness and inclusion.

Our rituals almost always include processions of drummers. Often the audience enters the place where the ritual will occur between two lines of tambourine players, while sage, cedar, and frankincense—ancient purifiers—smoke in censors. The ancient ritual procession toward a shrine or holy place mirrored the archetypal journey to the center of the self. It survives today in religious processionals, parades, and pilgrimages.

Though the Mob's ritual practices seemed to be developing naturally out of our drumming, my research into the history of goddess worship turned up astonishing parallels, like the images of drumming priestesses parading across the walls in Hathor's temple at Dendera. By chance, I also witnessed a modern version of this ritual when an Egyptian wedding party danced ceremonially through two lines of frame drummers. These were perfect complements to the Mob's opening processions. In some Mob rituals, I knelt to play my frame drum. Later I

The Mob of Angels, winter solstice celebration, Washington Square Church, 1992.

found ancient images of Anat and Hathor kneeling and playing their frame drums.

We created our public rituals at seasonally important times of the year, such as the summer and winter solstices and the spring and fall equinoxes. Today as in ancient times, collective rituals that re-create the origins of the world renew the community by reconnecting people with the rhythmic source of their being. Our rituals function as a gateway—an "in-trance-way"—into deeper realms of consciousness. The rhythms of our drums have the power to draw listeners away from the constraints of clock time back to the cyclical time of mythology.

Winter solstice celebration.

We also give some traditional American holidays a new focus. On Mother's Day, we acknowledge and honor the ancient Great Mother as well as our own mothers. On Valentine's Day, in recognition of the sacredness of sexuality, we read the sexually joyful texts of *The Courtship of Inanna and Dumuzi.* Halloween became our Day of the Dead.

RENEWAL

The Widow Jane Mine, a large cave in upstate New York, is the site of a number of unusual events. Because of its extraordinary acoustics, adventurous poets, singers, and musicians have staged performances in its cavernous depths. It seemed a perfect setting for a public celebration of the autumnal equinox of 1993. The equinox is the magical moment when the days and nights are of equal length and the magnetic fields of earth and sun are aligned. It's traditionally the time to celebrate renewal and balance.

More than seven hundred people from all over the East Coast and as far away as Chicago, Florida, and Los Angeles arrived to participate in the ritual. We began by playing in a field above the cave. Then we asked people to form a circle around us, and I led them in a pulse meditation, everyone moving and breathing in rhythm together.

I slipped away to a boat floating on the lake that flowed into the cave's interior. Meanwhile, the Mob led the guests to the mouth of the cave. Everyone entered in ritual fashion, through rows of drummers, past people burning sage and incense. Inside, they sat in concentric circles on bales of hay. The Mob came into the center of the circle, still drumming. Just as they gave a final shake of the tambourines, I started playing the bodhran, a twenty-two-inch frame drum, and my candlelit boat appeared around a cluster of rocks. There was a huge collective gasp as everyone was jolted by the archetypal quality of the moment.

After the ceremonies in the sacred enclosure of the earth, we hosted a celebratory feast on the grounds of the Snyder Estate. I found that our guests came from all walks of life, all religions and none, all ages. Everyone felt drawn to the event. We celebrated the autumnal equinox at the same site the following year, again with great success.

I think the popularity of this event speaks of our loss of connectedness to the rhythms of nature and our need for meaningful ritual. The cave is the oldest sacred precinct of our race. From the earliest times, to enter the cave was to leave the life of the outside world and enter upon a pilgrimage to the unconscious. The material trappings of life have changed many times throughout the last forty millennia, but our spiritual needs remain constant. People flocked to the mine instinctively in answer to these needs.

TRANSFORMATION

Our Rattlesnake Ritual uses the ancient archetype of the snake, a symbol associated with the goddess in most ancient cultures. The music I composed for it invokes the rattlesnake, who rises up and, with a great rattle, warns that any intruder violates her space at great peril. The ritual celebrates the shedding of outgrown selves, outmoded and dysfunctional family and social structures, and outworn religious thinking that devalues women.

The snake symbolizes the transformational energy of the earth. Shedding is a beautiful act, a purification and cleansing. It is a necessary stage in the passage to a new self. It is also painful and frightening. Birth, the first transformation, is accomplished through the agonizing pains of labor, the shedding of blood, and the tearing of flesh. Yet it is the oldest form of communion, the primal miracle at the heart of existence.

The snake constantly sheds her skin. Her message is that we, too, must constantly shed our old skin, even though it is familiar, and stand naked and exposed to accept whatever our lives offer next.

REVELATION

On Halloween, All Souls' Day, we honor our loved ones who have died. The ritual is based loosely on Mexican and Celtic traditions. Participants bring white flowers in remembrance of their beloved dead to place in vases at the center of the circle.

The Mob wears skull masks on the backs of our heads. As we perform in our traditional circle, we turn in and out so that we are seen alternately as living and dead, evoking the eternal cycles of nature.

This is also an opportunity for those of us who have been studying the frame drum to explore the reality of trance-revelation. Continuous drumming and dancing expands the parameters of our habitual mindsets, releasing the experience of undistracted awareness. It's as if a gateway between the conscious and unconscious minds were gradually and imperceptibly opening. Across this threshold flow new visions and heightened creativity. As we drum, the next step becomes apparent. Habitual patterns of thought are revealed for what they are and begin melting away. Blocks of information surface in the form of powerful archetypes. Drummers and dancers are fused in a place beyond conceptualization and conditioned patterns of behavior, entrained in a deeper awareness.

DEATH AND REBIRTH

Giving Birth to Ourselves retreat, Nantucket, 1993.

Recently we have created an intensive frame drum and ritual retreat for women drummers called Giving Birth to Ourselves. In these retreats we explore the history of the drum's use in initiations, blood mysteries, purifications, and ritual death-and-rebirth ceremonies.

Participants have already studied the frame drum prior to the retreat, and we have been able to create very powerful rituals. The retreat climaxes with each participant's symbolic death and release of her past life. We found that the sure knowledge that we will die can be a source of strength. It is like a wind that burns one clean. Everything pales in the face of our death. Our misunderstandings and confusions seem trivial. Habitual worries and anxieties evaporate, leaving each of us energized and inspired to proceed with the precious time we do have left to live.

We felt that we understood the rites of the ancient mystery schools, in which each initiate became the Mother of God, giving birth to the divinity within themselves. Often after these retreats the women have gone on to make major changes in their lives. One woman is now in her fourth year of Naturopathic Medical School. Another founded the Women's Rites Center in New York. Several women who were ordained ministers of traditional Christian churches went on to become pastors or associate pastors after the retreat.

THE EARTH AS THE GODDESS

If there was a fall from grace, it was a fall out of rhythm. The order of the universe is rhythmic, and we have a psychic and physiological need to be in sync with the earth's cycles.

I am not advocating a return to goddess worship. The past can never be recovered in so literal a sense. But my investigations of religions centered on the Divine Feminine have given me a glimpse of what is missing from contemporary culture. By divorcing ourselves from the natural world, we are doing violence to ourselves and to the planet.

In creating modern urban culture, we have left the ancient wisdom of natural cycles behind. The traditions we inherited from warrior nomads who viewed the natural world as an infinite source of new pastures to exploit and abandon have led to rampant materialism. Even now, when ecological crises have forced us to reassess our relationship to the environment, politicians take steps to "protect" our resources solely so that we may continue to exploit them. In the face of mounting evidence to the contrary, our culture persists in behaving as if nature exists to serve the desires of one species that values itself above all others.

Primordial religions placed the self in the context of nature as a whole, understanding her, recognizing her as the mother of all, identifying with her rhythms. No species had the right to exploit another. The concept of the earth as a living, sentient organism, lately redefined by James Lovelock and Lynn Margulis, is really a very old idea, and one that needs reviving. When the world and the self are equally expressions of divinity, every act becomes sacred.

SACRED SEXUALITY

As soon as someone speaks of restoring the Divine Feminine, there is a hue and cry about unleashing wild and uncontrollable sexuality. In fact, sexuality was sacred to the goddess. By devaluing the sanctity of the sexual act, patriarchal religions sowed the seeds for many of our contemporary social ills. The attempt by established religions of our time to confine expressions of sexuality within rigid religious constructs of guilt and fear has led to horrendous, escalating cycles of violence and rape against women and children.

The modern, secular mythology of sex glorifies the macho male, whose esteem is measured by the number of women he can engage in casual or forced sex or by the number of children he fathers (but doesn't necessarily care for). But the AIDS epidemic makes this skewed assessment of sexual worth insupportable. We find ourselves confronted with an urgent need to instruct our children in the sanctity of the sexual act. A return to this ancient understanding is crucial to their survival.

IN HER IMAGE

I am not a separatist. I have a deep and abiding love for the various men in my life—lovers, brothers, father, friends, musical and business partners. But I want to be considered their equal. If attacked, physically or verbally, I fight back, for which I've been condemned. I have been labeled a bossy girl, when in actuality I feel that I am a natural leader. Ever heard a male child derided for being bossy in a tone designed to make him change his behavior?

In our society, women live in a fog of denial and distortion. All around us, we can see women self-destructing. This is an inevitable consequence of cultural conditioning that exalts the masculine and degrades qualities defined as feminine.

We need to see ourselves as something more than the reflections of men's desires—their lovers, their wives, or the mothers of their children. We need to understand that our worth is not defined by our attractiveness to men. A knowledge of the ancient goddesses can counteract that image. We can learn to recognize ourselves as reflections of the divine—a view of the feminine that prevailed for many thousands of years.

Ancient religions acknowledged that women's power arises from an understanding of the interconnectedness of all people and all life, of the cycles of nature and the cycles of our bodies. Unearthing the goddess begins a journey back into the labyrinth of our feminine being, in search of the golden illumination at its center. By synthesizing her various archetypes, by pulling the fragments back into the whole, we can trace our way back to the sacred.

BEYOND SEXUAL ROLES

As much as we need feminine energy to right the balance of our culture, I know that the divine energy behind creation cannot be contained in any human-made image or mental concept. Ultimate reality—the force within the atoms of earth, air, water, and fire, the force that pulses through our veins—is far beyond the attributes we ascribe to femaleness or maleness. The ancients expressed the incomprehensible diversity of the divine in many deities of both human sexes and in animal, insect, bird, and plant form. We need to find our own ways to give divinity fuller expression.

The Mob of Angels is not exclusive to women. We have always had men as guest performers on instruments other than the frame drum—flutes, tambura, vocals. Then I began to get letters from men in their mid- to late twenties who wanted to study the frame drum with me. Eventually, we had four men playing with the Mob.

Interestingly, these young men had started out as rock drummers. They were now feeling a need to play with other drummers, instead of being the only drummer in the band. And they'd grown tired of the limitations of rock music and the less-than-spiritual milieu of audiences bent on getting as unconscious as possible.

But because of our history of repression over the last several thousand years, it's also important that women have nurturing environments where they can concentrate on recovering their archetypal female nature. The frame drum has historically been a vehicle for expressing female energy, and the Mob of Angels remains dedicated to helping women rediscover that heritage and become whole. Ritual drumming enables women to reclaim our ancient role as transmitters of the sacred. It returns us to who we were before we learned the patterns of self-destruction.

ACCEPTANCE

Although I've enjoyed professional recognition and success since striking out on my own, there's always the underlying impression that what I'm doing is weird. Marketable, but weird. Relating my music to goddesses and spirituality makes me suspect as a musician and as a person.

I made an instructional video, *Ritual Drumming*, for Interworld Music, a company that produces videos by some of the world's most respected percussionists, and I'm the first woman to have a signature series of drums created by Remo, Inc. *Since the Beginning*, the Mob's album of music drawn from our rituals, received excellent reviews. The *New York Times* wrote of one of our live concerts, "Layne Redmond is an excellent percussionist . . . she drew an astonishing variety of well-focused sounds from a tambourine, two frame drums and an African finger piano . . . the committed performers [the Mob of Angels] conveyed a refreshing energy, and the musical presentation was admirably honed." Yet the same critic labeled our work feminist and cultish.

In 1995, I was invited to perform as a soloist in the World Wide Percussion Festival in Bahia, Brazil. There, I was received in a way I have never experienced in the United States. In much of Latin America, the energy of goddesses and gods is still invoked through the power of the drum. There is nothing flakey about it. The drum plays a very powerful and sacred role in Brazil's culture.

Nana Vasconcelos, the Brazilian percussionist who was the artistic director for the 1995 festival, organized the program around an idea that came to him when he was featured in a documentary about the slave port of Goree in Senegal, Africa. He thought of his ancestors, who, by the time they had reached the waterfront to board the slave ships, had lost everything but the intangible qualities of their art and music. They survived the horrors of slavery by the spiritual power of their music, and brought the ancient rhythms of Africa to the New World. Nana was determined to pull these powerful, life-sustaining threads of rhythm together with rhythmic traditions from other parts of the world and present them to the people of Brazil.

I had been asked to conduct a workshop for about seventy Brazilian percussionists. Just before it was scheduled I attended a workshop conducted by Adama Drame on the *djembe*, a West African drum. He talked about the power of the drum to invoke divine energy and its powerful healing qualities. I thought, Well, if he's going to talk about that aspect of the drum, I will, too.

More than a little nervous (some of Brazil's most famous percussionists were in the room), I started speaking about the ancient goddesses who were connected with the drum and how it was used to alter consciousness. I demonstrated a number of different playing styles and techniques and then started answering questions. Someone remarked that I seemed to relate to the drum from a spiritual point of view and asked about its use in America. I told them about the rituals the Mob of Angels performs—some of which are not really that different from traditional Brazilian rituals. Someone else asked me to invite them into my music.

I led everyone in a breathing, walking, and singing meditation.

Then I asked that they join my frame drumming with their own improvised rhythms. The result was an extraordinarily beautiful impromptu performance, interwoven with bird whistles, chanting, singing, and hand-clapping. I felt transported to a golden place. At the end I knelt down and placed my drum on the floor, and these renowned percussionists lined up to thank me with hugs and kisses. Finally I felt fully acknowledged by people who placed the drum at the center of their lives.

NEW DIRECTIONS

At the festival, I encountered a contemporary tradition of frame drumming that I had no idea existed. Fogo de Mao (Hands of Fire), a group of drummers and dancers from the remote state of Maranhao in northeastern Brazil, combines African fire-hollowed wooden drums with Portuguese frame drums.

I learned that frame drums were introduced to Brazil by settlers from Portugal, where elderly women still play them in religious as well as secular contexts. In Portugal the drums are associated with the worship of the Virgin Mary. In the seventeenth century, an austere and conservative priest named Manual Bernardes banned their use in Portuguese village churches, but this did not stop the use of the frame drums in the ritual processions and ceremonies outside of the church grounds.

Each June at the Festival of St. John in Brazil, drummers and dancers enact the story of the Sacred Bull, who is sacrificed and magically brought back to life by the power of the frame drum. The saint's day coincides with the summer solstice, and the mythology of this rite stretches back through the Cretan story of the goddess and Dionysos to Çatal Hüyük and possibly back into the Paleolithic.

Writing this book has been the most difficult experience of my life. It has forced me to explore the very fabric of the mind, to trace the patterns of mythological thought, and to define the nature of divinity as it relates to myself. My curiosity about the female drummers of the ancient world unexpectedly opened up a door to a forgotten spiritual technology.

At the end, as at the beginning, stands the archetypal power of the Divine Feminine—the goddess. She is our future as she was our past. With her drum in hand, playing her sacramental rhythms, women can once again take their place in the world as technicians of the sacred.

In the pulse of my drum, in the beat of my heart, I erect an altar to her forever.

NOTES

CHAPTER ONE

IN SEARCH OF THE SACRED

Page 8 A number of scholars: Baring, Anne, and Jules Cashford. *The Myth of the Goddess: Evolution of an Image.* London: Penguin Books, 1991.

Drinker, Sophie. *Women and Music.* Toronto: Longmans, Green & Company, 1948.

Eisler, Riane. *The Chalice and the Blade: Our History, Our Future.* San Francisco: Harper & Row, 1987.

Gadon, Eleanor. *The Once and Future Goddess.* San Francisco: Harper & Row, 1989.

Gimbutas, Marija. *The Goddesses and Gods from Old Europe, 6500–3500 B.C.: Myths and Cult Images.* Berkeley: University of California Press, 1982.

―――. *The Language of the Goddess.* New York: HarperCollins, 1989.

Harrison, Jane Ellen. *Epilogomena to the Study of Greek Religion and Themis: A Study of the Social Origins of Greek Religion.* New Hyde Park, N.Y.: University Books, 1962.

―――. *Prolegomena to the Study of Greek Religion.* Princeton, N.J.: Princeton University Press, 1968.

Hirsch, Udo, James Mellaart, and Belkis Balpinar. *The Goddess from Anatolia.* Milan: Eskenazi, 1989.

Johnson, Buffie. *Lady of the Beasts: Ancient Images of the Goddess and Her Sacred Animals.* San Francisco: Harper & Row, 1988.

Neumann, Erich. *The Great Mother: An Analysis of the Archetype.* Princeton, N.J.: Princeton University Press, 1955.

Starhawk. *The Spiral Dance: A Rebirth of the Ancient Religion of the Great Goddess.* San Francisco: Harper & Row, 1979.

Stone, Merlin. *When God Was a Woman.* New York: Harcourt Brace Jovanovich, 1976.

Thompson, William Irwin. *The Time Falling Bodies Take to Light.* New York: St. Martin's Press, 1981.

Walker, Barbara G. *The Woman's Encyclopedia of Myths and Secrets.* San Francisco: Harper & Row, 1983.

This is only a partial list of important works dealing with the traditions of the goddess.

Page 10 learning to move and give voice: McNeill, William H. *Keeping Together in Time.* Cambridge, Mass.: Harvard University Press, 1995.

Page 10 Female performance ensembles of musicians: Drinker, Sophie, op. cit.

Galpin, F. W. *The Music of the Sumerians and Their Immediate Successors, the Babylonians and Assyrians.* Strasbourg: Strasbourg University Press, 1955.

Manniche, Lisa. *Music and Musicians in Ancient Egypt.* London: British Museum Press, 1991.

Rimmer, Joan. *Ancient Musical Instruments of Western Asia: In the Department of Western Asiatic Antiquities, the British Museum.* London: British Museum, 1969.

Page 11 Burying the Goddess: Baring, Anne, and Jules Cashford, op. cit.

Campbell, Joseph. *The Masks of God: Occidental Mythology.* New York: Viking Press, 1964.

Eisler, Riane, op. cit.

Gimbutas, Marija. "The Beginning of the Bronze Age in Europe and the Indo-Europeans: 3500–2500 B.C." *Journal of Indo-European Studies* 1 (1973): 166.

Lerner, Gerda. *The Creation of Patriarchy.* New York: Oxford University Press, 1986.

Mellaart, James. *The Neolithic of the Near East.* New York: Charles Scribner's Sons, 1975.

Stone, Merlin, op. cit.

Page 12 women were not even allowed to speak in church: "Women are ordered not to speak in church, not even softly, nor may they sing along or take part in the responses, but they should only be silent and pray to God." *Didascalia of the Three Hundred Eighteen Fathers,* circa A.D. 375. Referenced in Quasten, Johannes. *Music and Worship in Pagan and Christian Antiquity.* Washington, D.C.: National Association of Pastoral Musicians, 1973.

CHAPTER TWO

FIRST-PERSON FEMININE

Page 17 We earned some serious attention and good press: "Glen Velez, Steve Gorn and Layne Redmond are as close as anyone's come to the universal crossover group. Their pretty timbres and pure tuning attract the naive ear. Jazz fans and raga buffs alike enjoy following the variations they spin around their rhythmic patterns, which are complex enough to intrigue experimentalists. Their improvs are cleanly sculpted and motivically intricate enough to satisfy any lover of Brahms. Their rhythms are classic, their melodies romantic, their technique astounding. They probably don't make enough noise to please industrial band devotees; aside from that, they may be New York's most perfect musicians." Kyle Gann, *Village Voice*, October 24, 1989.

Page 19   **my search for answers:** There is no collected history of the frame drum or of the women who played this instrument for thousands of years. For years I searched for the images of the women drummers on temple walls, in the museum collections of Mediterranean countries, in books and journals. Much ancient art was taken from Greece and the Middle East by Europe and later by America in the eighteenth, nineteenth, and twentieth centuries. So not only did I drive for thousands of miles through Greece, Italy, Turkey, Syria, Egypt, and Morocco visiting large and small museums, I took every chance I could to search the major museums of Europe and the United States. I pored over art books, museum exhibition catalogs, and archaeological journals and was astonished at the thousands of images that survived intentional obliteration.

Pages 19–20   **symbolic meaning of drums:** *Funk and Wagnalls Standard Dictionary of Folklore Mythology and Legend.* Maria Leach, ed. Drum entry: Brakeley, Theresa C. New York: Funk & Wagnalls, 1972.

Pages 20–22   **ancient uses of the drum:** Galpin, F. W., op. cit.
    Hart, Mickey, and Fredric Lieberman. *Planet Drum.* San Francisco: Harper & Row, 1991.
    Manniche, Lisa, op. cit.
    Shafer, R. Murray. *The Tuning of the World.* New York: Alfred A. Knopf, 1977.

Page 21   **connection to sexuality and rebirth:** Manniche, Lisa, op. cit. "We may perhaps deduce that the angular harp, lyre, oboe and tambourine were so established in the cult of Hathor that they could not be played unless a sexual purpose was intended, be it procreation or rebirth." Women's power to give birth had been associated for thousands of years with the power to invoke rebirth, whether it be understood as a literal rebirth into a new human body or a spiritual rebirth achieved through initiations. The frame drum had always been her instrument of power to invoke this transformation of the spirit.

CHAPTER THREE

PRIMEVAL GODDESS OF RHYTHM

My thinking about the Paleolithic was heavily influenced by the work of:
    Eliade, Mircea. *A History of Religious Ideas*, vol. 1. Chicago: University of Chicago Press, 1978.
    Levy, G. Rachel. *The Gate of Horn: A Study of the Religious Conceptions of the Stone Age, and Their Influence on European Thought.* London: Faber & Faber, 1948.
    Marshack, Alexander. *The Roots of Civilization.* New York: McGraw-Hill, 1972.
    Thompson, William Irwin, op. cit.

Page 27   **The Paleolithic was also apparently a time of peace:** Ruspoli, Mario. *The Cave of Lascaux: The Final Photographic Record.* London: Thames and Hudson, 1987. "There is no real evidence of violence among the hunters of the Upper Palaeolithic: they seem not to have experienced tribal struggles, massacres, genocides and slavery. Nor does warfare appear to have been a part of their civilization."

Page 29   **representations of the vulva:** The dating methods used for the Paleolithic are varied, without a unifed sense of agreement among scholars. It is generally accepted that the reliefs of vulvas precede the mobilary sculptures and the paintings on the cave walls.

Page 30   **Thompson compares them to the pregnancy calendars:** Thompson, William Irwin, op. cit. "The implications of this association of women and the moon would suggest that women were the first observers of the basic periodicity of nature, the periodicity upon which all later scientific observations were made. Woman was the first to note a correspondence between an internal process she was going through and an external process in nature. . . . Out of the association of sexuality with the forces of nature, the females were to create our first religion, a religion of menstruation, childbirth mysteries, and the phases of the moon."

Page 30   **Paleolithic drumsticks:** Eliade in *A History of Religious Ideas*, op. cit., vol. 1. p. 19, cites Horst Kirchner's thesis ("Ein archaeologischer Beitrag zur Urgeschichte des Schamanismus," pp. 244 ff., 279 ff.) that the *batons de commandement* are drumsticks. Eliade states that if this is accepted, "it would mean that the Paleolithic sorcerers used drums [frame drums] comparable to those of the Siberian shamans." Eliade continues, "In this connection we may cite the fact that bone drumsticks have been found on the island of Oleny in the Barents Sea, in a site dated ca. 500 B.C."

Page 31 **Prudence C. Rice**: "Prehistoric Venuses: Symbols of Motherhood or Womanhood?" *Journal of Anthropological Research* 37 (4): 402–14.

Page 31 **Art historian George Weber**: Dr. Weber taught at Rutgers University in Newark, New Jersey, for many years, where I studied with him and completed a BA in Fine Arts in 1977.

Page 32 **When she doesn't bleed for ten cycles of the moon**: Alexander Marshack, op. cit., p. 336. "Perhaps Siberian peoples [of today] possess the key to that phenomenon; their women calculate child-birth by the phases of the moon. . . . Pregnancy has the duration of exactly 10 lunar months, and the woman keeps a sort of lunar calendar (it was always a woman who was the custodian of the lunar calendar among those nationalities)."

Page 32 **The horn is a very ancient symbol**: Thompson, William Irwin, op cit., pp. 105–106.

Page 33 **In classical mythology, women's menstrual periods**: Thompson, William Irwin, op. cit., pp. 96–97. He references Elise Boulding, *The Underside of History: A View of Women Through Time* (Boulder, Colo.: Westview Press, 1976), p. 106, and Martha K. McClintock, "Menstrual Synchrony and Suppression," *Nature* 299 (January 22, 1971): 171–79.

Page 34 **Eliade noted that**: Eliade, Mircea. *Patterns in Comparative Religion*, p. 154. New York: World, 1963.

Page 37 **Yet we don't find cave paintings glorifying the hunt**: Marshack, Alexander, op. cit. "Of the many human figures found with animals in Upper Paleolithic art none have weapons in hand, whereas many do have ceremonial and symbolic dress or objects."

Page 40 **Campbell recounts an ancient story of the Buriat people**: Campbell, Joseph. *The Way of the Animal Powers*, vol. 1, p. 176. San Francisco: Harper & Row, 1983.

Page 41 **Siberian and Altaic female shamans**: Ashe, Geoffrey. *Dawn Behind the Dawn: A Search for the Earthly Paradise*. New York: Henry Holt, 1992. "The term for female shamans is always a variant of the same word. A male Tungus shaman is simply that, but an Altaic one is a *kam*, a Buryat is a *bo*, a Yakut is an *oyun*. A female shaman is a *utygan* or a *udagan* or a *udaghan*, but never anything entymelogically different. We can infer that these tribes are descended from groups that were closer together, or in closer touch, and then all shamans were women, known by a single term—*utygan* or something like it—that stayed in use after the connections were broken. Male shamans appeared only after the separation, so the words for them were invented independently. . . . More can be said . . . about the possibility that male shamans began as smiths who made magical gear for female ones and gradually took over their powers, and also about the curious nostalgia that impels male shamans to dress like women and otherwise become feminized."

Page 41 **women as artists**: Johnson, Buffie, op. cit., p. 64–65. "The evidence points to women as the cave artists, as the size of the hand- and footprints found in the Paleolithic cave of Peche Merle fit the skeletal remains of women. . . . One would expect the stone and bone figurines to have been carved by men, the flintmakers who had dominated and perfected the use of tools. However, since the stone and ivory female figures, ranging from southern France to Siberian Mal'ta, are found largely in the women's quarters, it is likely that women were the sculptors."

CHAPTER FOUR

MOTHER OF THE FRUITED GRAIN

Page 44 **women developed the art of ceramics**: Both Erich Neumann and Robert Briffault have determined that women invented the craft and art of pottery. Neumann, Erich, op. cit. Briffault, Robert. *The Mothers*, vol. 1, pp. 474 ff. New York: Macmillan Company, 1927. "The art of pottery is a feminine invention: the original potter was a woman."

Page 45 **Skeletal remains reveal**: Hirsch, Udo, op. cit., vol 3. Mixed population of Çatal Hüyük: 59 percent Euro-Africans descended from Combe-Capelle Man from Upper Paleolithic, 17 percent were Proto-Mediterranian, 24 percent were Brachycephalic Alpine race.

Pages 45–46 **women as shrine painters**: Johnson, Buffie, op. cit., p. 64. "In Neolithic Catal Huyuk, Anatolia, painters' palettes were found among the female grave goods under the beds and floors of their houses. The palettes still bore color for painting the murals of the sacred rooms."

Page 46 **The development of agriculture**: Thompson, William Irwin, op. cit. "As a gatherer, woman was a botanist; as a cook and a potter, she was a priestess of the great Mother. . . . The origin of agriculture, rather than eliminating the religion of the Great Goddess of the Upper Paleolithic, ended by adding another miracle to the list of feminine wonders."

Page 47 **grain sieve and the frame drum**: Galpin, F. W., op. cit.
Budge, E. A. W. *Egyptian Hieroglyphic Dictionary*, vol. 2, p. 827. New York: Dover Publications, 1978.
The New Grove Dictionary of Music and Musical Instruments, vol. 1, pp. 243, 244. Stanley Sadie, ed. New York: Macmillan, 1984.

Pages 48–50 **bulls' heads as symbol of female power of birth**: Cameron, D. O. *Symbols of Birth and of Death in the Neolithic Era*. London: Kenyon-Deane, 1981.

Page 53 **priestesses were called melissae**: Harrison, Jane Ellen. *Prolegomena to the Study of Greek Religion*, op. cit., pp. 442–43. "They are in a word 'Melissae,' honey-priestesses, inspired by a honey intoxicant; they are bees . . . the priestesses of Artemis at Ephesus were 'Bees,' but also those of Demeter, and still more significant, the Delphic priestess herself was a Bee." She goes on to describe Aphrodite as a bee also.

Page 53 **Deborah as ruler and prophetess**: Judges 4:8 –9. Hastings, James, op. cit. Translates Deborah as "bee." "The fourth of the leaders or 'Judges' of Israel; called also a 'prophetess,' i.e., an inspired woman. . . . The Israelites came to her for guidance. . . . A personality of great power and outstanding character, she was looked up to as a 'mother in Israel.'"
Walker, Barbara G. *The Woman's Encyclopedia of Myths and Secrets*, op. cit., p. 407. San Francisco: Harper & Row,

1983. Walker describes her as "the Jewish Queen Deborah, priestess of Asherah, whose name also meant 'bee.'"

Page 59 **Excavations have unearthed a multitude of goddess figurines**: Lerner, Gerda. *The Creation of Patriarchy*. New York: Oxford University Press, 1986. "The pervasiveness of the veneration of the Mother-Goddess in the Neolithic and Chalcolithic periods has been confirmed by archaeological data. Marija Gimbutas reports that approximately 30,000 miniature sculptures in clay, marble, bone, copper, and gold are presently known from a total of some 3000 sites in southeastern Europe alone and that these testify to the communal worship of the Mother-Goddess."

Page 59 **In Sumerian, buru means both "vagina" and "river"**: Eliade, Mircea. *Myths, Dreams and Mysteries*, p. 169. New York: Harper & Row, Torch Books, 1975.

Page 60 **Egyptians could have been descendants of the Çatal Hüyük people**: Mellaart, James. *Çatal Hüyük and Anatolian Kilims*, vol. 2 of *The Goddess from Anatolia*. Milan: Eskenazi, 1989. "Egypt expresses early man's attitudes to religion and government in greater detail—through texts and pictures—than is available in Lower Mesopotamia in the third millennium B.C. Rightly or wrongly, however, one feels that the evidence from Çatal Hüyük comes closer to the Egyptian experience than it does to the Sumerian. Had the two been neighbours, few Egyptologists would have shown any hesitation in suggesting that the Çatal Hüyük people were the ancestors of the Ancient Egyptians."

Page 64 **Zimmer describes the damaru**: Zimmer, Heinrich. *Myths and Symbols in Indian Art and Civilization*. Princeton, N.J.: Princeton University Press, 1946.

Page 65 **Bhramaridevi**: Kinsley, David. *Hindu Goddesses: Visions of the Divine Feminine in the Hindu Religious Tradition*. Berkeley: University of California Press, 1988.

Page 66 **In the fourth and fifth centuries A.D., a form of Yoga now referred to as Tantra**: Mookerjee, Ajit, and Madhu Khanna. *The Tantric Way: Art, Science, Ritual,*

p. 10. New York: Thames and Hudson, 1977. "The earliest codified tantric texts date from the beginning of the Christian era. . . . Tantra literature took a long period to develop and no particular age can be assigned definitely."

Page 66 **Initiated priestesses known as Veshyas:** Jayakar, Pupul. *The Earth Mother: Legends, Goddesses, and Ritual Arts of India,* p. 25. San Francisco: Harper & Row, 1990.

Pages 67–70 **yantras and chakras:** Avalon, Arthur (Sir John Woodroffe). *The Serpent Power: The Secrets of Tantric and Shaktic Yoga.* New York: Dover Publications, 1974.
Johari, Harish. *Chakras: Energy Centers of Transformation.* Rochester, Vermont: Destiny Books, 1987.
———. *Tools for Tantra.* Rochester, Vermont: Destiny Books, 1986.
Mookerjee, Ajit, and Madhu Khanna, op. cit.

Page 69 **the vulva, or yoni, represents a "matrix of knowledge":** Fryba, Mirko. *The Art of Happiness: Teachings of Buddhist Psychology.* Boston: Shambhala, 1989.

Page 71 **"[Their] influence can be strong enough":** Danielou, Alain. *Music and the Power of Sound: The Influence of Tuning and Interval on Consciousness,* p. 188. Rochester, Vermont: Inner Traditions International, 1995.

Page 72 **The root word, bhrama:** Chatterjee, Amitava. Musician and teacher, in private conversation with the author.

Page 72 **"the significance of the drum":** Hamel, Peter Michael. *Through Music to the Self,* p. 77. Great Britain: Element Books Ltd., 1986.

....

CHAPTER SIX
....

THE QUEEN OF HEAVEN

Page 73 **The Sumerian city of Uruk:** Uruk is also translated as Erech.

Page 74 **Joseph Campbell describes the ziggurat:** Campbell, Joseph. *The Masks of God: Primitive Mythology,* p. 148. New York: Viking Press, 1959.

Page 74 **oval walls suggest the goddess's vulva:** Campbell, Joseph. *The Masks of God: Oriental Mythology,* p. 37. New York: Viking Press, 1962.

Page 75 **"The Link Between Heaven and Earth":** Eliade, Mircea. *Cosmos and History: The Myth of the Eternal Return.* New York: Harper, 1959.

Page 75 **A group of priestesses called the naditu:** Stone, Merlin, op. cit., p. 40.

Page 75 **Similarly, the Egyptian goddess of writing:** Lurker, Manfred. *The Gods and Symbols of Ancient Egypt: An Illustrated Dictionary,* p. 109. London: Thames and Hudson, 1980.

Page 75 **The en of the Ekishnugal was Lipushiau:** Drinker, Sophie. op. cit., p. 81.
F. Thureau-Dangin. *Les Inscriptions de Sumer et d'Addad,* p. 237. Paris: E. Leroux, 1905.

Pages 75–77 **Faces of the Goddess:** Jacobsen, Thorkild. *The Treasures of Darkness: A History of Mesopotamian Religion.* New Haven, Conn.: Yale University Press, 1976. A beautifully readable, exhaustive source based on textual evidence.

Page 77 **"I step onto the heavens":** Ibid, p. 136.

Pages 78–81 **Ritual Music:** Galpin, F. W., op cit.
Rimmer, Joan, op. cit.
Wiora, Walter. *The Four Ages of Music.* New York: W. W. Norton, 1965.

Page 80 **The balag-di, the small frame drum:** Cohen, Mark E. *Balag-compositions: Sumerian Lamentation Liturgies of the Second and First Millennium B.C.* Malibu, Calif.: Undena Publications, 1974. There was an entire category of liturgies composed to be chanted to the rhythms of this instrument.

Page 80 **This drum was named Nin-an-da-gal-ki:** Galpin, F. W., op. cit.

Page 80 **In a song describing how Inanna:** Wolkstein, Diane, and Samuel Noah Kramer. *Inanna, Queen of Heaven and Earth: Her Stories and Hymns from Sumer,* pp. 24, 26. New York: HarperCollins, 1983. From the poem "Inanna and the God of Wisdom." By kind permission of Diane Wolkstein.

Page 81 **A Hittite inscription describes**: Galpin, F. W., op. cit., p. 3.

Page 82 **"Blood fecundates the earth"**: Jayakar, Pupul, op. cit, p. 60.

Page 82 **"made the sacred cakes"**: Contenau, George. *Everyday Life in Babylon and Assyria*. London: E. Arnold, circa 1954.

Pages 82–83 **Grain rituals**: Black, Jeremy, and Anthony Green. *Gods, Demons and Symbols of Ancient Mesopotamia: An Illustrated Dictionary*, pp. 84, 128. Austin: University of Texas Press, 1992.

Page 82 **one of the Sumerian words for the frame drum, which also means "grain-measure"**: Galpin, F. W., op. cit. "The A-DA-PA (*adapu*) had a rectangular frame and perhaps skin-heads on both sides. A grain-measure of similar shape was called by the same name. The instrument was employed in the temples to accompany certain hymns and liturgies called after it."

Page 83 **the ancient recipe for brewing beer**: Katz, S. H., and F. Maytag. "Brewing an Ancient Beer." *Archaeology* (July/August 1991): 24–33.

Pages 84–85 **Sacred Sexual Priestesses**: Goldron, Romain. *Ancient and Oriental Music*. H. S. Stuttman Co.; distributed by New York: Doubleday, 1968. "Many female singers and dancers were associated with the temple as concubines of the god. Their domain was the sanctuary devoted to goddesses, where they formed a school of sacred courtesans. It seems that such an establishment was incorporated in the temple of the Egyptian goddess Hathor, sister of the Greek Aphrodite and the Babylonian Ishtar. It might be thought that an affiliation of this sort would have been shameful for young girls, but in fact the opposite was true. Our western morality, with all its hypocrisy, has made us draw a veil over these institutions, especially as we do not really understand their true significance.

"The courtesans, or handmaids of the goddess, solemnized the mysteries of carnal love by actively taking part in a magic rite. In doing so they maintained a psychic link, symbolized in bodily unity, with their goddess, and also transmitted the virtue of the goddess to those who joined with them in the performance of the sacrament. The maidens were variously called 'pure,' 'virginal' and 'saintly.' In principle, this union has the same function as the sacrament of the Eucharist; it represents man's communion with the *sacrum*, held and administered by the woman."

Page 84 **Evola, Julius**. *The Metaphysics of Sex*. New York: Inner Traditions International, reprinted 1983.

Pages 85–88 **Inanna's Descent**: Wolkstein, Diane, and Samuel Noah Kramer, op. cit.

Page 85 **In preparation, she instructs her minister**: Ibid. p. 149. Black, Jeremy, and Anthony Green, op. cit., pp. 141, 142. Ninshubar is Inanna's *sukkal*. "A sukkal is a servant who may act in many different capacities—as vizier, minister, chancellor, messenger, general, or warrior—a sukkal who carries out orders often has powers superior to his or her master. Inanna's sukkal Ninshubar, often referred to as the servant of the holy shrine of Uruk, seems to represent the inner spiritual resources of Inanna, which are intended for the greater good of Sumer." There also appears to be a god by the name of Ninsubur which sometimes confuses the translations in terms of the gender.

Page 87 **The ziggurat**: The ziggurats were built of sun-dried mud bricks which have greatly disintegrated over the millennia. Although it is unclear, archaeologists believe that ziggurats were built of three, five, six, or seven levels. Herodotus left a description of the ziggurat in Babylon in which he described the seven stages and their symbolic meanings.

....

CHAPTER SEVEN
....

THE GOLDEN ONE

Page 89 **"Egypt," Herodotus remarked**: Herodotus. *The Histories*. Trans. Evans, J. A. S. Boston: Twayne, 1982.

Page 91 **"ear" and "mind" are synonymous**: Lurker, Manfred, op. cit., p. 48.

Page 91 **Hathor, the Lady of the Horns, is the oldest depicted Egyptian deity**: Budge, E. A. W. *Gods of the Egyptians*. New York: Dover Publications, 1969. Amulets of Hathor's head have been found in predynastic graves. She was said to be the "mother of every god and goddess . . . never having been created."

Page 92 **In a text at the Hathor shrine at Djeser-Djeseru**: Pinch, Geraldine. *Votive Offerings to Hathor*, p. 176. Oxford: Griffith Institute Ashmolean Museum, 1993.

Page 92 **In the Coffin Texts**: Faulkner, R. O., trans. *The Ancient Egyptian Coffin Texts*. Warminster, England: Aris & Phillips, 1978. The Coffin Texts are a collection of magical incantations and rituals from the Middle Kingdoms. Faulkner is one of the most highly regarded sources.

Page 94 **Maat's Rules of Behavior**: Budge, E. A. W. *The Dwellers on the Nile*. New York: B. Blom, 1972.

Page 94 **played them as a djed pillar**: Sellers, Jane B. *The Death of Gods in Ancient Egypt*, p. 317. Harmondsworth, England: Penguin Books Ltd., 1992. "The Djed pillar is seen as a 'backbone' by Egyptologists. If it is indeed accurate to say that the ancient Egyptian used this analogy, might it not be because the vertebral column and ribs resemble a tree trunk with branches—a tree of life inside each human body?"

Page 95 **"Isis, Lady of the Sky, Mistress of [all] the Godesses"**: Manniche, Lisa. *Ancient Egyptian Musical Instruments*, p. 1. Berlin: Deutscher Kunstverlag, 1975.

Page 96 **Songs of Isis and Nephthys**: Translated from the Papyrus Bremner-Rhind, by R. O. Faulkner, quoted by Henry George Farmer in "The Music of Ancient Egypt" in *New Oxford History of Music*, vol. 1. Oxford and New York: Oxford University Press, 1990. Faulkner says: "Apart from a hymn to Osiris sung by the lector-priest in the middle of the ceremony, the songs consist of alternate duets by the two priestesses and solos on the part of her who represented Isis."

Page 97 **It is often inscribed with a lotus**: Barguet, P., p. 279. "L'origine de la signification du contrepids de collier-manat." *Bulletin de l'Institut Francais d'Archeologie Orientale du Caire* (1953). As referenced by Pinch, Geraldine, op. cit.

Page 97 **"This probably means that a kind of divine energy"**: Pinch, Geraldine, op. cit., p. 280.

Pages 97–98 **"the words mind, soul, and heart**: Lurker, Manfred, op. cit., p. 61. "The heart was a symbol of life. . . . A person's true character was revealed in his heart. . . . The heart was also the seat of the emotions and intellect."

Page 98 **"to wash the heart"**: Budge, E. A. W. *Egyptian Hieroglyphic Dictionary*, vol. 1, p. 28. New York: Dover Publications, 1978.

Page 101 **As historian Robert Lawlor points out**: Lawlor, Robert. "Ancient Temple Architecture." In *Homage to Pythagoras: Rediscovering Sacred Science*, pp. 35–132. Bamford, Christopher, ed. New York: Lindisfarne Press, 1982.

Pages 103–104 **Festival of the Reunion**: Lamy, Lucie. *Egyptian Mysteries: New Light on Ancient Knowledge*, pp. 80–81. New York: Thames and Hudson, 1981.

Page 107 **The ab was the most important**: Walker, Barbara G. *The Woman's Encyclopedia of Myths and Secrets*, op. cit. "*Ab* was the Egyptian word for heart-soul, most important of the seven souls bestowed by the seven birth-goddesses (Hathors). The *ab* was the soul that would be weighed in the balances of Maat after death."

Page 108 **"I am this one who escaped"**: From the Pyramid Texts, quoted in Sellers, Jane B., op. cit., p. 253.

CHAPTER EIGHT

THE MOTHER OF THE GODS

Page 110 **"Cybele, the All-Begetting Mother"**: Vermaseren, Maarten J. *Cybele and Attis*. London: Thames and Hudson, 1977.

Page 110 **Her lotus bowl, the patera**: Neumann, Erich, op. cit. "According to the Greek tradition, the first patera, or bowl, was modeled from Helen's (Helen of Troy) breast."

Page 112 **"The moon rose full"**: Wharton, Henry Thornton. *Sappho: Memoir, Text, Selected Renderings*. London: D. Stott, 1887.

Page 113 **In the Biblical Book of Revelations, Aphrodite's number**: Walker, Barbara G., op. cit., p. 523.

The Holy Bible, King James Version. Revelation, 13:18: "and his number is Six hundred threescore and six."

Revelation, 17:1–5: "1: And there came one of the seven angels which had the seven vials, and talked with me, saying unto me, Come hither; I will show unto thee the judgment of the great whore that sitteth upon many waters:

2: With whom the kings of the earth have committed fornication, and the inhabitants of the earth have been made drunk with the wine of her fornication.

3: So he carried me away in the spirit into the wilderness: and I saw a woman sit upon a scarlet coloured beast, full of names of blasphemy, having seven heads and ten horns.

4: And the woman was arrayed in purple and scarlet colour, and decked with gold and precious stones and pearls, having a golden cup in her hand full of abominations and filthiness of her fornication:

5: And upon her forehead was a name written, MYSTERY, BABLYON THE GREAT, THE MOTHER OF HARLOTS AND ABOMINATIONS OF THE EARTH."

Many of Inanna/Isis/Astarte/Aphrodite's symbols are illustrated in these verses: She was goddess of the water; of intoxication; of sacred sexuality; her high priestesses incarnated as the goddess herself performing the hieros gamos (sacred marriage rite) annually with the king of the city-states to ensure the fertility of the community; her priestesses wore robes of scarlet or purple; she held a golden patera in her hand; she rode on a lion; seven heads represented seven stages of awareness; and she almost always was associated with horned headdresses.

Pages 113–15   The Omphalos: The omphalos is a very important concept in the ancient world and was variously symbolized as a mound of earth or ashes, a mountain, a cone, a spike shape, a pillar, a beehive, a tomb, a Buddhist or Hindu stupa, or a navel. In Butterworth, E. A. S. *Some Traces of the Pre-Olympian World.* Berlin: Walter de Gruyter and Co., 1961, and *The Tree at the Navel of the Earth.* Berlin: Walter de Gruyter and Co., 1970, the relationship of the omphalos to ancient practices of shamanism, Yogic disciplines, and other techniques of altering consciousness is thoroughly explored.

Page 113   Deborah was the ancient Hebrew name: Lerner, Gerda, op. cit., p. 165.

Hastings, James, op. cit. "The date palm is identified in the Midrash Bereshith Rabba 15 as the 'tree of life' (Bn2:9); the prophetess Deborah 'sat' under a noted palm tree (Jg 4:5)." Inanna was the goddess of the date palm. The relationship here is to the goddess of the Tree of Life and the shamaness who through alignment with this power can know the future.

Page 114   In the Homeric Hymn to Hermes: The Thriae are three sisters who feed "on honey fresh, food of the gods divine, Then holy madness made their hearts to speak the truth. . . ." Fragment of Homer quoted in Harrison, Jane Ellen. *Prolegomena to the Study of Greek Religion,* op. cit.

Page 114   The Pythagoreans believed the nature of reality: Walker, Barbara G. *The Woman's Dictionary of Symbols and Sacred Objects,* p. 488. San Francisco: Harper & Row, 1988. Pythagoras (sixth century B.C.) was a mystic, philosopher, and sound healer whose works on mathematics are primarily what he is remembered for today. In the ancient world he was known as a great spiritual teacher who formed a religious school with initiates of both sexes. One of his disciplines for his students was a concentrated meditation on hexagons.

Page 114   In the Georgics, Virgil relates one of these stories: P. 85. David R. Slavitt, trans. Garden City, N.Y.: Doubleday, 1972. "They have their gifts from Jupiter as thanks from the grateful god. The myth is old, and bees were even then the agents of order, bringing hope on their fragile wings, thus: Cybele rebelled against the cruelty of Saturn, the condition of whose rule upon the earth was that he devour his sons. She fed him a stone, hid the baby, Jupiter, in a cave, and charged her Corybantes to beat their cymbals and dance to their noisy drums to hide the cries of the infant in the cave. A desperate plan, but the bees came. They fed the child with honey and kept him alive. He grew. He made his war to overthrow the Titans. And he remembered the kindness of the bees, for which his gifts: the civility of law; prosperity; the grandeur of cities; and delights of the countryside."

Page 116   The Honey Doctrine of Hinduism delineated: Avalon, Arthur (Sir John Woodroffe), op. cit.

Page 117   According to current scientific research: Theimer, Ernest. *Fragrance Chemistry: The Science of the Sense of Smell.* San Diego, Calif.: Academic Press, 1982.

Van Toller, Steve, and George Dodd. *Perfumery: The Psychology and Biology of Fragrance.* New York: Chapman & Hall, 1988.

Page 118 **Crete, a Greek word, means:** Graves, Robert. *The Greek Myths*, vol. 1, p. 295. New York: Penguin Books, 1960.

Page 119 **"playing on a brazen drum":** Ibid., p. 3.

Page 121 **Saint Paul demanded its destruction:** "So that not only this our craft is in danger to be set at nought; but also that the temple of the great goddess Diana should be despised, and her magnificence should be destroyed, whom all Asia and the world worshippeth" (Acts 19:27). Hastings, James, op. cit.

Page 123 **According to Robert Graves, the first shrine at Dephi "was made of bees' wax and feathers," symbols of the Great Mother as bee and dove goddess:** Ibid., p. 181.

....

CHAPTER NINE

....

THE GREAT PROTECTRESS

Page 126 **According to Livy, a Roman historian:** Livy, Titus Livius (59 B.C.–A.D. 17). *The War With Hannibal*, Books 21–30 of *The History of Rome from Its Foundation*. Aubrey de Selincourt, trans. Baltimore: Penguin Books, 1965.

Page 129 **"They called Demeter (the noisy)":** From the Ravenna scholiast on Aristoph. Ach. 709, Quoted in Cook, A. B. "The Gong at Donona." *Journal of Hellenic Studies*, 22 (1902).

Page 129 **"I have eaten from the drum":** Clement of Alexandria, in Butterworth, G. W., trans. *Exhortation to the Greeks*. Cambridge, Mass.: Harvard University Press, 1960, circa 1919. Versions of this verse are cited by the ancient writers Clement of Alexandria and Firmicus Maternus. It is agreed by scholars that it is a verse from the mysteries of the Great Mother; what is controversial is whether it is from Demeter and Persephone's mysteries or Cybele and Attis's mysteries.

Page 129 **"We know . . . that in the Greek rites":** Campbell, Joseph. *The Masks of God: Primitive Mythology*, op. cit., p. 189.

Page 130 **Dionysos's origins are something:** Harrison,

Jane Ellen. *Prolegomena to the Study of Greek Religion*, op. cit., pp. 551–62. "Dionysos . . . bears to the end, as no other god does, the stamp of his matriarchal origin. He can never rid himself of the throng of worshipping women, he is always the nursling of his Maenads. Moreover the instruments of his cult are always not his but his mother's." Harrison quotes Euripides' Bacchae. 126: "But the Timbrel, the Timbrel is another's. And away to Mother Rhea it must wend." (Timbrel is the Hebrew word for frame drum.)

Page 131 **"The association of red wine with blood":** Burkert, Walter. *Greek Religion: Archaic and Classical*. Oxford: Basil Blackwell, 1985.

Page 133 **"the leathern clamorous sieves":** Reference from Michaelides, Solon. Hesiod in *The Music of Ancient Greece: An Encyclopaedia*. London: Faber & Faber, 1978.

Page 134 **Cicero, speaking of the Eleusinian mysteries:** Burkert, Walter. *Ancient Mystery Cults*. Cambridge, Mass.: Harvard University Press, 1987.

Page 135 **"a tambourine nearly always":** Quasten, Johannes. *Music and Worship in Pagan and Christian Antiquity*. Washington, D.C.: National Association of Pastoral Musicians, 1973.

Page 136 **"Come, follow me to the house":** Catullus (Latin poet, 84(?)–54 B.C.) fragment quoted in Quasten, Johannes, op. cit., translated by J. Kroll.

Page 136 **According to Burkert, the cults:** Burkert, Walter. *Greek Religion: Archaic and Classical*, op. cit., p. 12. "The most intriguing, most impressive and most unambiguous discoveries are those from Çatal Hüyük. The Early Neolithic town here contains a series of sanctuaries, specially equipped chambers in the many-roomed houses: their distinctive features are secondary burials of the dead, cattle horns set into benches, figurative wall paintings and, most strikingly, wall reliefs of a Great Goddess with uplifted arms and straddled legs—clearly the birth-giving mother of the animals and of life itself. A female statuette is found accompanied by a boyish consort, another fulsome female figure enthroned between leopards is giving birth to a child, and a wall painting shows men masked as leopards hunting a bull; the association with the Asia Minor Great Mother of historical times, with her leopards or lions, her paredros, and with the society of men and bull sacrifice is irresistible. Here we have overwhelmingly clear proof of religious continuity over more than five millennia."

Page 137 **the Hilaria, a joyful procession**: Quasten, Johannes, op. cit. "In the *Martyrdom of Saint Theodotus* we read that each year in Ancyra the wooden statues of Artemis and Athena were taken to a nearby lake and bathed to the sound of drums and flutes. Ovid gives this same information in reference to similar baths of the cultic image of the Magna Mater in Almo near Rome and in the Phrygian river Gallos."

CHAPTER TEN

THE STORM GOD

Two extremely informative books that provided detailed sources for this chapter are Quasten, Johannes, op. cit., and Chuvin, Pierre. *A Chronicle of the Last Pagans*. B. A. Archer, trans. Cambridge, Mass.: Harvard University Press, 1990.

Pages 142–44 **The Huluppu Tree**: Kramer, Samuel Noah. *The Sumerians: Their History, Culture, and Character*, pp. 199–205. Chicago: University of Chicago Press, 1963.

Page 142 **pukku and mikku**: Some scholars translate these words as "puck" and "stick" and relate them to a sport game similar to modern hockey. Samuel Kramer translates these words as "drum" and "stick." Judging from the text in which Gilgamesh "made the drumming resound," and that he used them to summon men to war, it seems most likely to have been a drum.

Pages 145–46 **The People of the Storm God**: Jacobsen, Thorkild. *The Treasures of Darkness: A History of Mesopotamian Religion*, p. 179. New Haven, Conn.: Yale University Press, 1976. "As far as we can judge, the fourth millennium and the ages before it had been moderately peaceful. Wars and raids were not unknown; but they were not constant and they did not dominate existence. In the third millennium they appear to have become the order of the day. No one was safe."

Page 148 **Plotinus popularized a synthesis of the ideas of Plato**: In Cornell, Tim, and John Mathews, *Atlas of the Roman World* (New York: Facts on File, 1982), Neoplatonism is defined as "a systematization of platonic

thought in terms of a hierarchy of different levels of being and of reality through which the soul must by contemplation make its way in its return to the 'One,' the supreme principle from which it was derived."

Page 150 **Psalms 68:24–25**: *The Holy Bible, New International Version*. New York: International Bible Society, 1978.

Page 150 **Judith 16:1**: Ibid.

Page 150 **1 Samuel**: Ibid.

Page 151 **Exodus 15:20**: Ibid.

Page 151 **Amos 5:21–23**: Ibid.

Page 152 **A Church council in 826 prohibited**: Quasten, Johannes, op. cit., p. 177.

Page 152 **women who "dance in pagan fashion for their dead"**: Ibid. Barhebraeus's (died 1286) decree against the relics of the pagan cult of the dead known as his *Nomocanon*.

Page 153 **In the third century they were barred from funerals**: Ibid., pp. 176–77. "As early as the year 300 the Council of Elvira had forbidden women to hold vigils privately in cemeteries 'because they often secretly commit sins under the guise of praying.' . . . In the West the Third Council of Carthage in 397, along with many other later councils, maintained these prohibitions. . . . The Third Council of Toledo (589) took steps against dancing on the feasts of the martyrs with the following decree: 'The irreligious custom which the common people have of observing the solemnities of the saints—that is, that the people who should be attentive to the divine services try to keep themselves awake with dancing and the singing of songs of a low sort, thus not only harming themselves but disturbing the services of the monks—is to be entirely eradicated. The elimination of this from all of Spain is committed to the care of the sacred council of priests and judges.'"

CHAPTER ELEVEN

THE TRIUMPH OF THE VIRGIN

Marina Warner's book *Alone of All Her Sex: The Myth and the Cult of the Virgin Mary* (New York: Alfred A. Knopf, 1976) is one of the most thorough and interesting analyses of the Virgin Mary, and Jonathan Smith's *Drudgery Divine: On the Comparison of Early Christianities and the Religions of Late Antiquity* (London: School of Oriental and African Studies, University of London; Chicago: University of Chicago Press, 1990) is an extremely interesting analysis of the mythological origins of Roman Christianity. Although many scholars, including Joseph Campbell and Mircea Eliade, have thoroughly explored this topic, one of the earliest and most influential was Sir James George Fraser, in his series *The Golden Bough: A Study in Magic and Religion* (New York: Macmillan, 1974, c. 1950). Both of these books are meticulously scholarly, viewing their material without discernable bias while maintaining a provocative readability.

Pages 158–59   prohibitions against women speaking, praying, or singing aloud in church: "Women are ordered not to speak in church, not even softly, nor may they sing along or take part in the responses, but they should only be silent and pray to God" from the *Didascalia of the Three Hundred Eighteen Fathers*, trans. P. Batiffol, who dates it to A.D. 375. "The virgins should sing or read the Psalms very quietly during the liturgy. They should only move their lips, so that nothing is heard, for I do not permit women to speak in church" from the *Catechesis* by Cyril of Jerusalem (d. A.D. 386). "Christians are not allowed to teach their daughters singing" from *Commandments of the Fathers, Superiors and Masters* (A.D. 576), trans. W. Riedel. Quasten, Johannes, op. cit., pp. 81–83.

Page 159   By 603, even the choirs of virgins were silenced: Quasten, Johannes, op. cit., p. 86. "It is not permitted for choirs of virgins to sing in church or to prepare banquets in church," from the Council of Auxerre (573/603).

Pope Leo IV (847–855) ordered: "Forbid the singing of choirs of women in the church or in the vestibule of the church." Ibid. p. 86.

The Gnostics and Marcionites, along with other early sects of Christianity, did allow women to function as prophetesses, lectresses, teachers, deaconesses, and singers. As the early Roman church gained power, they slowly and surely moved to crush these other forms of Christianity that they labeled "heretical."

Page 161   "She is the flower, the violet, the full-blown rose": Gautier de Coincy. *Les chansons a la Vierge.* Jacques Chailley, ed. Paris: Heugel, 1959.

Page 162   Matthew 6:7: *The Holy Bible, King James Version*, op. cit.

Page 162.   For Saint Ursula she wrote: Lachman, Barbara. *The Journal of Hildegard of Bingen*, p. 166. New York: Bell Tower, 1993. *For the Benedictus Canticle at Lauds of the Vigil*: "O royal redness of blood." *At Matins for Her Feast*: "A dripping honeycomb." *Hildegard of Bingen.* New York: Bell Tower, 1993.

CHAPTER TWELVE

THE TECHNOLOGY OF RHYTHM

Page 170   Princeton physicist Edwart Witten: Davies, P. C. W., and J. Brown. *Superstrings: A Theory of Everything?*, p. 93. Cambridge, England: Cambridge University Press, 1988.

Page 170   Experiments performed by Hans Jenny: Jenny, Hans. *Cymatics.* Basel: Basilius Presse AG, 1974.

Pages 170–71   Fetal development and synchronization to physical sounds: Condon, William S. "Neonatal Entrainment and Enculturation." In *Before Speech: The Beginning of Interpersonal Communication.* M. Bullowa, ed. New York: Cambridge University Press, 1979.

Pages 171–72   The Pulse of Awareness: Hamilton, W. J., J. D. Boyd, and H. W. Mossman. *Human Embryology: Prenatal Development of Form and Function.* Cambridge, Mass. Heffer, 1972.

Hassett, James. *A Primer of Psychophysiology.* San Francisco: W. H. Freeman, 1978.

Hutchinson, Michael. *Megabrain.* New York: Beech Tree Books, 1986.

Kenyon, Tom. *Brain States.* Naples, Fla.: United States Publishing, 1984.

Pages 172–73   Right Brain, Left Brain: Johari, Harish. *Chakras: Energy Centers of Transformation.* Rochester, Vt.: Destiny Books, 1987.

Sagan, Carl. *The Dragons of Eden.* New York: Random House, 1977.

Page 173   Andrew Neher conducted a series: Neher, Andrew. "A Physiological Explanation of Unusual

Behavior in Ceremonies Involving Drums." *Human Biology* 34 (1962): 151–60.

Pages 174–75 **Entrainment:** Chapple, Eliot D. *Culture and Biological Man.* New York: Holt, Rinehart & Winston, 1970.

Condon, W. S., and W. D. Ogston. "Speech and Body Motion Synchrony of Speaker-Hearer." In *Perception of Language.* D. L. Horton and J. J. Jenkins, ed. Columbus, Ohio: Charles E. Merrill Press, 1971.

Leonard, George. *The Silent Pulse.* New York: Arkana, 1991.

Condon's work has been in research and is not easily accessible to a lay audience. Chapple, Leonard, and Hall's books are very readable, and I believe a completely new understanding of human behavior and cultural development in terms of rhythmic organization is now forming out of their work and other leading thinkers such as William H. McNeill.

Page 175 **The Third Eye:** Wosien, Maria-Gabriel. *Sacred Dance: Encounter with the Gods,* p. 23. New York: Thames and Hudson, 1974. "The 'frontal eye,' the square inch between the eyes, as the dwelling place of the primal spirit, is not represented as a bodily organ, but contains all reality; it represents the Present which is timeless and without extension."

Lamy, Lucie, op. cit., p. 17. "Thus the Eye evokes the means of the perception of light in all its forms, from the physical light of the sun and moon to the light of knowledge, and to the inner illumination of awakened Spirit."

Page 175 **a small organ called the pineal gland:** Eliot D. Chapple, op. cit., describes the pineal gland as translating "the energy of light into a fundamental secretion, melanin, which has biochemical impact on the whole regulatory or autonomic nervous system. It also acts directly on the hypothalamus, the autonomic coordinating center. The pineal body thus maintains the body's rhythms in phase with one another through the hypothalamus.

In Hebrew, *penuel,* or *peniel,* means "the Face of God." In Latin one of the definitions for pineal eye is "light atop the tree," which relates to the metaphor of the spine as the Tree of Life, with the light of the kundalini rising to the third eye.

Lucie Lamy, op. cit., p. 17, reports: "Certain authors around the time of Galen (A.D. 131–201) felt that 'it must serve as a sluice-gate regulating the quantity of spirit necessary to maintain psychic equilibrium.'"

In 1677 Descartes described the pineal as the seat of the rational soul. In Hindu and Buddhist traditions it is the sixth chakra or energy center in the human body.

Page 176 **modern Western medicine ignores the concept of biorhythms:** Sollberger, Arne. *Biological Rhythm Research.* Amsterdam, New York: Elsevier Publishing Co., 1965. "A peculiar static thinking of the medical mind (in spite of the clear recognition of such dynamic functions as the heartbeat, the respiratory rhythm or bowel movements by the physiologists) caused a solid reaction against the concept of biological rhythms. The medical profession was strongly opposed and more prepared to regard the 24-hour variations as simple reflexes and effects of the feeding habits. This resistance has continued more or less up to the present day. In no field has the lack of interest been stronger than in pharmacology."

Page 176 **Edward T. Hall:** Hall, Edward T. *The Dance of Life: The Other Dimension of Time.* New York: Anchor Books, 1984.

CHAPTER THIRTEEN

GIVING BIRTH TO OURSELVES

Page 180 **As Campbell says:** Campbell, Joseph. *The Masks of God: Occidental Mythology.* New York: Viking Press, 1964.

SELECTED BIBLIOGRAPHY

Adams, Robert M. "The Origin of Cities." *Scientific American*, vol. 203, no. 3 (September 1960): 153–68.

Anderson, R. D. *Musical Instruments*, vol. 3 of *Catalogue of Egyptian Antiquities in the British Museum*. London: British Museum Publications, 1976.

Ashe, Geoffrey. *Dawn Behind the Dawn: A Search for the Earthly Paradise*. New York: Henry Holt, 1992.

Avalon, Arthur (Sir John Woodroffe). *The Serpent Power: The Secrets of Tantric and Shaktic Yoga*. New York: Dover Publications, 1974.

Bachofen, Johann Jakob. *Myth, Religion and Mother Right*. Princeton, N.J.: Princeton University Press, 1967.

Baring, Anne, and Jules Cashford. *The Myth of the Goddess: Evolution of an Image*. London: Penguin Books, 1991.

Barnard, Mary. *Sappho: A New Translation*. Berkeley: University of California Press, 1958.

Batto, Bernard Frank. *Studies on Women at Mari*. Baltimore: Johns Hopkins Near Eastern Studies, 1974.

Begley, Vimala, and R. D. De Puma, ed. *Rome and India: The Ancient Sea Trade*. Madison, Wis.: University of Wisconsin Press, 1991.

Berger, Pamela. *The Goddess Obscured: Transformation of the Grain Protectress from Goddess to Saint*. Boston: Beacon Press, 1985.

Bernal, Martin. *The Fabrication of Ancient Greece, 1785–1985*, vol. 1 of *Black Athena: The Afroasiatic Roots of Classical Civilization*. London: Free Association Books, 1987.

———. *The Archaeological and Documentary Evidence*, vol. 2 of *Black Athena: The Afroasiatic Roots of Classical Civilization*. London: Free Association Books, 1991.

Bianchi, Ugo. *The Greek Mysteries*. Leiden, the Netherlands: E. J. Brill, 1976.

Black, Jeremy, and Anthony Green. *Gods, Demons and Symbols of Ancient Mesopotamia: An Illustrated Dictionary*. Austin: University of Texas Press, 1992.

Blacker, Carmen, and Michael Loewe. *Oracles and Divination*. Boulder, Colo.: Shambhala, 1981.

Blades, James. *Percussion Instruments and Their History*. London: Faber & Faber, 1984.

Boardman, John. *Athenian Red Figure Vases: The Archaic Period*. London: Thames and Hudson, 1975.

———. *The Greek Overseas: Their Early Colonies and Trade*. London: Thames and Hudson, 1980.

Bohm, David. *Wholeness and the Implicate Order*. London: Routledge & Kegan Paul, 1980.

Bouzek, Jan. *The Aegean, Anatolia and Europe: Cultural Interrelations in the Second Millennium b.c.* Prague: Academia, 1985.

Briffault, Robert. *The Mothers*, 3 vols. New York: Macmillan Company, 1927.

Budge, E. A. W. *The Book of the Dead*. London: Routledge & Kegan Paul, 1977.

———. *The Dwellers on the Nile*. New York: B. Blom, 1972.

———. *Egyptian Hieroglyphic Dictionary*, vol. 1 and 2. New York: Dover Publications, 1978.

———. *Gods of the Egyptians*. New York: Dover Publications, 1969.

Burkert, Walter. *Ancient Mystery Cults*. Cambridge, Mass.: Harvard University Press, 1987.

———. *Greek Religion: Archaic and Classical*. Oxford: Basil Blackwell, 1985.

———. *Homo Necans: The Anthropology of Ancient Greek Sacrificial Ritual and Myth*. Berkeley: University of California Press, 1983.

Burn, Lucilla. *The Meidias Painter*. Oxford: Clarendon Press; New York: Oxford University Press, 1987.

Butterworth, E. A. S. *Some Traces of the Pre-Olympian World*. Berlin: Walter de Gruyter and Co., 1961.

———. *The Tree at the Navel of the Earth*. Berlin: Walter de Gruyter and Co., 1970.

Cameron, Averil, and Amelie Kuhrt, ed. *Images of Women in Antiquity*. Detroit: Wayne State University Press, 1985.

Cameron, D. O. *Symbols of Birth and of Death in the Neolithic Era*. London: Kenyon-Deane, 1981.

Campbell, Joseph. *The Hero with a Thousand Faces*. Princeton, N.J.: Princeton University Press, 1968.

———. *The Masks of God: Creative Mythology*. New York: Viking Press, 1970.

———. *The Masks of God: Occidental Mythology*. New York: Viking Press, 1964.

———. *The Masks of God: Oriental Mythology*. New York: Viking Press, 1962.

———. *The Masks of God: Primitive Mythology*. New York: Viking Press, 1959.

———. *Myths to Live By*. New York: Viking Press, 1972.

———. *The Way of the Animal Powers*, vol. 1. San Francisco: Harper & Row, 1983.

Cassuto, Umberto. *The Goddess Anath*. Jerusalem: Magnes Press, Hebrew University, 1971.

Chapple, Eliot D. *Culture and Biological Man.* New York: Holt, Rinehart & Winston, 1970.

Chuvin, Pierre. *A Chronicle of the Last Pagans.* B. A. Archer, trans. Cambridge, Mass.: Harvard University Press, 1990.

Cohen, Mark E. *Balag-compositions: Sumerian Lamentation Liturgies of the Second and First Millennium b.c.* Malibu, Calif.: Undena Publications, 1974.

Condon, William S. "Neonatal Entrainment and Enculturation." In *Before Speech: The Beginning of Interpersonal Communication.* M. Bullowa, ed. New York: Cambridge University Press, 1979.

Condon, W. S., and W. D. Ogston. "Speech and Body Motion Synchrony of Speaker-Hearer." In *Perception of Language.* D. L. Horton and J. J. Jenkins, ed. Columbus, Ohio: Charles E. Merrill Press, 1971.

Contenau, George. *Everyday Life in Babylon and Assyria.* London: E. Arnold, circa 1954.

Cook, A. B. "The Gong of Donona." *Journal of Hellenic Studies* (1902): 22.

Cumont, Franz. *Oriental Religions in Roman Paganism.* New York: Dover Publications, 1956.

Daly, Mary. *Gyn/Ecology: The Metaethics of Radical Feminism.* Boston: Beacon Press, 1978.

————. *Pure Lust: Elemental Feminist Philosophy.* Boston: Beacon Press, 1984.

Danielou, Alain. *Shiva and Dionysus, Gods of Love and Ecstasy.* Rochester, Vt.: Inner Traditions International, 1982.

————. *Music and the Power of Sound. The Influence of Tuning and Interval on Consciousness.* Rochester, Vt.: Inner Traditions International, 1995.

Davies, P. C. W., and J. Brown. *Superstrings: A Theory of Everything?* Cambridge, England: Cambridge University Press, 1988.

de Moor, Johannes C., ed. *An Anthology of Religious Texts from Ugarit.* Leiden, the Netherlands, and New York: E. J. Brill, 1987.

Diallo, Yaya, and Mitchell Hall. *The Healing Drum: African Wisdom Teachings.* Rochester, Vt.: Destiny Books, 1989.

Dickson, D. Bruce. *The Dawn of Belief: Religion in the Upper Paleolithic of Southwestern Europe.* Tucson: University of Arizona Press, 1990.

Dodds, E. R. *The Greeks and the Irrational.* Berkeley: University of California Press, 1951.

Drinker, Sophie. *Women and Music.* Toronto: Longmans, Green & Company, 1948.

Durdin-Robertson, Lawrence. *The Goddesses of Chaldea, Syria and Egypt.* Enniscorthy, Eire: Cesara Publications, 1975.

Eisler, Riane. *The Chalice and the Blade: Our History, Our Future.* San Francisco: Harper & Row, 1987.

Eliade, Mircea. *Cosmos and History: The Myth of the Eternal Return.* New York: Harper, 1959.

————. *A History of Religious Ideas,* 3 vols. Chicago: University of Chicago Press, 1978–85.

————. *The Myth of the Eternal Return.* Princeton, N.J.: Princeton University Press, 1971.

————. *Myth and Reality.* New York: Harper & Row, 1963.

————. *Myths, Dreams and Mysteries.* New York: Harper & Row, Torch Books, 1975.

————. *Patterns in Comparative Religion.* New York: World, 1963.

————. *Rites and Symbols of Initiation.* New York: Harper & Row, Torch Books, 1975.

————. *Shamanism: Archaic Techniques of Ecstasy.* Princeton, N.J.: Princeton University Press, 1972.

————. *Yoga: Immortality and Freedom.* Princeton, N.J.: Princeton University Press, 1969.

Evans, Sir Arthur. *The Mycenaean Tree and Pillar Cult.* London: Macmillan, 1901.

————. *The Palace of Minos,* 6 vols. London: Macmillan, 1930.

Evans, Arthur. *The God of Ecstasy: Sex-Roles and the Madness of Dionysos.* New York: St. Martin's Press, 1988.

Evola, Julius. *The Metaphysics of Sex.* Reprint, New York: Inner Traditions International, 1983.

Farnell, L. R. *The Cults of the Greek States,* vol. 1–4. Oxford: Clarendon Press, 1896–1909.

Faulkner, R. O., trans. *The Ancient Egyptian Coffin Texts.* Warminster, England: Aris & Phillips, 1978.

Faulkner, R. O., trans. *Pyramid Texts (The Ancient Egyptian Pyramid Texts).* Warminster, England: Aris & Phillys, 1969.

Ferron, Jean. "Les Statuettes au Tympanon des Hypogees Puniques." *Antiquites Africaines,* 3 (1969) 11–33.

Frankfort, Henri. *Kingship and the Gods.* Chicago: University of Chicago Press, 1948.

Fraser, Sir James George. *The Golden Bough: A Study in Magic and Religion.* New York: Macmillan, 1922.

Fraser, Peter Marshall. *Ptolemaic Alexandria.* Oxford: Clarendon Press, 1972.

Fryba, Mirko. *The Art of Happiness: Teachings of Buddhist Psychology.* Boston: Shambhala, 1989.

Funk and Wagnalls Standard Dictionary of Folklore Mythology and Legend. Maria Leach, ed. Drum entry: Brakeley, Theresa C. New York: Funk & Wagnalls, 1972.

Gadon, Eleanor. *The Once and Future Goddess.* San Francisco: Harper & Row, 1989.

Galpin, F. W. *The Music of the Sumerians and Their Immediate Successors, the Babylonians and Assyrians*. Strasbourg: Strasbourg University Press, 1955.

Gautier, de Coincy. *Les chansons à la Vierge*. Jacques Chailley, ed. Paris: Heugel, 1959.

Getty, Adele. *Goddess: Mother of Living Nature*. London: Thames and Hudson, 1990.

Gimbutas, Marija. "The Beginning of the Bronze Age in Europe and the Indo-Europeans: 3500–2500 B.C." *Journal of Indo-European Studies* 1 (1973): 166.

———. *The Goddesses and Gods of Old Europe, 6500–3500 B.C.: Myths and Cult Images*. Berkeley: University of California Press, 1982.

———. *The Language of the Goddess*. New York: Harper-Collins, 1989.

Goldron, Romain. *Ancient and Oriental Music*. H. S. Stuttman Co; distributed by New York: Doubleday, 1968.

Goodman, F. D., J. H. Henney, and E. Pressel. *Trance, Healing, and Hallucination: Three Field Studies in Religious Experience*. New York: A Wiley-Interscience Publication, 1974.

Graves, Robert. *The Greek Myths*, vol. 1 and 2. Rev. ed. New York: Penguin Books, 1960.

Gurney, O. R. *The Hittites*. London: Allen Lane, 1975.

Hall, Edward T. *The Dance of Life: The Other Dimension of Time*. New York: Anchor Books, 1984.

Hamel, Peter Michael. *Through Music to the Self*. Great Britain: Element Books Ltd., 1986.

Hamilton, W. J., J. D. Boyd, and H. W. Mossman. *Human Embryology: Prenatal Development of Form and Function*. Cambridge: Heffer, 1972.

Harding, Esther. *Woman's Mysteries: Ancient and Modern*. New York: Harper & Row, 1971.

Harner, Michael. *The Way of the Shaman: A Guide to Power and Healing*. New York: Bantam Books, 1980.

Harrison, Jane Ellen. *Epilogomena to the Study of Greek Religion and Themis: A Study of the Social Origins of Greek Religion*. New Hyde Park, N.Y.: University Books, 1962.

———. *Prolegomena to the Study of Greek Religion*. Princeton, N.J.: Princeton University Press, 1968.

Hart, Mickey, and Fredric Lieberman. *Planet Drum*. San Francisco: Harper & Row, 1991.

Hart, Mickey, and Jay Stevens. *Drumming at the Edge of Magic*. San Francisco: Harper & Row, 1990.

Hassett, James. *A Primer of Psychophysiology*. San Francisco: W. H. Freeman, 1978.

Hastings, James. *Dictionary of the Bible*. New York: Charles Scribner's Sons, 1963.

Hawkes, Jacquetta. *Dawn of the Gods*. London: Chatto & Windus, 1968.

Herodotus. *The Histories*. J. A. S. Evans, trans. Boston: Twayne, 1982.

Hickmann, Hans. *Orientalische Musik*. Leiden, the Netherlands: E. J. Brill, 1970.

Hillers, D. H. "The Goddess with the Tambourine." *Concordia Theological Monthly* 41: 606–19.

Hirsch, Udo, James Mellaart, and Belkis Balpinar. *The Goddess from Anatolia*, vol. 1–4. Milan: Eskenazi, 1989.

The Holy Bible, King James Version. Grand Rapids, Mich.: Zondervan Corp., 1984.

The Holy Bible, New International Version. New York: International Bible Society, 1978.

Hooke, S. H. *Babylonian and Assyrian Religion*. London: Hutchinson, 1953.

———. *Middle Eastern Mythology*. Harmondsworth, England: Penguin Books, Pelican, 1963.

———. *Myth, Ritual and Kingship*. London: Oxford University Press, 1958.

———. *Origins of Early Semitic Ritual*. London: Oxford University Press, 1935.

Hornung, Erik. *Conceptions of God in Ancient Egypt*. Ithaca, N.Y.: Cornell University Press, 1971.

Hutchinson, Michael. *Megabrain*. New York: Beech Tree Books, 1986.

Inayat Khan, Hazrat. *Music*, vol. 2 of *The Sufi Message of Hazrat Inayat Khan*. London: Barrie & Jenkins, 1973.

Jacobsen, Thorkild. *The Treasures of Darkness: A History of Mesopotamian Religion*. New Haven, Conn.: Yale University Press, 1976.

James, E. O. *The Ancient Gods: The History and Diffusion of Religion in the Ancient Near East and the Eastern Mediterranean*. London: Weidenfeld and Nicolson, 1960.

———. *The Cult of the Mother Goddess*. London: Thames and Hudson, 1959.

———. *Prehistoric Religion*. London and New York: Barnes & Noble, 1957.

Jayakar, Pupul. *The Earth Mother: Legends, Goddesses, and Ritual Arts of India*. San Francisco: Harper & Row, 1990.

Jenny, Hans. *Cymatics*. Basel: Basilius Presse AG, 1974.

Johari, Harish. *Chakras: Energy Centers of Transformation*. Rochester, Vt.: Destiny Books, 1987.

———. *Tools for Tantra*. Rochester, Vt.: Destiny Books. 1986.

Johnson, Buffie. *Lady of the Beasts: Ancient Images of the Goddess and Her Sacred Animals*. San Francisco: Harper & Row, 1988.

Johnson, Sally G. *The Cobra Goddess of Ancient Egypt: Predynastic, Early Dynastic, and Old Kingdom Periods*.

London and New York: Kegan Paul International, 1990.

Jung, C. G., and C. Kerenyi. *Essays on a Science of Mythology: The Myth of the Divine Child and the Mysteries of Eleusis*. Princeton, N.J.: Princeton University Press, renewed copyright, 1978.

Katz, S. H., and F. Maytag. "Brewing an Ancient Beer." *Archaeology* (July/August 1991): 24–33.

Kenyon, Tom. *Brain States*. Naples, Fla.: United States Publishing, 1984.

Kerenyi, Carl. *Dionysos: Archetypal Image of Indestructible Life*. Princeton, N.J.: Princeton University Press, 1976.

———. *Goddesses of Sun and Moon: Circe, Aphrodite, Medea, Niobe*. Irving, Tex.: Spring Publications, 1979.

Kessler, Evelyn. *Woman: The Anthropological View*. New York: Holt, Rhinehart & Winston, 1976.

Kinsley, David. *Hindu Goddesses: Visions of the Divine Feminine in the Hindu Religious Tradition*. Berkeley: University of California Press, 1988.

Kraemer, Ross. "Ecstasy and Possession: The Attraction of Women to the Cult of Dionysus." *Harvard Theological Review* 72 (1979): 55–80.

———. *Her Share of the Blessings: Women's Religions Among Pagans, Jews, and Christians in the Greco-Roman World*. New York: Oxford University Press, 1993.

———. *Maenads, Martyrs, Matrons, Monastics: A Sourcebook on Women's Religions in the Greco-Roman World*. Philadelphia: Fortress Press, 1988.

Kramer, Samuel Noah. *History Begins at Sumer*. London: Thames and Hudson, 1958.

———. *The Sacred Marriage Rite: Aspects of Faith, Myth and Ritual in Ancient Sumer*. Bloomington, Ind.: Indiana University Press, 1969.

———. *The Sumerians: Their History, Culture, and Character*. Chicago: University of Chicago Press, 1963.

Lachman, Barbara. *The Journal of Hildegard of Bingen*. New York: Bell Tower, 1993.

Lamy, Lucie. *Egyptian Mysteries: New Light on Ancient Knowledge*. New York: Thames and Hudson, 1981.

Larsen, Stephen. *The Shaman's Doorway*. Barrytown, N.Y.: Station Hill Press, 1988.

Lawlor, Robert. "Ancient Temple Architecture." In *Homage to Pythagoras: Rediscovering Sacred Science*, pp. 35–132. Bamford, Christopher, ed. New York: Lindisfarne Press, 1982.

Leonard, George. *The Silent Pulse*. New York: Arkana, 1991.

Lerner, Gerda. *The Creation of Patriarchy*. New York: Oxford University Press, 1986.

Leroi-Gourhan, Andre. *Treasures of Prehistoric Art*. New York: Harry N. Abrams, 1967.

Levy, G. Rachel. *The Gate of Horn: A Study of the Religious Conceptions of the Stone Age, and Their Influence on European Thought*. London: Faber & Faber, 1948.

Livy, Titus Livius (59 B.C.–A.D. 17). *The War With Hannibal*, Books 21–30 of *The History of Rome from Its Foundation*. Aubrey de Sélincourt, trans. Baltimore: Penguin Books, 1965.

Luce, Gay Gaer. *Biological Rhythms in Psychiatry and Medicine*. Chevy Chase, Md.: U.S. National Institute of Mental Health, 1970.

Lucian (attributed to Lucian, second century A.D.). *The Syrian Goddess*. Missoula, Mont.: Scholars Press for the Society of Biblical Literature, 1976.

Lurker, Manfred. *The Gods and Symbols of Ancient Egypt: An Illustrated Dictionary*. London: Thames and Hudson, 1980.

Manniche, Lisa. *An Ancient Egyptian Herbal*. Austin: University of Texas, 1993.

———. *Ancient Egyptian Musical Instruments*. Berlin: Deutscher Kunstverlag, 1975.

———. *Music and Musicians in Ancient Egypt*. London: British Museum Press, 1991.

———. "Rare Fragments of a Round Tambourine in the Ashmolean Museum." Oxford, England: *ACTA Orientalia*, no. 35, 1973.

Marinatos, Nanno. *Art and Religion in Thera: Reconstructing a Bronze Age Society*. Athens: D. & I. Mathioulakis, 1985.

Marinatos, Nanno, and Robin Hagg, ed. *Sanctuaries and Cults in the Aegean Bronze Age*. Sweden: Svenska Institutet i Athens, 1981.

Marshack, Alexander. *The Roots of Civilization*. New York: McGraw-Hill, 1972.

Marshall, Sir John Hubert. *Mohenjo-Daro and the Indus Civilization*. Delhi: Indological Book House, 1973.

McNeill, William H. *Keeping Together in Time*. Cambridge, Mass.: Harvard University Press, 1995.

Mellaart, James. *Çatal Hüyük: A Neolithic Town in Anatolia*. London: Thames and Hudson, 1967.

———. "Excavations at Çatal Hüyük: First Preliminary Report." *Anatolian Studies* 12 (1962): 41–65.

———. "Excavations at Çatal Hüyük: Second Preliminary Report." *Anatolian Studies* 13 (1963): 43–103.

———. "Excavations at Çatal Hüyük: Third Preliminary Report." *Anatolian Studies* 14 (1964): 39–119.

———. "Excavations at Çatal Hüyük: Fourth Preliminary Report." *Anatolian Studies* 16 (1966): 165–91.

————. *Excavations at Hacilar*. Edinburgh: Edinburgh University Press, 1970.

————. *The Neolithic of the Near East*. New York: Charles Scribner's Sons, 1975.

Meyer, Marvin W., ed. *The Ancient Mysteries: A Sourcebook*. San Francisco: HarperCollins, 1987.

Meyer-Baer, Kathi. *Music of the Spheres and the Dance of Death: Studies in Musical Iconology*. Princeton, N.J.: Princeton University Press, 1970.

Meyers, Carol L. "Of Drums and Damsels: Women's Performance in Ancient Israel." *Biblical Archaeologist* 54, no. 1 (March 1991): 16–27.

Michaelides, Solon. *The Music of Ancient Greece: An Encyclopaedia*. London: Faber & Faber, 1978.

Mookerjee, Ajit, and Madhu Khanna. *Kali: The Feminine Force*. Rochester, Vt.: Destiny Books, 1988.

————. *The Tantric Way: Art, Science, Ritual*. New York: Thames and Hudson, 1977.

Mukherjee, B. N. *Nana On Lion*. Calcutta: Asiatic Society, 1969.

Neher, Andrew. "A Physiological Explanation of Unusual Behavior in Ceremonies Involving Drums." *Human Biology* 34 (1962): 151–60.

Neumann, Erich. *The Great Mother: An Analysis of the Archetype*. Princeton, N.J.: Princeton University Press, 1955.

The New Grove Dictionary of Music and Musical Instruments, 3 vols. Stanley Sadie, ed. New York: Macmillan, 1984.

New Oxford History of Music, vol. 1. Oxford and New York: Oxford University Press, 1990.

Nilsson, M. P. *The Minoan-Mycenaean Religion and Its Survival in Greek Religion*. London: Lund, 1927.

Noble, Vicki. *Shakti Woman*. New York: HarperCollins, 1991.

Oliveira, Ernesto de. *Instrumentos Musicais Populares Portugues*. Lisboa: Fundcao Calouste Gulben Kian, 1982.

Parke, H. W. *Sibyls and Sibylline Prophecy in Classical Antiquity*. B. C. McGing, ed. London and New York: Routledge, 1988.

Palmer, John D. *An Introduction to Biological Rhythms*. New York: Academic Press, 1976.

Paris, Ginette. *Pagan Meditations: The Worlds of Aphrodite, Artemis and Hestia*. Dallas, Tex.: Spring Publications, 1986.

Patai, Raphael. *The Hebrew Goddess*. Detroit: Wayne State University Press, 1990.

Pelletier, Kenneth R. *Toward a Science of Consciousness*. New York: Dell, 1978.

Perera, Sylvia Brinton. *Descent to the Goddess: A Way of Initiation for Women*. Toronto: Inner City Books, 1981.

Pinch, Geraldine. *Votive Offerings to Hathor*. Oxford: Griffith Institute Ashmolean Museum, 1993.

Pomeroy, Sarah B. *Goddesses, Whores, Wives and Slaves*. New York: Shocken Books, 1975.

Preston, James J. *Mother Worship: Theme and Variations*. Chapel Hill: University of North Carolina Press, 1982.

Pritchard, James B., ed. *The Ancient Near East: An Anthology of Texts and Pictures*, 2 vols. Princeton, N.J.: Princeton University Press, 1958.

————. *Palestinian Figurines in Relation to Certain Goddesses Known Through Literature*, vol 24 of *American Oriental Series*. New Haven, Conn.: American Oriental Society, 1943.

Quasten, Johannes. *Music and Worship in Pagan and Christian Antiquity*. Washington, D.C.: National Association of Pastoral Musicians, 1973.

Ransome, H. M. *The Sacred Bee in Ancient Times and Folklore*. Burrowbridge, Bridgewater (Somerset): Bee Books New & Old, 1986.

Renfrew, Colin. *The Emergence of Civilisation: The Cyclades and the Aegean in the Third Millennium B.C.* London: Methuen, 1972.

Rice, Prudence C. "Prehistoric Venuses: Symbols of Motherhood or Womanhood?" *Journal of Anthropological Research* 37 (4): 402–14.

Rimmer, Joan. *Ancient Musical Instruments of Western Asia: In the Department of Western Asiatic Antiquities, the British Museum*. London: British Museum, 1969.

Robins, Gay. *Women in Ancient Egypt*. London: British Museum Press, 1993.

Rose, H. J. *Religion in Greece and Rome*. New York: Harper Torchbooks, 1959.

Rothmuller, Aron Marko. *The Music of the Jews*. New York: A. S. Barnes, 1954.

Rouget, Gilbert. *Music and Trance: A Theory of the Relations Between Music and Possession*. Chicago: University of Chicago Press, 1985.

Rundle Clark, R. T. *Myth and Symbol in Ancient Egypt*. London: Thames and Hudson, 1978.

Ruspoli, Mario. *The Cave of Lascaux: The Final Photographic Record*. London: Thames and Hudson, 1987.

Sachs, Curt. *The History of Musical Instruments*. New York: W. W. Norton, 1940.

————. *Rhythm and Tempo: A Study in Music History*. New York: W. W. Norton, 1953.

————. *The Rise of Music in the Ancient World, East and West*. New York: W. W. Norton, 1943.

Sagan, Carl. *The Dragons of Eden*. New York: Random House, 1977.

Salvatore, Gianfranco. *Can Archtypes Be Heard?* Severine Hamilton, trans. Private paper, 1985.

Sellers, Jane B. *The Death of Gods in Ancient Egypt.* Harmondsworth, England: Penguin Books Ltd., 1992.

Settegast, Mary. *Plato Prehistorian.* Cambridge: Rotenberg Press, 1987.

Shafer, R. Murray. *The Tuning of the World.* New York: Alfred A. Knopf, 1977.

Showerman, Grant. *The Great Mother of the Gods.* Chicago: Argonaut, 1969.

Slavitt, David R. *The Eclogues and the Georgics of Virgil.* Garden City, N.Y.: Doubleday, 1972.

Smith, Jonathan. *Drudgery Divine: On the Comparison of Early Christianities and the Religions of Late Antiquity.* London: School of Oriental and African Studies, University of London; Chicago: University of Chicago Press, 1990.

Sollberger, Arne. *Biological Rhythm Research.* Amsterdam, N.Y.: Elsevier Publishing Co., 1965.

Spretnak, Charlene. *Lost Goddesses of Early Greece.* Boston: Beacon Press, 1984.

Starhawk. *The Spiral Dance: A Rebirth of the Ancient Religion of the Great Goddess.* San Francisco: Harper & Row, 1979.

Stone, Merlin. *When God Was a Woman.* New York: Harcourt Brace Jovanovich, 1976.

Talbot, Michael. *The Holographic Universe.* New York: HarperCollins, 1992.

Tame, David. *The Secret Power of Music.* New York: Destiny Books, 1984.

Temko, Allan. *Notre-Dame of Paris: The Biography of a Cathedral.* New York: Viking Press, 1955.

Terrill, Barbara Ann. *The Shaman's Drum.* Unpublished masters in ethnomusicology thesis, State University of New York at Albany, 1993.

Theimer, Ernest. *Fragrance Chemistry: The Science of the Sense of Smell.* San Diego, Calif.: Academic Press, 1982.

Thompson, Robert Farris. *Flash of the Spirit: African and Afro-American Art and Philosophy.* New York: Vintage, 1984.

Thompson, William Irwin. *The Time Falling Bodies Take to Light.* New York: St. Martin's Press. 1981.

Thureau-Dangin, F. *Les Inscriptions de Sumer et d'Addad.* Paris: E. Leroux, 1905.

Trendall, A. D. *Red Figure Vases of South Italy and Sicily.* London: Thames and Hudson, 1989.

Ucko, P. J., and A. Rosenfeld. *Anthropomorphic Figurines of Predynastic Egypt and Neolithic Crete with Comparative Material from the Prehistoric Near East and Mainland Greece.* London: A. Szmidla, 1968.

———. *Paleolithic Cave Art.* New York: McGraw-Hill, 1967.

Van Gennep, Arnold. *The Rites of Passage.* Chicago: University of Chicago Press, 1960.

Van Toller, Steve, and George Dodd. *Perfumery: The Psychology and Biology of Fragrance.* New York: Chapman & Hall, 1988.

Vermaseren, Maarten J. *Cybele and Attis.* London: Thames and Hudson, 1977.

———. *Corpus Cultus Cybelae Attidisque,* 7 vols. Leiden, the Netherlands: E. F. Brill, 1977.

Walker, Barbara G. *The Woman's Dictionary of Symbols and Sacred Objects.* San Francisco: Harper & Row, 1988.

———. *The Woman's Encyclopedia of Myths and Secrets.* San Francisco: Harper & Row, 1983.

Warner, Marina. *Alone of All Her Sex: The Myth and the Cult of the Virgin Mary.* New York: Alfred A. Knopf, 1976.

Weiss, Harvey, ed. *Ebla to Damascus: Art and Archaeology of Ancient Syria. An Exhibition from the Directorate General of Antiquities and Museums [of the] Syrian Arab Republic.* Washington, D.C.: Smithsonian Institution, 1985.

West, John Anthony. *Serpent in the Sky: The High Wisdom of Ancient Egypt.* Wheaton, Ill.: Quest Books, 1993.

———. *The Traveler's Key to Ancient Egypt: A Guide to the Sacred Places of Ancient Egypt.* New York: Alfred A. Knopf, 1989.

Wharton, Henry Thornton. *Sappho: Memoir, Text, Selected Renderings and a Literal Translation.* London: D. Stott, 1887.

Wheeler, Robert Eric Mortimer. *The Cambridge History of India.* Delhi: S. Chand, 1955–58.

Wiora, Walter. *The Four Ages of Music.* New York: W. W. Norton, 1965.

Wolkstein, Diane, and Samuel Noah Kramer. *Inanna, Queen of Heaven and Earth: Her Stories and Hymns from Sumer.* New York: HarperCollins, 1983.

Woolley, Sir Charles Leonard. *The Excavations at Ur.* New York: Thomas Crowell, 1965.

Wosien, Maria-Gabriel. *Sacred Dance: Encounter with the Gods.* New York: Thames and Hudson, 1974.

Zabkar, Louis V. *Hymns to Isis in Her Temple at Philae.* Hanover, N.H.: Published for Brandeis University Press by University Press of New England, 1988.

Zimmer, Heinrich. *Myths and Symbols in Indian Art and Civilization.* Princeton, N.J.: Princeton University Press, 1946.

Zimdars-Swartz, Sandra. *Encountering Mary: From La Salette to Medjugorje.* Princeton, N.J.: Princeton University Press, 1991.

Discography

Since the Beginning. Layne Redmond and the Mob of Angels, featuring Steve Gorn on flute, Vicki Richards on violin, Amitava Chatterjee, vocals (Interworld Music CD-20904, 1992).

Internal Combustion. Glen Velez with Layne Redmond (CMP CD 23, 1985).

Seven Heaven. Glen Velez with Steve Gorn and Layne Redmond (CMP CD 30, 1987).

Assyrian Rose. Glen Velez with Steve Gorn, Layne Redmond, and special guests John Clark and Howard Levy (CMP CD 42, 1989).

Handdance. Glen Velez with Layne Redmond (NMD 50301, 1983).

Ramana. Glen Velez with Layne Redmond, Howard Levy, and Jan Hagiwara (Music of the World CDH-307, 1991).

VIDEO AND AUDIO INSTRUCTIONAL TAPES

Ritual Drumming: Instructional Video. Layne Redmond and the Mob of Angels (Interworld Music, 1992).

The Fantastic World of Frame Drums: Instructional Video. Glen Velez with special guest Layne Redmond (Interworld Music, 1990).

Tambourine Practice Tape #1, audiocassette, Layne Redmond, 1996.

MEDITATION TAPES

Pulse of the Earth and Sun. Layne Redmond with Tommy Brunjes, 1996.

The First Sound—The Pulse of the Mother's Blood. Layne Redmond with Tommy Brunjes, 1996.

For information on frame drum retreats, workshops, percussion instruments, and links to all kinds of cutting edge rhythmic sources see this website:

http://www1.mhv.net/~lredmond/

ILLUSTRATION CREDITS

Frontispiece, page x   Detail of red-figured Greek vase. Museo Nazionale, Naples.

page xvi   Carthage Museum. Photo by Andrew Myatt.

page 6   Photo by Steve Silverstein.

page 8   Reproduced with the permission of the Master and Fellows of Corpus Christi College and of the Fitzwilliam Museum, Cambridge. Copyright Fitzwilliam Museum, Cambridge.

page 9   Courtesy of Museu D'Arqueologia De Catalunya.

page 10   The Art Museum, Princeton University, Museum purchase. Photo by Bruce M. White.

page 11   Carthage Museum. Photo by Andrew Myatt.

page 12   Manisa Museum, Turkey.

page 13   Staatliche Museen, Berlin.

page 18, top   Babylonian Collection, Sterling Memorial Library, Yale University, YBC 10002, by permission.

page 18, below   Istanbul Arkeoloji Museleri, #4787.

page 19   Rijksmuseum Van Oudheden, Leiden, the Netherlands, by permission.

page 20   Drawing after E. Prisse D'Avennes. Plate N. II.7, Tomb #129 of Amenmose, Thutmose III.

page 21   Utica Museum. Photo by Andrew Myatt.

page 22, above   Copyright British Museum.

page 22, below   Damascus Museum, No. 1614/3528.

page 23   The Metropolitan Museum of Art, Rogers Fund, 1912 (12.181.196).

page 24   National Museum, Athens.

page 29, above   Drawings after Alexander Marshack.

page 31   Neg. No. 326475, Courtesy Department Library Services, American Museum of Natural History.

page 32   Courtesy of Museum National d'Histoire Naturelle, Musee De L'Homme.

page 40   The Nelson-Atkins Museum of Art (Purchase: Nelson Trust). Photo by Robert Newcombe.

page 42   Courtesy of Cambridge University Museum of Archaeology and Anthropology.

page 44, above   Drawing after Miss Raymonde Enderle Ludovici, north wall of the Hunting Shrine at Level V, Çatal Hüyük.

page 46, bottom   Drawing after Grace Huxtable with reference to photograph from Mellaart's excavations, from Shrine VII, Çatal Hüyük.

page 47, below   Drawing after Mellaart, Level III, Çatal Hüyük.

page 48, below left   Drawing after Mellaart, Shrine E VI, Çatal Hüyük.

page 49, above right   Drawing after Mellaart, Shrine VII, 21, Çatal Hüyük.

page 50, above   Collection of the J. Paul Getty Museum, Los Angeles, California.

page 50, below   Drawing after Mellaart, Level VII, 8, Çatal Hüyük.

page 52   Musee du Louvre, Paris.

page 54, left   Museum of Anatolian Civilization, Ankara, Turkey.

page 54, right   Alinari/Art Resource, New York.

page 55   Drawing after reconstruction painting by Gaynor Chapman.

pages 56 and 71   Staatliche Museen zu Berlin–PreuBischer Kulturbesitz Museum fur Indische Kunst, Inv. N. I 5570. Credit Pahari-Gebiel Bosohli/Bilaspur circa 1750. Foto/Jahr.

page 61, above   Aleppo Museum, Hama Excavations.

page 61   Drawing after Mackay 1938, pl. LXXVI, 6.

page 64   Damaru, collection of Dr. Raam Pandey.

page 65, below   Drawing after J. Fergusson, *Tree and Serpent Worship*, second ed., 1873, pl. XVI, 2.

page 68, above   Victoria and Albert Museum/Art Resource, New York.

page 70   The Metropolitan Museum of Art, The Crosby Brown Collection of Musical Instruments, 1889 (89.4.214).

page 71, left and right   Staatliche Museen zu Berlin–PreuBischer Kulturbesitz Museum fur Indische Kunst. Foto/Jahr.

page 72, above and below   Photos courtesy of Air India.

page 74, above   Copyright British Museum.

page 74, below   University of Pennsylvania Museum, Philadelphia.

page 75   Istanbul Arkeoloji Museleri.

page 76   Musee du Louvre.

page 77   Copyright British Museum.

page 78   Staatliche Museen, Berlin.

page 79   Photo by Snouck Hurgronje, formerly in the Bonfils Collection, Visual Collections, Fine Arts Library, Werner Otto Hall, Harvard University.

page 80, below   The Metropolitan Museum of Art, purchase, 1955. Joseph Pulitzer Bequest (55.137.1).

page 81, above   Istanbul Arkeoloji Museleri, #2571.

page 81, below   Copyright British Museum.

page 84   Copyright British Museum.

page 85   University of Pennsylvania Museum, Philadelphia (neg. #54-142159), object no. CBS 7054.

page 87   Copyright British Museum.

page 91   Department of Egyptian and Classical Art, The Brooklyn Museum, Museum Collection Fund.

page 92   Egyptian Museum, Cairo.

page 95, center   Department of Egyptian and Classical Art, The Brooklyn Museum, Charles Edwin Wilbour Fund.

page 96, above   Musee du Louvre.

page 96, center   Drawing after E. Prisse D'Avennes, plate N. II.7.

page 96, below   Drawing after E. Prisse D'Avennes, plate N. II.45.

page 97, below   The Metropolitan Museum of Art, Rogers Fund, 1950 (50.99).

page 106, above   Drawing after I. Rosellini, Monumenti dell' Egitto e della Nubia, Pisa, 1832, pl. cxxiv, detail.

page 106, below   Department of Egyptian and Classical Art, The Brooklyn Museum, Charles Edwin Wilbour Fund.

Page 108, below   Department of Egyptian and Classical Art, The Brooklyn Museum, Charles Edwin Wilbour Fund.

page 109   Courtesy of Allard Pierson Museum, Amsterdam. Inv. n. 3986.

page 110, center left   The Metropolitan Museum of Art, Rogers Fund, 1962 (62.11.1).

page 110, below   Archaeological Museum of Thessaloniki.

page 111, center   Carthage Museum, Tunisia. Photo by Andrew Myatt.

page 111, below   Department of Antiquities, the Republic of Cyprus, No. 1970/V-28/1.

page 112, top left   The Metropolitan Museum of Art, The Cesnola Collection; purchased by subscription, 1874–1876 (74.51.2502).

page 112, top right   Copyright British Museum.

page 112, bottom right   Department of Antiquities, the Republic of Cyprus, Inventory B.190, neg. C.6973.

page 112, bottom left   Department of Antiquities, the Republic of Cyprus, T.276/253. neg. B56.203 and neg. B56 204.

page 113, top   The Metropolitan Museum of Art, The Cesnola Collection; purchased by subscription, 1874–1876 (74.51.1679).

page 113, center   Drawing after Arthur Evans, The Palace of Minos, Vol. IV, Part 1, page 344.

page 115, top   Drawing after Arthur Evans, The Palace of Minos, Vol. IV, Part 1, page 164.

page 115, bottom   Drawing after Greek vase, Hermitage Museum (Hermitage Cat. 1807).

page 116, top   Copyright Fitzwilliam Museum, Cambridge.

page 117   Collection of the J. Paul Getty Museum, Los Angeles, California.

page 118, top   Copyright British Museum.

page 118, bottom   Musee du Bardo, Tunisia. Photo by Andrew Myatt.

page 121   Archaeological Museum of Thessaloniki.

page 122   Courtesy of Ny Carlsberg Glyptotek, Copenhagen.

page 124 bottom   The Metropolitan Museum of Art, Samuel D. Lee Fund, 1937 (37.11.23).

page 125   The Metropolitan Museum of Art, Gift of Henry G. Marquand, 1897 (97.22.24).

page 126, top   Il Museo Eoliano Di Lipari.

page 126, bottom   Copyright British Museum.

page 127   Alinari/Art Resource, New York.

page 128, top   Alinari/Art Resource, New York.

page 128, bottom   Staatliche Museen, Berlin.

page 129, center   Drawing from Hydria from Capua, Lyons Museum.

page 129, bottom   Drawing from Apulian vase, Museo National Napoli.

page 130, top   Il Museo Eoliano Di Lipari.

page 130, bottom   Drawing from Greek vase, Museo Nazionale, Naples. Frontispiece illustration is the other side of this vase.

page 131   Drawing from Roman relief of maenads, Nach Clara, Musee de Sculpture.

page 132   Royal Museum of Art and History, Brussels, A3456 (photo A.C.L.).

page 133, top   The Metropolitan Museum of Art, Purchase, 1953, Joseph Pulitzer Bequest (53.11.5).